Statesmanship, Character, and Leadership in America

Statesmanship, Character, and Leadership in America

Terry Newell

palgrave
macmillan

STATESMANSHIP, CHARACTER, AND LEADERSHIP IN AMERICA
Copyright © Terry Newell, 2012.

First published in 2012 by PALGRAVE MACMILLAN® in the United States—
a division of St. Martin's Press LLC, 175 Fifth Avenue, New York,
NY 10010.

Where this book is distributed in the UK, Europe and the rest of the world,
this is by Palgrave Macmillan, a division of Macmillan Publishers Limited,
registered in England, company number 785998, of Houndmills,
Basingstoke, Hampshire RG21 6XS.

Palgrave Macmillan is the global academic imprint of the above companies
and has companies and representatives throughout the world.

Palgrave® and Macmillan® are registered trademarks in the United States,
the United Kingdom, Europe and other countries.

ISBN: 978–1–137–33092–5

The Library of Congress has cataloged the hardcover edition as follows:

Newell, Terry.
    Statesmanship, character, and leadership in America / Terry Newell.
      pages cm
    Includes bibliographical references.
      ISBN 978–0–230–34108–1
      1. Political leadership—United States—History. 2. Character—
Political aspects—United States—History. 3. Political culture—United
States—History. 4. Washington, George, 1732–1799. 5. Jefferson,
Thomas, 1743–1826. 6. Lincoln, Abraham, 1809–1865. 7. Anthony,
Susan B. (Susan Brownell), 1820–1906. 8. Marshall, George C. (George
Catlett), 1880–1959. 9. King, Martin Luther, Jr., 1929–1968. 10. Ford,
Gerald R., 1913–2006. I. Title.

E183.N54 2012
306.20973—dc23   2011048405

A catalogue record of the book is available from the British Library.

Design by Newgen Imaging Systems (P) Ltd., Chennai, India.

First PALGRAVE MACMILLAN paperback edition: May 2013

10 9 8 7 6 5 4 3 2 1

Transferred to Digital Printing in 2013

For Ashton and Trevor
May your generation find the
statesmanship it needs

Character is the only secure foundation of the state.

—Calvin Coolidge

A politician is interested in the next election.
A statesman is concerned about the next generation.

—Gerald Ford

Contents

Figures

Preface

xvii

> *These are the times in which a genius would wish to live. It is not in the still calm of life, or the repose of a pacific station, that great characters are formed... Great necessities call out great virtues. When the mind is raised, and animated by scenes that engage the Heart, then those qualities which would otherwise lay dormant, wake into Life, and form the Character of the Hero and the Statesman.*
>
> —Abigail Adams to John Quincy Adams,
> January 19, 1780

Writing to her 12-year-old son, reluctantly accompanying his father to the Netherlands where the elder Adams was trying to secure funding for the revolution, Abigail Adams, suggested that the boy could chart his own path to greatness. That path could, with "attention, diligence and steady application" form a character suited for statesmanship.[1] On September 11, 2001, as American Airlines flight 11 and United Airlines flight 175 tore into the Twin Towers, another plane hit the Pentagon, and a fourth plummeted into a field in rural Pennsylvania, the United States could be said to have entered its own time in which "great necessities call out great virtues." The decade would be marked by two wars, the near dismantling of New Orleans by hurricane Katrina, the worst financial crisis since the Great Depression, the burgeoning costs of health care, a massive Gulf oil spill, increasing concerns about global warming, and a massive federal debt.

Some of these problems were "Black Swans," the term coined by Nassim Nicholas Taleb[2] for seemingly unpredictable, high-impact events. Either we couldn't connect the dots of events or we missed the dots themselves. Some of these problems were foreseeable. The same could be said for our future. We know about the potential for another financial meltdown, the skyrocketing health care demands of an aging population, religious fundamentalism, tsunamis, and nuclear proliferation. We may not anticipate a new virus, a revolution in another strategic country we thought was stable, or a war launched over arable land.

Of course, Abigail Adams sought to prepare her son not only for problems but for great opportunities—of which American independence was foremost in her mind. In the same letter, she reminded him that "with the blessing of heaven [we] will transmit this inheritance to ages yet unborn." America, in the twenty-first century, faces astounding opportunities as well.

Yet predictable or not, the problems and opportunities we will face demand "the Character of the Hero and the Statesman." They will occur in a world, made smaller and more combustible by technology—a world that seems harder to understand, and lead, than ever.

We hunger for leadership equal to such challenges. An August 2011 Reuters/Ipsos Poll showed that 73 percent of Americans think "things in this country are on the wrong track."[3] Yet, despite the need, a July 2010 Gallup Poll found that only 16 percent of Americans had "a great deal of confidence" in the presidency. By comparison, only 15 percent had "a great deal of confidence" in the Supreme Court, 4 percent in Congress, and 7 percent in big business.[4]

A November 2009 poll by the Center for Public Leadership at Harvard's Kennedy School of Government found that 68 percent of respondents agreed that "we have a leadership crisis in the country today." Americans expressed more than average confidence in only military, medical, and nonprofit/charity leaders. In short, leadership seems illusive on Main Street, Wall Street, and Pennsylvania Avenue.[5]

Why? What do we want from leaders anyway? For decades, Americans have sought take-charge, supremely confident, no-nonsense, charismatic leaders. Either we are not finding them or that model of leadership is not the answer we thought it was.

This book takes the view that America needs leaders who practice what we have historically called "statesmanship."[6] Yet Americans seem to think such people are more the stuff of legend than life. They look at leaders today and find too many of them arrogant, isolated, partisan, divisive, and/or rigid. They want leaders who put the country above personal interests. They want what Abigail Adams wanted, but they despair of getting it.

We need not be so pessimistic. As a nation, we forget that, in their time, Washington, Adams, Jefferson, and others faced problems equally complex, in an environment equally divisive and uncertain. Yet they practiced statesmanship and were recognized for doing so by many (not all, of course) while they lived. They led 13 diverse, rural colonies with no professional army and wrestled independence from the greatest military power on earth. Then they built a republican government that has lasted over 200 years.

Nor was statesmanship just the province of the eighteenth century. Lincoln saved the union and called, in his Second Inaugural, for "malice toward none; with charity for all," as profound an act of statesmanship as we may ever see. Even in the twentieth century, when we wondered if we could recover from a second world war, statesmanship came forward in the form of a man from Uniontown, Pennsylvania. George Marshall helped create an economic structure in Europe that brought material wealth and collective security to hundreds of millions.

Leaders who engage in statesmanship have made, do make, and can still make a difference. But there are no guarantees we'll have them. We dare not trust to providence that they will emerge. We must seek out and foster statesmanship. Our pessimism may be due in part to the fact that we don't know how. That is what propelled the writing of this book.

Elusive Statesmanship

What is this thing called statesmanship? Books defining leadership seem endless, with lists upon lists of requisite skills. Statesmanship seems harder to define. It draws on leadership skills, but the recipe seems somehow beyond our grasp.

In *Statesmanship, Character, and Leadership in America*, the aim is to suggest that recipe. To the extent that statesmanship requires the application of certain skills, the goal is to illuminate what they are.

Yet statesmanship requires more than skills. Leaders in government may be rated highly on conflict management, delegation, and managing diversity, for example, but their organizations may still fail to meet citizens' expectations, or they may produce near-term gains at the expense of the long-term health of the nation at large. Leaders in corporate America no doubt might have scored high in the past decade on skills such as decisiveness, oral communication, and resourcefulness. But many of their firms tanked nonetheless, often due to ethical failures. We would hardly grace their behavior with the label of statesmanship. Far less scrupulous leaders—a Hitler, Stalin, or Hussein—also had certain highly tuned skills.

What's missing from leadership skill lists is attention to character. Statesmanship is defined as much by *who* leaders are as the skills they possess. Leaders who forge good societies are not just clever tacticians. Their skills rest on a foundation of moral values and a deep understanding of history. Such leaders face the twenty-first century with a moral compass and at least one foot firmly planted in centuries past.

To raise the bar still higher, even this is not enough. Acts of statesmanship also call forth moral character in others. Leaders don't just apply skills to a measurable goal in some strategic plan. They have an understanding of what constitutes a good society. While they cannot command it, they can expect it. Indeed, it is their capacity to elicit higher character in others in pursuit of the good society that turns statesmanship in theory into statesmanship in practice. To paraphrase an old army recruiting slogan, those who would practice statesmanship must not only "be all they can be" they must invite us to "be all we can be."

This is not a call for philosopher-kings. The acts of statesmanship in this book were not by people uniformly revered or faultless in their time. We are not in search of perfect beings, just human ones. Washington lost more battles in war than he won and was pilloried by an opposition press during his second term. He could be hard to approach and overly concerned with deference from others. Jefferson's terms as governor were troubled enough that the legislature asked for an investigation of his conduct, and his failure to work for the abolition of slavery leaves no doubt that his character had flaws. Lincoln's conversion to emancipation came late in his political career. Susan B. Anthony was reviled by much of America for most of her life. Sacrificing all for suffrage, she ignored the pleas of black women in the South so as not to offend the whites whose support she craved more.

But each of them raised the bar on themselves and their followers. No one acts as a statesman all the time. The pressures of politics, career advancement, and personality make this impossible. What we seek are not statesmen but acts of statesmanship, times when leaders rise above more selfish interests to accomplish something positive for our future.

The thesis is that the skills and character essential to statesmanship can be both described and developed. Statesmanship then becomes attainable not only in the mythic past but in the troubled present and in the Black Swan future.

The Plan for This Book

Life can only be understood backwards, but it must be lived forwards.

—*Soren Kierkegaard*

History is our vehicle. Statesmanship is very visible, not to mention interesting, at turning points in American history—times characterized by some combination of high stakes, contending values, ambiguity about the situation, disagreement about what to do, and high stress and personal exposure for the leader. At turning points, statesmanship matters, and the direction of society can hang in the balance. At turning points, statesmanship helps shape though it clearly cannot control who we are and what we become.

By choice, the focus is *not* on contemporary leaders. The full record of the turning points they faced and their actions is not yet available. Sufficient evidence, and distance, to make sound judgments about them is impossible.

Also, due to the understandably limited time and patience of readers, the focus is on a small number of leaders. This sacrifice of breadth for depth necessarily limits the book's conclusions. The aim is to provide some actionable ideas, not an intellectually complete theory of statesmanship. The goal is to contribute to that conversation, a conversation we seem to need.

In my work at the Federal Executive Institute, a residential leadership education center for senior government officials, the focus on leaders at turning points has proven to be a productive approach. Leaders love history. The case method, a modified form of which forms the core of this book, is a well-regarded learning approach. Historical case studies have the added advantage of being fascinating stories, and the power of stories to spur thinking and learning is well known.[7]

Historical cases are an appropriate vehicle for another reason. Too many leaders, public and private, don't understand the American experience. In the productive years of midlife, they face the road ahead partially blind to our collective past, as if one could drive properly without ever checking the rearview mirror. Many have not studied the Constitution since high school and didn't much enjoy the experience then. Few have ever read any of the *Federalist Papers*, not to mention the major anti-Federalist writings, despite how profoundly these shape our public discourse. Few have spent any time with other major historical documents that have shaped the ideas and ideals that constitute who we are and what we want. It's not that they don't relish such learning when it comes their way. But their education, filled with dates and facts rather than understanding, didn't provide it. Without adequate historical understanding, leaders miss the lessons of the past or even worse, they apply with false analogies what they thought those lessons were.[8]

A Constitution Day 2010 quiz administered by the Intercollegiate Studies Institute (ISI) illustrates the dimensions of this problem. Only 44 percent of respondents correctly understood the meaning of "federalism," and only 50 percent knew why the Federalist Papers were written.[9] A civic literacy survey administered by ISI to college students in 2006 revealed that college graduates don't do much better than the general public: fewer than half of college seniors (47.9 percent) recognized that the line "We hold these truths to be self-evident, that all men are created equal," is from the Declaration of Independence.[10]

This book is not, however, a history text. The goal is more modest: to bring the past alive at a small number of historical turning points so that contemporary leaders can benefit from what took place, how people prepared themselves to lead, what they said and did, and the impact they made—or did not make.

The leaders in this book are all people in public roles. Some were presidents. One was a civil servant. Two were leaders of social movements. There are no private sector leaders, but I believe most of the conclusions have value for them. Recent history suggests that, while there is certainly a distinction between the public and private sectors, and public and private sector leaders, the distinction is not as clear as we might have thought. BPs former CEO, Tony Haywood, learned quickly (but too late) during the 2010 Gulf oil spill that he was a public servant as well as a private sector leader. Bill Gates made his fortune as Microsoft's CEO but has now dedicated much of his life to philanthropy in a very public role. As we witnessed the fallout from the financial collapse of 2008, few would suggest that the leaders of our nation's major financial institutions are not "public" figures who could do with a heavy injection of statesmanship.

The book is laid out in eight chapters. Seven focus on a turning point and leader. The eighth defines statesmanship across all the case studies and summarizes the leadership skills and traits of character upon which our leaders drew.

Each of the turning point chapters begins by plunging the reader into a specific historical moment and provides context for the crisis in which the leader had to act. The focus is then placed on a speech or document the leader gave at the turning point, because, as Disraeli said, "With words we govern men."[11] After that, the chapter provides an analysis: what was the leader trying to do? Why did he or she choose this approach? How did statesmanship emerge? Interwoven with textual analysis are biographical details that provide insight into the leader's skills and character. Each chapter concludes by addressing the historical impact of what the leader said and did.

Here, briefly, is a description of each turning point.

Chapter 1: Washington Steps Down: The Farewell Address

In September 1796, George Washington was concluding his second term as president. Nothing prevented him for serving a third term, and he was the only figure who seemed able to unite the nation, increasingly torn by emerging political battles. Yet he longed to return to Mount Vernon. He sought escape from the disapproval that even he seemed unable to avoid as factions contended for power. So he stepped down. The move surprised Americans and shocked the crowned heads of Europe. Would the nation come apart? Was there anything he could do to help assure a successful transition of power, the first under the Constitution? Washington chose to explain his decision in a "farewell address." But what could he say that would help the nation through this critical turning point?

Chapter 2: The Electoral Crisis of 1801: Jefferson's First Inaugural

In the election of 1800, President John Adams, a Federalist, faced Thomas Jefferson, the leader of the second of two emerging political parties, the Republicans, in a scathingly partisan contest. Jefferson defeated Adams but not his own vice presidential running mate, Aaron Burr. The election was thrown into the House of Representatives. The deadlock lasted for 35 ballots. Some Republicans threatened to march on Washington if Jefferson was denied the presidency. Some

Federalists plotted to remove the New England states from the union if he was elected. When Jefferson finally won, he had to unite a divided nation and preside over the first transfer of power between political parties in American presidential history. What could he say to build unity yet assume the power needed to forge ahead with his vision for America?

Chapter 3: Healing the Wounds of Civil War: Lincoln's Second Inaugural

In March 1865, a war that had claimed over 600,000 lives finally appeared to be ending. Abraham Lincoln had led the divided nation in war. Now he had to unite it in peace. As his second inaugural approached, how could he speak to both the North and the South to offer a way forward? Would a vengeful North and an angry South even listen? How could he engage both in forging the "United" States that emerged from the conflict?

Chapter 4: The Struggle for Woman Suffrage: The Trial of Susan B. Anthony

On November 5, 1872, Susan B. Anthony voted and was arrested for breaking the law. Despite the rising tide of democracy in America that saw near-universal male suffrage and the emancipation of slaves, women were left behind. In most states, they could not own property, testify in court, ask for a divorce, or even keep their children should their marriage end. And they could not vote. Convinced that the Fourteenth Amendment's guarantee of rights to all "citizens" meant that women could vote, Anthony cast her ballot. When tried, she sat idly by (refused permission to testify) and was declared guilty by the judge. Asked if she wished to address the court before sentencing, her chance to speak finally came. What could she say to propel the movement for woman suffrage forward?

Chapter 5: Saving Postwar Europe (and America): The Marshall Plan Speech

In 1947, Europe faced seemingly insurmountable economic, political, and social challenges. Its infrastructure had been devastated by war. Widespread food shortages created conditions ripe for political unrest. The threat of Soviet expansion hung over the struggling continent. Alone among the major powers in its intact industrial and agricultural base, America could play an important role in the reconstruction of Europe, but the nation had always retreated into isolationism when its wars ended. Secretary of State George C. Marshall knew that doing so would be a tragic mistake. In a speech at Harvard on June 5, 1947, he laid out the rationale for what became known as the Marshall Plan. How could he convince Americans to sacrifice to rebuild war-torn nations?

Chapter 6: The Movement in Crisis: King's Letter from Birmingham Jail

After a failed effort in Albany, Georgia, Martin Luther King Jr.'s leadership of the struggle for African American equality was in jeopardy. His direct action campaign in Birmingham in early 1963 would be a critical turning point. Could he build enough support among both resistant black moderates and the hesitant Kennedy administration to overcome massive white resistance? Shortly after the Birmingham protests began, King was arrested for defying a court injunction against marching. In jail, he read a letter written by eight Alabama clergy, charging his protest effort with being untimely, unlawful, and extreme. With almost no access to the outside world, he wrote one of the most profound leadership documents of the twentieth century. What could he say to a nation that had neither selected him as a leader nor asked him to foster civil disobedience?

Chapter 7: Constitutional Crisis: Ford Assumes the Presidency and Pardons Nixon

As Watergate shredded the Nixon presidency, the nation plunged into turmoil. Spiro Agnew had been forced to resign the vice presidency in October 1973, and Gerald Ford was nominated by Nixon and approved by Congress as vice president in December. Nixon continued to stonewall Congress and the Watergate Special Prosecutor, who sought the tapes that would eventually force him to resign. In late July 1974, the House voted three articles of impeachment, and on August 9, Nixon resigned. How could Ford build legitimacy in his transition to the presidency, an office to which he had not even been elected? How could he heal the nation? Should he pardon Nixon, and, if it was the right thing to do, how could he explain it to a nation determined to seek justice—and revenge—through Nixon's trial and imprisonment?

These seven cases are by no means exhaustive. There are other leaders that could have been chosen. John Adams as president, avoiding war with France; Andrew Jackson confronting the nullification crisis; FDR giving the nation hope in the depths of the Great Depression; Harry Truman relieving the wildly popular Douglas MacArthur of command in the Korean War; Margaret Chase Smith confronting Senator Joe McCarthy on his un-American use of the investigate powers of his office—are just a few others we might have chosen. If this volume stimulates your desire to learn about statesmanship at those turning points as well, it will have accomplished even more than hoped.

What the Book Asks of You

The best way to learn from history and study leadership is to engage with both. Please be an active reader. Each of the first seven chapters will invite you to engage in four ways:

1. First, each turning point is set in its historical *context* to generate a sense of the tension and import of the moment. Read the first part of the chapter and project yourself into the situation. If you were the leader, what would be on your mind? Who do you want to lead and what are their interests? What would you want to accomplish? What would you say?
2. Second, read the words the leader used—the speech or document he or she gave at the turning point. These (or links to them) are in the appendices. As you read, think about the *challenge* that the speech or document faced. How well do you think the leader met that challenge? Answer this for yourself before you return to the chapter.
3. Third, read the chapter's analysis of the leader's words as they demonstrate her or his *character* and *competence*. This includes both a textual analysis and what actions the leader took to bring words to life. Ponder as well what distinctive traits and skills the leader brought to the problem he or she faced.
4. Finally, the chapter examines the historical impact—the *consequences*—of the leader's words and actions. Did the leader succeed or fall short, and how can we explain either outcome? What else might the leader have done?

Honoring a Debt

I am indebted to many for their support in preparing this book. This includes executives who were my students, especially at the Federal

Executive Institute where most of these leaders and their words were the subject of a series of short seminars. These remarkable career civil servants grappled with the texts and the history and taught me many of the lessons shared in these pages. I also want to thank my colleague, Declan Murphy, who pioneered these seminars with me and who helped me learn, from his experience as an Aspen Institute moderator, how to help executives discover their own insights in the texts.

I owe a debt to the staff of several research libraries and foundations as well as to colleagues who kindly reviewed my work. This includes Paul Barron, Director of Library and Archives and Jeffrey Kozak, Assistant Librarian and Archivist of the George C. Marshall Foundation; Stacy Davis, Archivist of the Gerald Ford Presidential Library; Ann Gordon, editor of The Papers of Elizabeth Cady Stanton and Susan B. Anthony at Rutgers University; Robert Maranto, 21st Century Chair in Leadership at the Department of Education Reform at the University of Arkansas; Jack Robertson, Foundation Librarian of the Thomas Jefferson Library at Kenwood; and Jim Sofka, Jefferson Scholar at the Thomas Jefferson Memorial Foundation. Their guidance stimulated my work and thinking, but any errors in either are of course entirely my own.

I owe a debt to my wife, Carol, for never losing faith that this book had something important to say and that it would have an audience to read it.

I owe a debt to my editors, Robyn Curtis and Matthew Kopel, whose enthusiastic support and gentle guidance helped me turn the dream of this book into reality. I would also like to thank the copyeditor from Newgen Knowledge Works, Geetha Ajay, for her diligent copyediting on my book and Abby Naqvi and Noelle Fair of Palgrave Macmillan for their diligent marketing efforts to help this book find its audience.

And I owe a debt to those who shaped the history, ideas, and ideals that form the core of this book—and to rising leaders whose acts of statesmanship, love of country, character and skills will become the subject for future books that honor their deeds.

TERRY NEWELL
Earlysville, Virginia

Washington Steps Down: The Farewell Address

Up before dawn on September 19, 1796, George Washington signed 147 ships' passes and half a dozen naval commissions, reviewed the rest of the day's paperwork, and then met with his new minister to France, Charles Cotesworth Pinckney, before climbing into his carriage to leave the capital. Anxious to get to Mount Vernon, he felt no need to wait to see the publication of what would become known as his Farewell Address.[1] The address, titled simply "To the People of the United States," appeared on page 2 of the *American Daily Advertiser.* Washington informed his "Friends and Fellow-Citizens" that on March 4, 1797, they would have a new president. The man who had seen them through the revolution, was part of the creation of a republican form of government, and who served two terms as "First Magistrate" had earned, nearing 65, an honorable retirement. He was determined to have it.

Reluctant President

Washington had always answered his nation's call—as Commander in Chief of the Continental Army in 1775, as president of the Constitutional Convention in 1787, and as its unanimously elected first president in 1789. Being a gentleman, duty and honor left him little choice. Yet he seldom did so without reservations. As when he served in uniform, he had accepted the presidency with diffidence, declined a salary, and asked only that his expenses be paid.[2]

He was not pleased to risk his reputation for an infant government, but declining seemed a worse choice. "Be assured," he had told wartime general and friend Benjamin Lincoln in October 1788, after 11 states had ratified the Constitution: "Every personal consideration conspires to rivet me...to retirement...nothing in this world can ever draw me from it, unless it be a *conviction* that the partiality of my Countrymen had made my services absolutely necessary, joined to a *fear* that my refusal might induce a belief that I preferred the conservation of my own reputation and private ease, to the good of my Country."[3] At 57, with a family history of men who died early, Washington was sensible of his own mortality but cared more about his character.

As in commanding the army, when he became president he entered a position he had to define. "I walk on untrodden ground. There is scarcely any part of my conduct which may not hereafter be drawn into precedent," Washington had written.[4] Being a nationalist, he had set about forming a nation. From the selection of his cabinet (e.g. Alexander Hamilton from New York for Treasury, Thomas Jefferson from Virginia for State, Henry Knox from Massachusetts for Secretary of War) to his travels (a New England tour followed by a southern tour) to his efforts to tie the frontier West to the more established East, Washington had sought to unify the nation, not just his cabinet. The "united States" in the Declaration of Independence would not for quite some time be the "United States."

His desired cabinet unity lasted about a year. When Hamilton proposed that the national government assume state war debts, Jefferson and James Madison accommodated him in exchange for support to locate the national capital on the Potomac River (Jefferson would later claim he was "duped"). But in late 1790, when Hamilton proposed the creation of a "Bank of the United States" to service the debt and make loans for major projects, Jefferson and Madison feared an everstrengthening, "monocratic" national government. Charging that the Constitution contained no enumerated power to charter a bank, they urged a Washington veto. Hamilton convinced Washington that a veto would render the national government impotent to meet future needs, and a week after Washington signed the bill, Jefferson quietly took steps to launch an opposition newspaper.

Hamilton responded in kind, leading a distraught Washington to plead with his secretaries for civility amid attacks that were "harrowing and tearing our vitals."[5] Used to being respected if not revered, by 1792 Washington had had enough. On May 5, he asked to see Madison, a trusted confidant, Constitutional architect, and drafter of previous presidential messages, for advice on how and when to tell the public he would not serve a second term. On May 20, he asked Madison's help in drafting a "plain and modest" valedictory. According to Madison's account, the president "found himself in the decline of life" and "that it was evident...that a spirit of party in Government was becoming a fresh source of difficulty."[6]

Madison delivered a draft but pleaded with Washington to reconsider. Jefferson chimed in, telling the president that only he could prevent "violence or secession" and that "North and South will hang together, if they have you to hang on"[7] Hamilton agreed, appealing to Washington's honor by telling him that retirement would be seen as a blow "critically hazardous to your own reputation."[8] Torn between personal yearning and public duty, Washington did nothing, accepting unanimous election again by the Electoral College on February 13, 1793.

His Second Inaugural, on March 4, 1793, is still the shortest on record. Perhaps he had little more to say. Perhaps he preferred republican simplicity. Perhaps he was in no mood to celebrate. In 135 words, he acknowledged his election and that he would be held accountable if he failed. On March 17, he learned that Louis XVI had been executed by Parisian revolutionaries, an early signal that his second term would live out his worst fears.

Pressed by Jeffersonian Republicans to side with wartime ally France and Hamiltonian Federalists to side with commercial partner England, arguments that held more peril when those two nations resumed fighting each other on the high seas, Washington issued a formal proclamation of neutrality in 1793 to keep America out of a war it was not prepared to fight. The British ignored it, and the French sent an ambassador bent on establishing "Democratic Societies" partial to France among the American people and outfitting American ships as privateers. In Washington's mind, these societies fomented disunion, including a revolt of western Pennsylvania farmers against Hamilton's excise tax on liquor, requiring an armed force to put down the "Whiskey Rebellion" in October 1794.

In a bid to buy time and avert war, Washington sent Supreme Court Chief Justice John Jay to England. Jay's treaty pleased no one. While it secured Britain's agreement to leave frontier posts, which it still occupied in violation of the Treaty of Paris ending the Revolutionary War, it seemed to accomplish little else. Washington was pilloried in the Republican press, but he signed the treaty. It had the singular advantage of ending the threat of a second war with

England. Yet his letter to Jefferson of July 6, 1796, showed the level of his frustration:

> I had no conception that Parties would, or even could go, the length I have been witness to; nor did I believe until lately, that...while I was using my utmost exertions to establish a national character of our own, independent, as far as our obligations, and justice would permit, of every nation of the earth; and wished, by steering a steady course, to preserve this Country from the horrors of a desolating war, that I should be accused of being the enemy of one Nation, and subject to the influence of another; and to prove it, that every action of my administration would be tortured, and the grossest, and most insidious misrepresentations of them be made...and that too in such exaggerated and indecent terms as could scarcely be applied to a Nero; a notorious defaulter; or even to a common pickpocket.

With Jefferson and Hamilton having by then left the cabinet, to take up their battles unhindered by national office, with his reputation suffering, with his character impugned, with flagging energy after more than four decades of public service, Washington retrieved Madison's 1792 draft and set out again to prepare a parting address.

The United States under the Constitution was only eight years old. If 1792 had been a dangerous time to leave the presidency, 1796 was no better. There had never been a transfer of power, and many wondered if a peaceful transition was possible in a world where violence most often attended a change in rulers. The presidential election following his departure would pit the Federalist Adams against the Republican Jefferson, representing dramatically different views of the future of America—manufacturing vs. agrarian, national vs. state sovereignty, the spirit of '87 vs. the spirit of '76. The fledgling United States lacked a credible army and navy. It could neither defend itself against foreign dangers nor with certainty counter domestic threats of secession. It was not an auspicious moment for the one man who could unify America to step down, but as Washington told John Jay on May 8, "nothing short of events of such imperious circumstances" that "might render a retreat dishonorable" would prevent him from leaving office.[9]

Drafting the Address

In a move politically deft (since the Republican, Madison, had drafted the 1792 version) and fitting with his trust and perhaps increasing agreement with (the Federalist) Hamilton, Washington added some ideas, which he described as "ardent wishes of my heart," to the former's work and sent all of it to Hamilton on May 15, 1796, with a request for his thoughts. Washington made clear that, for his valedictory, he wanted "the whole to appear in a plain stile...and be handed to the public in an honest;—unaffected;—simple garb."[10]

Washington lacked Jefferson's felicity of expression, and this may have led him to rely on trusted aides for help in crafting major state papers. Unlike his two stepbrothers and his father, he was not educated in England, a goal that was lost when his father died when Washington was only 11.[11] Washington was mostly self-taught, with but a few months of tutoring in subjects such as geography, composition, and math.[12] Years later, the biting realist John Adams would say of him "[T]hat he was too illiterate, unlearned, unread for his station and reputation is...past dispute"[13]

Washington was anxious to receive Hamilton's reworked draft, which the latter sent him on July 30. Always deferential to his former military as well as civilian chief, Hamilton urged the president to use it as he wished. Hamilton had stayed faithful to Washington's sentiments but had enhanced the content, expression, and structure of the message.

On August 10, Washington wrote to Hamilton that he found "the Sentiments therein contained...extremely just & such as ought to be inculcated."[14] On September 1, he wrote to Hamilton expressing a desire to include a proposal for a unifying, national university where youth from all parts of the nation might come together to learn. Hamilton replied that he thought such detail more appropriate for Washington's final report to Congress in December but that he would add a general statement supportive of education. While he never did, Washington included such a passage in the final address that he prepared, in his own hand, in early September.[15]

On September 15, he shared his address with confidants in his cabinet and requested a meeting with David Claypoole, editor of the *American Daily Advertiser*. Claypoole confirmed he could print the address the following Monday. He sent a proof to Washington and after that "two different Revises, to be examined by the President; who made but few alterations from the original, except in punctuation, in which he was very minute."[16]

Thus satisfied, Washington prepared to depart. The nation would now have to prepare for his departure as well.

Washington's Intent

By 1796, Washington already had a history of farewells. In this sense, the Farewell Address is neither remarkable nor surprising. But his reasons for this message offer a window on his leadership. Washington believed it his duty to leave a legacy. His last *Circular Letter* to state executives in 1783, as he left command of the Continental Army, had asked that they share his sentiments with their legislatures "as the Legacy of One, who has ardently wished, on all occasions, to be useful to his Country, and who, even in the shade of Retirement, will not fail to implore the divine benediction upon it."[17]

As much as he wished to provide a legacy, Washington also believed Americans needed to hear one. Writing to Hamilton on May 8, 1796, he had said that: "I am *sure* the mass of Citizens in these United States *mean well*—and I firmly believe they will always *act well,* whenever they can obtain a right understanding of matters," but then went on to add that political passions made a right understanding difficult. The address was designed to help them see things correctly.

For Washington, duty was always connected to reputation. So an address was needed, as he had told Hamilton a week later when he sent him his draft, "to blunt, if it does not turn aside, some of the shafts which it may be presumed will be aimed at my enunciation of this event;—among which—conviction of fallen popularity, and despair of being re-elected, will be leveled at me with dexterity & keenness."[18]

Finally, as historians Matthew Spalding and Patrick Garrity have noted, "Washington...was the sole spokesperson for the people as a whole and the official representative of the nation for the rest of the world...His words and deeds would be considered a timeless legacy to his country and the supports of republican government everywhere."[19]

Given Washington's intent, we can examine his leadership in the Farewell Address from two vantage points. The first is what he set out to say and how he did so. The second is what his words reveal about leadership.

The Focus and Structure of the Address

Washington's chief concern, his core message, is the critical need for national union. In war and peace, Washington devoted his professional life to that idea. He intended that to be his legacy, however fragile union still was.

Unlike most of the founders, Washington had spent eight years in the field. This gave him a national perspective that many who spent the war closer to home lacked. He came to think like a continental as he practiced national and international politics. The new Constitution offered a way to strengthen national ties among the states, but few took for granted that this would be the natural result. Individual states jealously guarded their sovereignty. Without a stronger union, republican government could well founder.

To limit the message's contribution to political divisiveness, Washington offered no specific policy or programmatic proposals. He was concerned with legacy, not legislation. He refused to name political parties, people, issues, or even nations in an effort to ensure his advice would be judged against the cool standard of reason, not the hot passion of factions. Washington was intent on timely advice encased in timeless truths.

His testament has a clear, logical structure, and we can begin to understand the address—and its author—by seeing the flow of his argument.[20] He began by informing the reader that he would not serve another term (the presenting reason for the statement). The timing of the address was important—had he waited much longer, his silence might have led to his election for another term, as it had in 1792. He then prefaced most of the major topics of the address: union, the Constitution, and the necessity for sound administration, wisdom, and virtue. He did not address these topics immediately; there was something more important to do first.

Humility and the Obligations of Citizens

The opening of the address demonstrates Washington's humility— not uncommon for speakers of the day and especially typical of him. When Congress unanimously elected Washington on June 15, 1775, to take command of a Continental Army that existed in name only, he confessed his lack of qualifications. Perhaps this was also a hedge against defeat, but it would typify him even after victory. He warned Congress that day: "But, lest some unlucky event should happen unfavorable to my reputation, I beg it may be remembered by every gentleman in the room that I this day declare with utmost sincerity that I do not think myself equal to the command."[21]

At the same time, he had told Martha that: "It was utterly out of my power to refuse this appointment, without exposing my character to such censures, as would have reflected dishonour upon myself."[22] Humility was joined to duty. The early lines of the address return to these traits. His words are an announcement but also a thoughtful, almost pleading appeal for understanding and approbation. He had his character to preserve.

Washington wanted it clear that his parting message was driven by patriotism, not self-interest: "The acceptance of, and continuance hitherto in, the office to which your suffrages have twice called me have been a uniform sacrifice of inclination to the opinion of duty and to a deference for what appeared to be your desire." So he would "recommend to your frequent review, some sentiments...offered to you with the more freedom, as you can only see in them the disinterested warnings of a parting friend, who can possibly have no personal motive to bias his counsel." That he had earned the right to step down and that his words would be without personal agenda were central to the receptivity to his message.

Perhaps less central and more subtle was Washington's lesson on citizenship. If his duty was to serve, to answer the call of his nation, and if he needed the firmest of justifications to lay down the mantle of responsibility, what might this imply is the duty of others? It is, after all, a "citizen" who will next "administer the executive government." There is a "relation which binds a dutiful citizen to his country." Washington made "a uniform sacrifice of inclination to the opinion of duty." Might not others be expected to do the same—by both acknowledging that he has earned the right to retire and that others are obligated now to step forward as a requirement of being citizens?

"Here, perhaps, I ought to stop" signals the end of the section based on Madison's 1792 draft. Of course he has no intention of stopping. What follows is the first of six major topical sections. The order proceeds from domestic to foreign affairs, and he begins with the central, integrating message.

Union

"The unity of government...is a main pillar in the edifice of your real independence," Washington said. "The immense value of your national union to your collective and individual happiness" makes it the "palladium of your political safety and prosperity." Washington had seen how disunity among the states (concerned more with their own defense than the needs of the Continental Army) nearly led to failure in the field. In the immediate postwar period, he had seen the impotent nation under the Articles of Confederation laughed at in the courts of Europe—and sometimes ignored by its own people. In eight years as president, he had seen disunity encourage French and English depredations on the high seas. Fearing the intensification of already-bitter partisanship, he warned against anything that would "enfeeble the sacred ties" of union. For Washington, union was not a by-product or companion of liberty but a precondition. By raising national unity to a *sacred* obligation, he sought to cement an essential attachment—to a civic religion for a republican government.

If union could not be maintained, nothing else Washington had to say would matter. To complement his opening, he thus cited two further arguments. First, citizens with "slight shades of difference" shared "the same religion, manners, habits, and political principles." They shared "a common country...that has a right to concentrate your affections." These cultural and emotional ties Washington called the "inducement of sympathy." He wanted the people to think of themselves first as Americans.

He knew, however, that they would be guided by self-interest more than by filial affection. Thus, in an argument as long as the entire 1792 draft, he reminded his audience that the sections of the nation gained much from each other as each contributed to the other's economic development and common security. They would all be safer because they "cannot fail to find in the united mass of means and efforts greater strength, greater resource, proportionably greater security from external danger."

Constitution

Washington turned next to the form of union the nation had chosen and, in strong and demanding language, declared support of the Constitution, "the offspring of our own choice," "sacredly obligatory upon all."

As Commander in Chief, Washington made no secret of his belief that the United States, under the Articles, lacked unifying strength. States issued their own currencies and erected trade barriers against neighbors. James Madison, Alexander Hamilton, and others, convinced of the need for a stronger national government, had engineered the convention in Philadelphia in May 1787, which Washington reluctantly agreed to attend (he feared the loss of reputation if the convention failed, attending only when convinced his reputation would suffer more if failure was attributed to his absence).

Silent through most of the proceedings, a skill that increased his authority when he spoke, Washington nevertheless played a powerful role. After the convention, he first held the view that he should say nothing to support ratification, lest it look like he was concerned with gaining power. In time, he became more active, leading James Monroe to say in a letter to Jefferson: "Be assured, his influence carried this government."[23]

Yet the American founding was not on solid ground. Americans did not identify with the national government in a distant capital literally still under construction on the banks of the Potomac. Other than Washington himself, the Constitution was the sole embodiment of the potential of "a more perfect Union." Yet many had opposed its ratification. Fidelity to it was by no means the given it is today. Accordingly, Washington demanded "*Respect* for its authority, *compliance* with its laws, *acquiescence* in its measures" (emphasis added). He reminded citizens that they chose the government and now "the *duty* of every individual" is "to *obey*" (emphasis added). If 1776 had overturned one government, Washington believed that 1787 had established the next. The man who led a revolution declared that now it must end.

Controlling Factions and Parties

Sympathy, interest, and the Constitution are major centripetal forces. Countering them were the centrifugal forces of faction and party. As their leader, he felt impelled to warn of this danger. A party, for Washington, was antirepublican: "often a small but artful and enterprising minority" whose triumph could "make the public administration the mirror of ill-concerted and incongruous projects of faction." The spirit of party was, Washington admits, "inseparable from our nature," yet uncontrolled it would wreak havoc that will "incline the minds of men to seek security and repose in the absolute power of an individual." It is "A fire not to be quenched" and thus "demands a uniform vigilance to prevent its bursting into a flame." Washington was well aware of world history, where internal division fueled calls for strength, order, and absolute power in a single individual—a process just repeated in the French Revolution.

Cautious Public Administration

In two sections, slightly separated, Washington next expressed his concern with the reciprocal obligations of rulers and ruled in the daily administration of public affairs. Honored, these obligations would help

check the spirit of party and the concentration of power. He coun-
seled public officials to "confine themselves within their respective
constitutional spheres" as he had done. Washington, for example,
saw the executive veto justifiable only when an act of Congress was
unconstitutional—not to be used just because he disagreed with
Congressional policy. He reminded his readers as well that there was
a process to amend the Constitution, making "usurpation" inexcus-
able. It was time for evolutionary, not revolutionary change.

In a section seemingly added by Hamilton, Washington also
described the necessity to "cherish public credit" and reminded both
rulers and ruled that they had an obligation to raise and pay taxes
to meet inevitable needs, forestall greater expenditures later, and to
avoid "ungenerously throwing upon posterity the burden we ourselves
ought to bear."

Virtue and Morality

Washington ended the domestic section of the address with the final
bulwark for union: "religion and morality are indispensable supports." Sympathy and interest, the Constitution, and a cautious public
administration could bolster union from the outside in. But they were
unlikely without a force operating from the inside out. All his previous admonitions would mean little unless citizens were raised with
"these firmest props." In his view, the government dared not give a
blind eye to the virtues of its people. Unlike Jefferson, Washington
had no qualms in saying that national morality could not "prevail in
exclusion of religious principle."

While this section of the address is short and often overlooked, it
demonstrates the careful observations Washington had made about
human nature and the importance of public character to the success
of republican government.

But character must be assisted by right understanding. Washington's
plea to promote "institutions for the general diffusion of knowledge"
was as specific as he would get about his cherished aim for a national
university. Hamilton's advice to avoid specifics would be followed and
thus lends the call for education to inform public opinion a broader
and more lasting tone.

Foreign Affairs

Washington reserved the last third of the address for foreign affairs.
The placement is deliberate. Without union, the states would be at the

mercy of foreign powers. Still further, since foreign affairs was so divisive in itself, to have raised it earlier in the address may have invited ignoring all of the arguments for union.

Affairs with other nations should be guided by duty and interest, Washington insisted. Mindful of pro-British and pro-French factions, he argued for a neutral foreign policy to buy the young nation time until "the period... not far off when we may defy material injury from external annoyance." But that period was not yet at hand, and so the president advised the nation to "steer clear of permanent alliances."

Washington was not urging isolationism. Indeed, he argued both for "good faith and justice" to all nations in honoring commitments already made, and he supported commercial treaties. He saw such economic arrangements (somewhat naively for the relatively impotent and still-agrarian United States) as a lever to control other nations. It was political treaties that might embroil the nation in the foreign wars that Washington was trying to prevent, as he urged his countrymen to have "as little political connection as possible" with the nations of Europe.

Reflecting on His Legacy

Concluding, Washington acknowledged the tentativeness of his legacy: "I dare not hope they [his counsels] will make the strong and lasting impression I could wish; that they will control the usual current of the passions, or prevent our nation from running the course which has hitherto marked the destiny of nations." Ending with the same characteristic humility with which he began, he wrote in the manner of a father hoping his children would prove him wrong. Washington thus acknowledged the limits of his leadership and ended his farewell.

The Farewell Address and the Tasks of Leadership

Aside from its substantive message, the Farewell Address can be seen as an exercise in leadership.

Offering a Leadership Philosophy

The address stands as an "Executive Summary" of Washington's leadership philosophy, even though he was, at heart, a man of practical affairs, a student in the world of experience not theory.

One could argue, of course, that there was nothing really new in the address. Much of what he said, he had said before. His concern for a strong union was well known, for example. In his 1783 *Circular Address*, he had championed the need to "cultivate a spirit of subordination and obedience to Government, to entertain a brotherly affection for one another." Indeed, that circular covered much of the territory he covers in 1796. In regard to foreign affairs, writing to Gouverneur Morris in December 1795, he had made clear that "My policy has been...to be on friendly terms with, but independent of, all the nations of the earth" and added "for sure I am, if this country is preserved in tranquility twenty years longer, it may bid defiance, in a just cause, to any power whatever."[24] Commenting on aid from France during the revolution, he made clear that "It is a maxim founded in the universal experience of mankind, that no nation is to be trusted further than is bound by its interest."[25]

Yet in the address, Washington offers a nearly *comprehensive* statement of his core values and principles, something he had done in only separate pieces before. In presenting this in one place, in a public forum, at a time designed to draw maximum attention and offered with no personal agenda, he provides both testimony and a testament to core beliefs essential for a republican nation. If leaders have a responsibility to their institutions beyond their own tenure, and Washington believed he did, articulating a leadership philosophy is essential work. Having shared major points in private correspondence was not enough. Washington understood the importance of communicating—not just having—a leadership philosophy.

Seeing Clearly

Having a credible leadership philosophy depends on one's ability to see the world clearly. The address is nothing if not a demonstration of Washington's insightful reading of four decades of the American experience.

Washington demonstrated that capacity early in his career, not because he was unerring but because he learned from mistakes in the world of action not books. At 20, as historian Joseph Ellis notes, "[I]nstead of going to college, Washington went to war."[26] It was in the field, not in the classroom, that Washington came to understand human behavior and an emerging America.

As a young provincial officer, he was given to impetuousness—he preferred to attack. As his biographer, James Thomas Flexner, noted: "Although, in moments of reflection conscious of his inadequacies, in action he could be rash, brash, impolitic, over-self-confident. He made dreadful mistakes." Yet he learned, Flexner concludes: "As his character and his world view expanded, more meanings became clear to him. He accurately defined his failures and worked out the reasons why he had failed."[27]

As Commander in Chief of the Continental Army, Washington lost more battles than he won. Yet amid dying men at Valley Forge, the lessons of experience became clear. He realized he could not win a war with militia alone—they were hard to train and their enlistments too short. He saw that he could not win open battles against British regulars, and he understood the need for officers trained and loyal to the nation not just their state. He might not be able to win the war, he decided, but he could avoid losing it—if he could keep his army in the field. Since he could not count on the Continental Congress to supply his needs—they lacked the power to tax or enforce their requests of the states—he realized he needed the support of the local population. This he could gain only by refraining from taking supplies at gunpoint as the British did. Finally, he learned that his reputation and bearing were crucial. As the embodiment of the nation, he must project steadfastness and authority.

Indeed, the entire address is a reflection on the lessons of Washington's experience and on their importance in guiding behavior. Early on, he told his audience that his sentiments "are the result of much reflection, of no inconsiderable observation." In discussing the importance of union, after raising the question about whether the national government could "embrace so large a sphere," he answered his own question by saying: "Let experience solve it. To listen to mere speculation in such a case were criminal." Yet again, "reason and experience both forbid us to expect that national morality can prevail in the exclusion of religious principle." If Jefferson saw the world as he hoped it could be, Washington saw the world as it was. In Aristotle's terms, he had "practical wisdom," which was superior to theoretical wisdom—and more useful.

Part of learning from experience was a willingness to experiment, and Washington used that phrase frequently to refer to America's effort at self-government. "It is well worth a fair and full experiment," he suggested. Indeed, the address can be viewed as Washington's effort to extract the lessons from the American experiment.

Embodying the Message

A leadership philosophy anchored in experience but unmatched by admirable behavior is no more useful than a field manual is to troops without a respected officer to lead them. Leaders must embody their legacy, and this depends as much on *who* they are as on *what* they accomplish. The most powerful legacies come from leaders we admire for their character as well as their achievements. Washington was always conscious of modeling his leadership ideal.

As a young militia officer, he was a taskmaster yet earned the love of his men even in defeat. He asked nothing that he would not do. He put their needs at the forefront of his leadership. He protested to Virginia royal governor Dinwiddie that his colonial regiment deserved the same pay as British regulars, and he insisted on breaking with British tradition by basing promotions on merit.[28] One of his men wrote of him that: "Your steady adherence to impartial justice, your quick discernment and invariable regard to merit...first heightened our natural emulation and desire to excel."[29]

As Commander in Chief of the Continental Army, he endured the hardships of long campaigns and winter encampments, staying in the field when he could easily have spent winters at Mount Vernon. After Yorktown, he stayed in the field for two years, mostly without pay, until a treaty with Great Britain was executed. In May 1782, when one of his officers suggested he accept the mantle of king, he rebuked him: "I must view with abhorrence and reprehend with severity" an idea that is "big with the greatest mischiefs that can befall my country."[30]

Embodying leadership meant as well the need to be seen as a selfless servant. This shows up in a full paragraph he struck out near the end of the text when preparing it for printing. Among the lines removed were: "May I, without the appearance of affectation, say that the fortune with which I came into office is not bettered otherwise than by that improvement in the value of property, which the quick progress & uncommon prosperity of our country have produced?" Washington wanted to make sure the nation knew he did not personally profit from public service, but he took the lines out because he cared more about what saying them would say about him. His marginal note explaining the deletion said: "This paragraph may have the appearance of self distrust and mere vanity."[31]

The fact that he gave up power is the greatest embodiment of his leadership legacy. He had modeled this when he resigned his

Revolutionary War commission. Writing from London in 1784, the American painter John Trumbull would say that Washington's resignation "excites the astonishment and admiration of this part of the world. Tis a Conduct so novel, so unconceivable to People, who, far from giving up powers they possess, are willing to convulse the empire to acquire more." And Jefferson noted that same year that "the moderation and virtue of a single character...probably prevented this revolution from being closed, as most others have been, by a subversion of that liberty it was intended to establish."[32]

In stepping down, Washington modeled Cincinnatus, the Roman general who gave up command to return to his farm. Conscious of every act as a precedent, Washington established one that would last for nearly 150 years and that would ultimately be enshrined in the Twenty-Second Amendment.[33]

Printing the Farewell Address is also a powerful leadership act. He does not deliver a speech to Congress or any public gathering. He delivers the words on the inside page of a newspaper. His ability to use what John Adams once called the "gift of silence" was a behavior that he had demonstrated before. As a delegate to the First Continental Congress, Washington said little but was noticed, leading Patrick Henry to say of him that "if you speak of solid information and sound judgment, Colonel Washington is by far the greatest man on the floor."[34]

Indeed, Washington understood that public speaking was not his strength and that silence could be used as a leadership tool. Years later, writing to his nephew, he would advise him to: "Speak seldom, but to important subjects...and make yourself master of the subject. Never exceed a decent warmth, and submit your sentiments with diffidence."[35] Knowing this, Washington delivered his address in the mode most calculated to lend it weight.

The Language of Leadership

"With words we govern men," Disraeli said, and the address demonstrates the powerful use of language.[36] While not a master wordsmith, Washington certainly understood the importance of word choice. This explains, in part, both the various drafts and the extent to which he labored over the final version.

One major thread of the address illustrates the point. A believer in the power of reason, Washington nevertheless appealed strongly to the emotions to keep the union intact. Early on, he cited the importance of "your union and brotherly affection" and shortly thereafter that: "Interwoven as is the love of liberty with every ligament of your hearts, no recommendation of mine is necessary to fortify or confirm the attachment." Arguing further for the importance of union, Washington tells Americans that they "should cherish a cordial, habitual and immovable attachment to it" and that the "country has a right to concentrate your affections." This is the "inducement of sympathy" that must hold them together. Additional use of such terms as "fraternal affection," "brethren," and "intimate union" illustrate that Washington intended words to represent and help strengthen the interpersonal bonds of union. A leader must appeal to the heart as well as the head. As Washington said to Secretary of War Henry Knox in 1787, "the people must *feel* before they will *see*."[37]

Washington also used the power of the question. While much of the address is declarative—Washington had advice to give—he also asked the audience to think. Nothing does this better than a powerful question. Perhaps the most powerful one, historian Matthew Spalding suggests, is that posed by the address itself: can the people of the United States govern themselves, or are they destined to destroy the republican experiment and achieve the "ruins of liberty"?[38]

Washington also asked rhetorical questions. When arguing the importance of union, even for so large a geographic entity as the new United States, Washington recalled the question Madison had raised in Federalist #10: "Is there a doubt whether a common government can embrace so large a sphere?" When extolling the importance of religion to fostering virtue in citizens, Washington asked: "Where is the security for property, for reputation, for life, if the sense of religious obligation desert the oaths which are the instruments of investigation in courts of justice?" And in urging the nation to base foreign policy on its own interests, Washington asked several questions, whose power increased by their rapid succession: "Why forego the advantages of so peculiar a situation? Why quit our own to stand upon foreign ground? Why, by interweaving our destiny with that of any part of Europe, entangle our peace and prosperity in the toils of European ambition, rivalship, interest, humor or caprice?"

A Leader's View of Human Nature

Washington's experiences also served as a classroom for lessons about human nature. Leaders always have a "theory" about human nature, even if they do not articulate it. Jefferson, for example, based his view of limited government on the belief that each person had a "moral sense"—people would mostly do right and thus government could mostly do little. Adams harbored less pleasant assumptions and feared "mob" rule might emerge if democracy were unleashed. Washington, neither philosopher nor lawyer, fell in between, and this more balanced view of human nature is evident in the address.

He took pains to draw on the best in human nature (as we have seen from his appeal to fraternal affection, sympathy, and attachment). Yet he knew the dark side: "This spirit," [of party] "unfortunately, is inseparable from our nature, having its root in the strongest passions of the human mind." The Farewell Address, as a reflection on human nature, concluded that the best in us can control the worst in us if the core principles of the republican experiment are learned and practiced. As Washington told John Jay, "I am *sure* the mass of Citizens in these United States *mean well*—and I firmly believe they will always *act well*, whenever they can obtain a right understanding of matters"(emphasis in original)[39] The address aimed to foster that "right understanding."

Mentoring the Next Generation of Leaders

Washington understood that his life was entering its final phase (he would die less than three years later) and that the nation might enter a new century without his active guidance. In part, he knew, delegation was destiny. He delegated to trusted officers during the war, some of whom had far more battlefield success than he did. He assembled perhaps the strongest cabinet in presidential history. And, in leaving the presidency, he would have to delegate again.

Effective delegation in the address comes from the attention he gave to articulating core values and beliefs. You can't be there to tell people how to act, but if they are instilled with what in modern military terms we call "Commander's Intent," they are empowered to lead well. Though Washington began the address with "I" language, he shifted mostly to "you" language as he guided followers to assume the responsibility for leadership since he must soon be consigned "to the mansions of rest."

Leadership through Story

Effective leaders are powerful storytellers. The best leadership stories paint a vivid picture of a desired future and engage followers in achieving it. Washington had three stories to tell.

One was about himself, his obligation to serve, his best efforts despite a "fallible judgment," and his compelling—yet certainly acceptable—decision to return to private life. Washington knew he was the progenitor of a hoped-for race of republican leaders, so his opening to the address traced that story. He closed with it as well, reminding his followers that "after forty five years of my life dedicated to its service with an upright zeal, the faults of incompetent abilities will be consigned to oblivion."

The two remaining stories, in the core of the address, offer two visions of the future. They recall that the biblical Moses, who brought his people to the Promised Land, will not enter it, and of course cannot guarantee they will live up to the promise.

These two stories are the dream and the nightmare,[40] and which story prevails will depend on the virtue of the people. The dream is captured early in the address, as Washington's wish:

> [T]hat heaven may continue to you the choicest tokens of its beneficence; that your union and brotherly affection may be perpetual; that the free Constitution, which is the work of your hands, may be sacredly maintained; that its administration in every department may be stamped with wisdom and virtue; that, in fine, the happiness of the people of these States, under the auspices of liberty, may be made complete.

But opposed to this is a darker vision if virtue and morality do not underlie American behavior:

> All obstructions...serve to organize faction, to give it an artificial and extraordinary force; to put, in the place of the delegated will of the nation the will of a party, often a small but artful and enterprising minority of the community; and, according to the alternate triumphs of different parties, to make the public administration the mirror of the ill-concerted and incongruous projects of faction...they are likely, in the course of time and things, to become potent engines, by which cunning, ambitious, and unprincipled men will be enabled to subvert the power of the people and to usurp for themselves the reins of government.

Whether Washington was conscious of his role as storyteller is debatable. That he saw two contrasting futures for the United States is not. In the *Circular Address of 1783*, he had already etched these options in prophetic language:

> At this auspicious period, the United States came into existence as a Nation, and if their Citizens should not be completely free and happy,

the fault will be intirely [sic] their own...This is the time of their political probation, this is the moment when the eyes of the whole World are turned upon them, this is the moment to establish or ruin their national Character forever...it is yet to be decided, whether the Revolution must ultimately be considered as a blessing or a curse: a blessing or a curse, not to the present age alone, for with our fate will the destiny of unborn Millions be involved.[41]

The Obligations of Followers

Washington accepted that leadership is a relationship that depends on leaders and led playing their roles well. He had a lot to say about the leader-follower relationship, especially in the first half of the address.

The nation, Washington believed, required what in our time Robert Greenleaf calls "servant-leaders"—delegates guided by obligations to followers.[42] That is why Washington felt impelled to inform his audience of his decision to leave and begged them to acknowledge that he had their best interests at heart. He acknowledged that he owed them much: "[M]y feelings do not permit me to suspend the deep acknowledgment of that debt of gratitude which I owe to my beloved country for the many honors it has conferred upon me; still more for the steadfast confidence with which it has supported me." A leader was called to duty and served honorably. That was *his* job.

But followers also had obligations—*their* job. They must cherish union, constrain self-interest, obey the Constitution and laws, and let reason guide their public affairs. They were not just people; they were citizens. His salutation to "Friends and Fellow-Citizens," suggested both a familial and a formal connection. As citizens, they had reciprocal obligations. In our modern context, the duties of citizens are often lost in our tendency to treat Americans as customers of government, whose only duties are to vote and pay taxes.

The tasks of leadership are nearly impossible unless leaders and followers enact their roles, and so the address is not just a set of guidelines on how to *act* in specific situations but a set of traits on how to *be* a citizen and a leader in a republican government. Given the nation's youth, and the conflicting passions and attachments of the people, Washington saw the need to establish habits conducive to liberty. Virtue, as Aristotle said, comes from the habitual practice of right behavior. The Farewell Address was Washington's primer on republican virtue.

Spalding and Garrity make this point excellently in *A Sacred Union of Citizens*. "For Washington," they note, "there was an inseparable relationship between individual character or virtue and the national character."[43] "The first transactions of a nation, like those of an individual upon his entrance into life make the deepest impression, and are to form the leading traits in its character," Washington had written to Congressmen John Armstrong in 1788.[44] Washington was intent on establishing a national character, and that required building character in its people. This may seem quaint today, but developing the character of the next generation of leaders and followers is a task that is ignored at great risk, as any number of public and private sector ethical scandals demonstrate.

Finally, the address demonstrated the need for moral courage. Washington was interested in securing his reputation, but he was also risking it one last time. As historian Roland Usher observed: "For us who have been accustomed to think of the Farewell Address as delivered to a patriotic and affectionate nation, eager to receive from its most honored and revered statesman his parting words of counsel, it is a shock to learn that Washington meant it to be his justification before posterity for a policy which had been roundly abused and more generally disapproved by his contemporaries than any other ever initiated by an American statesman."[45] While Usher's tone may be a bit hyperbolic and while Washington had other aims that went beyond self-justification, there is no question that he could have simply left office without an attempt to affect the future. As it was, and as he knew would be the case, the address had mixed results.

The Impact of the Farewell Address

Washington was interested in how his address was received, and it did not take long to find out.[46] Predictably, initial reactions followed partisan lines. His Secretary of War, James McHenry, wrote to him from Philadelphia on September 25 that he had complied "with your request" to observe reactions and that "Your address on the first day of its publication, drew from friends of government, through every part of the City, the strongest expressions of sensibility."[47] On September 30, Washington received the first of a flock of tributes from citizens from various communities, and on October 27, the Vermont legislature sent him an engrossed address that said, in part:

> We receive your address to your fellow citizens, as expressive of the highest zeal for their prosperity, and containing the best advice to ensure its continuance...We shall recollect you with filial affection— your advice as an inestimable legacy.[48]

Daniel Webster stated that the address "was full of truths important at all times."[49]

It was hard to tell, in some cases, whether tributes were honoring the man or the message—though an effective legacy will blur this distinction. On the day after the address first appeared, *Gale's Independent Gazetteer* of Philadelphia ran an editorial saying:

> However the spirit of Party may have depreciated the conduct of President Washington on one hand, or exalted it above the failings of humanity on the other, all parties must acknowledge that to have fought and conquered for his country in War, to have been twice elected to the Presidency by the almost unanimous voice of his country in Peace—and to know the precise moment to retire with dignity, are advantages which few men could so honorably (have) availed themselves of as Mr. Washington.[50]

Not all were so kind. As Victor Hugo Paltsits notes in his extensive collection of documentation on the address, "some of the anti-administration newspapers were as silent as a sphinx—they did not even damn Washington with a feint of praise; others would not condescend so much as to reprint editorials or other comment favorable to him."[51]

Others were not silent. A newspaper in South Carolina printed "A Humble Address to George I, Perpetual Dictator of the U.S."[52] One reviewer described the address as "the loathings of a sick mind"[53] while the *Boston Gazette* and the *Weekly Republican Journal* carried an editorial, under the signature "Watchman," that said, in part:

> The President in his Address to the People upon Government, frequently notices the Necessity of obeying the Rulers, but does not even hint that Rulers have no right, as such, to speculate upon the Rights and Property of the PEOPLE.—But this has been almost an exclusive Right for eight Years past, and executed by means of a magic Charm attached to a Name.[54]

James Madison, writing to James Monroe, said the "the valedictory address of the president...shews that he [is] compleatly in the snares of the British faction."[55] Twelve members of the House of Representatives, young freshman Republican Andrew Jackson among them, refused to sign a formal reply praising Washington as "firm, wise, and patriotic."[56]

The *American Telegraph & Fairfield County Gazette* of Newfield, Connecticut, signaled that Washington's hope for diminished party animosity was not likely:

> The Electioneering campaign will undoubtedly be a busy, if not a bloody one. The party papers have already entered the field, and much ink will probably be shed in praising certain favorites, and in blackening the character of their rivals. We could heartily wish....that a man divested of prejudices, like our present Chief Magistrate, might be chosen. But alas! Where can that man be found?[57]

The ensuing campaign suggested that such a man could not be found. John Adams, who had faithfully served Washington for two terms as vice president, garnered 71 electoral votes to Thomas Jefferson's 68 in a predominantly North-South split of electors. Since the Constitution's framers did not anticipate political parties, this led to the Federalist Adams and the Republican Jefferson serving together. Washington's Farewell Address aside, they did not get along, leading Jefferson to recall that, after their first six months in office, they did not speak for the remaining three and one-half years.

Washington's hope for constraint of factions and parties seemed a distant dream for the next four years as the Republicans plotted their electoral strategy for 1800. Factions even within the Federalists made Adams's tenure a waking nightmare, though his efforts to chart a course to keep the nation out of war with both England and France were fully in the Washington tradition. Adams's steadfast effort to stamp out a growing clamor for war with France was especially courageous as it involved standing firm against his supposed Federalist friends. His statesmanship, however, cost him enough Federalist support to allow Jefferson to become chief magistrate in 1801—the first transition in party control of the presidency.

Jefferson paid homage to Washington's Farewell Address in his own inaugural. While he would be more partisan in action than in rhetoric, Jefferson's words would have given Washington, who died on December 14, 1799, some comfort: "We have called by different names brethren of the same principle. We are all Republicans, we are all Federalists." Jefferson, heretofore a firm Francophile, also adopted Washington's neutrality policy—that the United States sought: "peace, commerce, and honest friendship with all nations, entangling alliances with none" (coining the phrase often mistakenly attributed to Washington).[58] And both Jefferson and Madison included the address on the required reading list for the new school of law when the University of Virginia opened in 1825.

While faction and party continued to animate national politics after the Farewell Address, the union held. Neutrality continued as the policy of the young nation for the two decades Washington sought, until 1812, when, as he predicted, the United States was finally strong enough to protect its independence in its second war with England.

If people were not always guided by virtue and morality, and if the union was not always held together by sympathy and interest, Washington had expected that his counsels would not "control the usual current of the passions." If his hope and his leadership in the Farewell Address fell short, the fault surely cannot be laid at his feet alone.

Still, Washington was an eighteenth-century gentleman ill-adapted by temperament to an emerging, nineteenth-century, two-party democracy. He played no role in seeing to his succession, preferring to remain as much out of partisan politics as he could. By temperament, Washington took conflict hard; attacks on him hurt deeply.

Neither had he addressed the single issue that most divided the nation. Slavery, perhaps ignored in the Farewell Address as in the Constitution in order to preserve unity, intensified party and sectional animosities in the first half of the nineteenth century. This was an outcome Washington might well have anticipated yet, short of freeing his own slaves in his will (after Martha's death) and providing for their financial support, he played no part in addressing the issue in or outside of Virginia. As the nation lurched towards Civil War, compromise voices such as Daniel Webster tried to draw on the address: "Liberty and Union, now and for ever, one and inseparable," he urged in 1830.[59] Henry Clay, the "Great Compromiser," introduced a motion in the Senate in 1850 to purchase the original manuscript of the Farewell Address when its owner, David Claypoole, died. Clay's rationale, in part, was that the address should be preserved and read "amid the discordance and ungrateful sounds of disunion and discord which assail our ears."[60] Daniel Webster seconded Clay's motion. It was eventually approved, but too late for the purchase, allowing the address to go into private hands. Opponents included Senator Jefferson Davis, later the Civil War president of the Confederacy, who said that government funds did not need to be spent on a speech for which many copies already existed.

In the midst of the Civil War, following a petition introduced by Tennessee senator Andrew Johnson (one of the few Southern politicians to remain faithful to the Union and who would become Lincoln's second-term vice president), the Farewell Address was read to both House of Congress on February 22, 1862, to commemorate Washington's 130th birthday and as a symbol of the importance of unity.

After the Civil War, with the question of union answered in blood, references to the address focused more on its attention to foreign affairs. Washington's advice guided foreign policy throughout the nineteenth century.[61] Indeed, right up until Pearl Harbor, some used it to argue for isolationism while others, such as Woodrow Wilson, interpreted it to permit alliances that did not entangle us in the ambitions of other nations. Whichever side one took, there seemed a need to demonstrate Washington's blessing.

Even though President Roosevelt, in his State of the Union address on January 4, 1939, said, "We have learned that when we deliberately try to legislate neutrality, our neutrality laws may operate unevenly and unfairly—may actually give aid to an aggressor and deny it to the victim," the message fell mostly on deaf ears as the nation clung to the belief that it could avoid involvement in foreign wars.[62]

After World War II, Washington's dictum to "steer clear of permanent alliances" seemed increasingly suspect, a throwback to a world where great distances could provide safety from global politics. Harry Truman, in his memoirs, recalled as a senator continually coming up against the address: "It served little purpose," he said, "to point out to the isolationists that Washington had advised a method suitable under the conditions of his day to achieve a great end of preserving the nation." But in the Cold War, Truman concluded, "'Fortress America' notions could only result in handing to the Russians vast areas of the globe now denied to them."[63]

Sadly, the focus on isolationism vs. alliances missed Washington's central message. He was opposed only to alliances that engaged the nation inimical to its interests.

A Testament to a Legacy

Perhaps the best measure of the power of Washington's legacy in the Farewell Address is to pose the questions he did. Is union essential to maintain liberty? Is the Constitution sacredly obligatory upon all citizens? Do factions and parties pose threats to the public good and sound public administration? Are virtue and morality essential foundations to public happiness? Is education necessary to inform public opinion? Should foreign affairs be guided by duty and interest? Do rulers and ruled have reciprocal obligations guided by duty, honor, and selfless service?

If these questions are still provocative, the arms of Washington's legacy have spread across the centuries. This may be why the practice of reading the Farewell Address on his birthday resumed in 1893 and continues in the Senate today. Washington would be pleased that the honor is rotated among political parties and that each senator is allowed to sign a black, leather-bound book, including her or his own thoughts on the address.[64] Toward the end of it, Washington had said that he hoped his counsels "may be productive of some partial benefit, some occasional good." We can certainly grant him this, and a legacy that still provokes our study and admiration more than two hundred years later may grant him a great deal more.

2

The Electoral Crisis of 1801:
Jefferson's First Inaugural

On the snowy morning of Wednesday, February 11, 1801, Vice President Thomas Jefferson, as president of the Senate, began to announce the electoral vote for the bitterly contested election of 1800. The crowded Senate chamber, barely finished the previous November, the only part of the Capitol constructed thus far, offered the setting for a constitutionally routine and simple task being exercised in anything but a routine and simple situation. He knew the result, as did everyone else in the chamber, before the ballots were opened: Jefferson–73, Aaron Burr–73, John Adams–65, Charles Cotesworth Pinckney–64, and John Jay–1.

Indeed, Jefferson had known since mid-December that he would beat his rival, sitting president John Adams, but would tie his own Republican running mate, New Yorker Aaron Burr. Since the Constitution provided no mechanism for designating ballots as either for president or vice president, under Article II, Section 1, the House would decide the contest. The voting would begin later that morning. Each state delegation would have one vote.

Midway through the count, when the teller handed him Georgia's ballot, Jefferson saw immediately that it was improperly completed. As everyone else, he knew the electors' intent—four votes for Jefferson and four for Burr—so he announced that result. If those votes were subtracted from his total, the Constitution stated that the House would choose not just between the two Republicans but among Federalists' Adams and Pinckney as well, none of the four having a majority of electors. A bad situation would get much worse. The Federalists, aware of the problem yet realizing it was a mechanical not a substantive error, remained silent. They would not be silent on much else.

Congress had resolved earlier to go into immediate session, doing no other business until a choice for president was final. Yet, despite the fact that the Republicans had captured a 69–36 majority in the House (as well as an 18–13 margin in the Senate), *that* Congress would not (in another Constitutional quirk) convene until December. The lame-duck, Federalist Congress would choose a president. To the Republicans' advantage, despite their minority in numbers, they controlled 8 of 16 state delegations, the Federalists controlled 6. Two were evenly divided. Nine states were needed for election.

Not every Federalist felt honor bound to the Constitution's stipulation that the choice be Jefferson or Burr. The fate of the republic was in their hands, they believed, and both sides lacked the fidelity to Constitutional practice we take as given. Federalist "machinations" considered many possibilities. Some argued for continuing the deadlock to enable the president pro tem of the Senate or Speaker of the House, both Federalists, to assume the presidency, at least until December. Some suggested a new law to make someone else—perhaps Supreme Court chief justice (and Federalist) John Marshall—interim president. Others proposed invalidating enough Republican electoral votes to make Adams president. Their most likely option was to elect Burr. At least he was a *New York* Republican—and not Jefferson.

By 6 p.m., 15 ballots had produced no change in the result: eight states for Jefferson. The nation seemed on a collision course with itself. It had been for the past dozen years.

The 1790s had seen a growing schism in the founding generation. Though modern political parties had not yet formed—the founders neither anticipated nor would have condoned them if they had— political differences were striking and passionate, especially between Jefferson and Alexander Hamilton. Both had served in Washington's cabinet, the former as Secretary of State and the latter as Secretary of the Treasury. They and their followers had dramatically different visions for America. Hamilton saw a manufacturing nation, requiring a strong central government, a National Bank, and a powerful financial structure to fund internal improvements and tie the wealthy to the government. Jefferson saw an agrarian nation with a weak central government, believing that the independent yeoman farmer, with his own small plot, was a bulwark against the centralized power that Hamilton sought. Despite such differences, Jefferson had earlier scoffed at the notion that he might identify with a party, writing to Francis Hopkinson from Paris in 1789 that he had "never submitted the whole system of my opinion to the creed of any party of men...Such an addiction is the last degradation of a free and moral agent. If I could not go to heaven but with a party, I would not go at all."[1]

Yet by 1791, he and his protégé, Virginian James Madison, were organizing political opposition in New York and New England, and in 1796, after Washington stepped down, Jefferson lost the presidency to Adams by only three electoral votes. The penalty for defeat was to serve four years as vice president under a man whose political views he increasingly detested.

Jefferson and Adams held contrasting assumptions on the nature of man. The former's belief that a "moral sense" guides people into right action contradicted the latter's reading of history, in which selfish men required restraint by government. Adams felt that liberty required an energetic central government; Jefferson that the national government destroyed liberty, like wolves devouring sheep. Everywhere he looked, he saw Federalists moving toward monarchical and aristocratic forms and away from the "spirit of 76." Adams saw Republicans flirting dangerously with democracy, which Federalists equated with mob rule.[2]

In Jefferson's view, the "long train of abuses" by Federalists peaked in 1798, when they passed and Adams signed the Naturalization, Alien, and Sedition Acts. These increased the length of time it took to become a citizen (a boon to Federalists as it kept Republican-leaning immigrants from voting), empowered the president to deport aliens considered dangerous, and allowed for the arrest and trial of those who published "false, scandalous, and malicious writing" against the government or the president (the vice president was, perhaps not surprisingly, not protected). Republican writers were promptly tried and jailed.

Jefferson led the counterassault. He secretly drafted (being public risked arrest) what would become the Kentucky Resolutions, arguing that a state could decide for itself if the national government had acted unconstitutionally and, if it had, nullify an act of Congress. Yet, ever optimistic, he was convinced that Federalists had overreached, noting in a June 1798 letter to his Virginia friend John Taylor that "the body of our countrymen is substantially republican through every part of the union" and that "a little patience and we shall see the reign of witches pass over."[3]

Though both Jefferson and Adams had remained at home through the summer of 1800 (it was unseemly for gentlemen to campaign) they followed developments closely. The contest was not so sedate. In 1799, Jefferson had quietly supported a scurrilous journalist, James Callender, in publishing *The Prospect Before Us*, an attack on Adams for which he was jailed for sedition. Republican and Federalist newspapers pounded their opponents, the former going after not just Adams but Hamilton, reminding readers that he had endorsed a monarchical form of government in the Constitutional Convention. Strangely—perhaps not so strangely if one believes that he wanted to see Pinckney president—Hamilton published his own diatribe against Adams, who was just not Federalist enough.[4] As for Jefferson, historian John Ferling notes that he and Republicans were labeled as: "artful and ambitious demagogues" who led "discontented hotheads," "democratic blockhead[s]," and "cold-hearted Jacobin[s]." Jefferson was called a "howling atheist and infidel."[5]

Ill will continued to blast an ill wind through the House as the ballots—and days—dragged on. The continuing tie between Jefferson and Burr, through another 20 ballots and five days demonstrated what Jefferson had told James Monroe, "we remain in the hands of our enemies."[6]

Jefferson refused to offer concessions for Federalist support. When he visited Adams, the president refused to intervene without assurances on the direction of a Jefferson administration. Jefferson alluded to the possibility of armed force if the Federalists tried to steal the election and suggested that Republicans might convene another Constitutional Convention in December, a prospect he correctly judged would alarm the opposition. While Burr stayed in New York, he did not remove his name from consideration, even though he had earlier claimed no designs on the presidency.

Federalist unity eventually weakened. Even Hamilton argued that Jefferson would be better than Burr, whom he called "without Scruple," and "unprincipled."[7] On February 17, during the 36th ballot, Delaware Federalist James Bayard, the lone vote in his state's delegation, abstained as did his colleagues in Maryland and Vermont. This was sufficient to elect Jefferson—with ten states now in his favor. Claims of a "deal" by Bayard and denial of one by Republicans lasted for years. The Federalists had sought assurances that the Bank of the United States would be continued, the national debt discharged, the navy kept intact, and Federalist officeholders retained. In practice,

Jefferson would honor the first two and to some extent the last two but insisted that he "would not receive the government on capitulation, that I would not go into it with my hands tied."[8]

Seeking a New Kind of Presidency

It is one thing to campaign and another to govern. With less than three weeks to prepare an inaugural address, Jefferson's hope of effective leadership was compounded by the two minds with which he approached his task. On one hand, he was angry, writing to Madison that the Federalists, rather than choosing "to come over in a body to go with the tide," chose instead to allow him to be narrowly elected through abstentions. "We consider this," he said, "as a declaration of war on the part of this band."[9] On the other hand, he saw the result as an affirmation that the nation was truly Republican. Which Jefferson would speak on March 4?

Being of two minds was vintage Jefferson, a duality that has intrigued his biographers. The titles of many of their books showcase their quandary: *American Sphinx, A Strange Case of Mistaken Identity, The Inner Jefferson*.[10] While his Federalist audience prepared for the worst, and his Republican loyalists prepared for dramatic change, Jefferson prepared to surprise both.

The first public signal came as he emerged, about 11 a.m. from his room at Conrad and McMunn's. Having lived at the boarding house since late November, he began his short walk up Capitol Hill dressed "as a plain citizen," without the sword that Washington and Adams had worn at their inaugurations—and without the horse-drawn carriage that marked their processions. The Alexandria militia led the way, and Jefferson, just a month shy of his fifty-eighth birthday, was also accompanied by U.S. marshals, a smattering of his predecessor's cabinet, and Republican members of Congress. After a discharge of artillery, he entered the Capitol, where 1,140 people had gathered in the dimly lit Senate chamber. Absent was the outgoing president; Adams had left on the 4 a.m. stage.[11]

Present were Burr, now vice president, and Chief Justice John Marshall, Jefferson's cousin, who would administer the oath. Elevated to the post a month earlier by a defeated president intent on packing the judiciary with Federalists, the only remaining bulwark against the Republican tide, Marshall had his own misgivings about the man he was about to swear in.

As the first president to be inaugurated in Washington City, the first in the new century, the first after Washington's death, and the first to represent a change of political "party," Jefferson faced huge and conflicting expectations. He was known to have a fine pen. He would need it.

The Nation in 1801

Political turmoil was just one drama unfolding as Jefferson prepared his address. The nation was also grappling with two demographic identities. From 4 million in the 1790 census, the nation had grown over 25 percent to 5.3 million by 1800. The farmer, the Jeffersonian ideal, was being joined by the merchant and small manufacturer. Most Americans still lived in rural areas, but cities were growing.[12] Philadelphia and New York had nearly 100,000 people, at least double their size during the revolution.[13] Americans were flooding over the Appalachians. North and South would soon be engaged politically and economically by an increasingly vocal West. The land mass of the United States itself was nearly double that of France, Spain, and Great Britain combined.[14]

The democratic spirit was on the loose. The success of the revolution made Americans less deferential to the very gentlemen who had won it. Average men could now aspire to hold office, and many shopkeepers and tradesmen did. Indeed, the generation that crafted a republic was on the verge of handing it over to a generation of the "middling" sort who would turn it into a democracy. In 1800, only 4 of the 16 states had presidential electors chosen by popular vote instead of state legislatures. By 1824, this would be the case in 18 of 24 states.

Amid the political, demographic, and social fervent that was "teenage" America, Jefferson, at nearly six feet, three inches, rose to speak. He carried a text of 1,655 words in 5 paragraphs, written on 4 sides of 2 sheets of paper, each approximately 6-and-a-half by 5-and-a-half inches.[15]

A Private Man Crafts a Public Role

An intensely private man, Jefferson was comfortable in small groups but retiring in large ones. A capable writer, he drew back from public speaking, lacking a strong voice and oral spontaneity. Indeed, when he delivered his inaugural address, he could not be heard in the back of the room, a fact also attributable to the Senate chamber itself.[16] But he was more concerned with projecting ideas than utterances. Among these was his view of the presidency.

His conception of presidential power, of course, is what worried Federalists. The nominally nonpartisan Washington was their model. The potential for abuse by someone who lacked Washington's public virtue scared them. South Carolina framer Pierce Butler, writing to a relative in May 1788, had said that the powers of the presidency were "greater than I was disposed to make them" and that "they would not have been so great had not many of the members [of the Convention] cast their eyes toward General Washington as President."[17]

Washington honored this expectation in his First Inaugural, showing deference to the Constitution and Congress, refusing to "recommend to your consideration" measures and pledging, even on the contentious subject of a Bill of Rights, to be guided by their "discernment and pursuit of the public good." He took the oath in a public ceremony but then went inside New York City's Federal Hall to give his address to a joint session of Congress—they were the people's representatives. In 1793, he again addressed just Congress.

In 1797, Adams broke no new ground. He also addressed just a joint session of Congress in a speech that traced the history of the republic, paid homage to the Constitution, praised Washington, and contained nothing memorable—except perhaps a demonstration that Jefferson could indeed write "ten times better," as Adams had said when he prevailed upon the Virginian to draft the Declaration of Independence. He even kept Washington's cabinet in place (to his eventual regret), thinking that continuity rather than imagination was his task. Jefferson's own address to the Senate after taking the vice presidential oath was equally pedestrian. He promised to apply the rules of the Senate with rigor and diligence and attach himself to the Constitution.

Jefferson would now break with the past in words as he had already by his dress and walk to the Capitol. He considered his election an affirmation of the Constitution and the principles his predecessor had violated. He intended to clothe himself in the first and enunciate the second—in front of the public not just Congress. In his practice of the presidency, he would redefine it. But first he faced four tasks. He had to heal the nation, establish his legitimacy, enunciate a vision, and isolate his remaining political opposition.

Healing the Partisan Divide

Jefferson's salutation, to "Friends and Fellow-Citizens," was the first clue that he sought to build bridges with but also beyond Congress. In writing to Monroe about his inaugural address he had stated its "leading objects to be conciliation and sound principle."[18] This made political sense and was consistent with his lifelong distaste for overt public conflict: near the end of his life, he would list as one of a "Decalogue of Canons" for the son of a friend that one should "Take things always by the smooth handle."[19]

A conciliatory approach required softening emotions that had almost derailed the republic. As customary, he began humbly, expressing "grateful thanks," acknowledging that the job was "above my talents" and that he approached it with "the weakness of my powers." Jefferson would conclude in a similar tone, eschewing "pretensions to that high confidence you reposed in our first and greatest revolutionary character [Washington]." This was the deferential Jefferson, in contrast to the demagogue the Federalists had told the nation to fear.

Jefferson would soon get more direct. At the start of the second paragraph, he summarized the past year as "the contest of opinion through which we have passed," a rather polite—and conciliatory—reference to vicious partisan warfare. The call for reconciliation was put forcefully, and artfully, in the address's most memorable lines:

> Let us, then, fellow-citizens, unite with one heart and one mind. Let us restore to social intercourse that harmony and affection without which liberty and even life itself are but dreary things. And let us reflect that, having banished from our land that religious intolerance under which mankind so long bled and suffered, we have yet gained little if we countenance a political intolerance as despotic, as wicked, and capable of as bitter and bloody persecutions...But every difference of opinion is not a difference of principle. We have called by different names brethren of the same principle. We are all republicans, we are all federalists."

Jefferson thus signaled his belief that political harmony was possible because Americans shared the same governing principles. Though printed editions of the speech often capitalized "republicans" and "federalists," he did not. He had won under the Republican banner, but he was not at heart a party man. Two days later he would write to the "financier of the Revolution," Pennsylvanian Robert Morris, that: "I hope to see them [the people] again consolidated into a homogeneous mass, and the very name of party obliterated from among us."[20]

In three drafts of the speech, Jefferson made changes that demonstrate his intent on reconciliation. The term "engaged in commerce" in the first paragraph had been changed from "entangled in commerce," which could have come across as an attack on New England Federalists with close ties to the British. In the fourth paragraph of the first draft he had called for "alliance with none" of the European powers, but he softened that in the final version to "entangling alliances with none," again keeping New England's interests in mind.

Whether his approach represented political naiveté, high statesmanship, or just crafty politics is hard for us, witnesses of two centuries of party politics, to judge. The ambiguity of his reasons nevertheless enhanced the leadership of the words, and it made a direct attack on him difficult. The belief that party conflict might actually improve the republic was foreign in 1801. At the same time, it was characteristic of this apostle of human freedom who was a lifelong slaveholder to hold two opposing ideas in his head without necessarily seeing them in irreconcilable conflict. He could plan a Republican presidency while believing that "Republicans" and "Federalists" were labels no longer needed. His words would give some Federalists pause, and in that pause he would seize the initiative.

Establishing Legitimacy

While reconciliation aimed at social harmony, it was designed to smooth the path to deference as well. The Republicans, after all, had won. Jefferson was intent on reminding the nation that he was the legitimate embodiment of Article II. He did so gently at first. Using the passive voice, he reminded his audience in his first sentence that he was "[C]alled upon to undertake the duties of the first executive office." (It was unseemly to *want* the presidency but acceptable to be *called upon*.) Before the paragraph would end, he would also note that he was present with "the other high authorities provided by our Constitution," showing deference to the Congress and cloaking himself with the same "high authority."

Jefferson was on record as having mixed feelings about constitutions. He had sought to shape the constitution of Virginia, even drafting one to send to Williamsburg in 1776. During the Federal Convention of 1787, he was abroad as minister to France yet expressed reservations that the proposed charter lacked a bill of rights and enabled the executive to be reelected, potentially for life. As the ratification debate intensified, however, he lent support. Yet to Madison, in 1789, he suggested that the national Constitution should last no longer than about 19 years, under the principle that each generation should be able to decide for itself how it wished to be governed.[21] In early 1800, watching the French Revolution spinning out of control, he had written to Dr. William Bache of Philadelphia that Americans should "rally firmly & in close bands round their constitution; never to suffer an iota of it to be infringed.[22] Yet in 1798 he had proposed nullification of acts of Congress, and in early 1801 he had threatened to call a new convention if the Federalists persisted in blocking his election, though this itself admitted that the Constitutional process for amendment must be followed. All of that was history. As president, he needed to reestablish the "sacredly obligatory" nature of the Constitution that Washington had called for in his Farewell Address.

This was central to his legitimacy, and he put it forcefully in the second paragraph:

> ...now decided by the voice of the nation, announced according to the rules of the Constitution, all will, of course, arrange themselves under the will of the law, and unite in common efforts for the common good. All, too, will bear in mind this sacred principle, that though the will of the majority is in all cases to prevail, that will to be rightful must be reasonable; that the minority possess their equal rights, which equal law must protect, and to violate would be oppression.

This was a clear message, especially to the Ultra-Federalists, who must hear "the voice of the nation," and follow "the will of the law." Jefferson took pride, both personally and as a matter of political philosophy, as he put it years later to Judge Spencer Roane that his election was a mandate: "not effected indeed by the sword" but rather "by the rational and peaceable instrument of reform, the suffrage of the people."[23]

In reality, the electoral totals for Adams and Jefferson in 1800 were only slightly different than they had been in 1796, and evidence suggests that Republicans in national and state races won only about 52 percent of the votes cast in the election. Yet as John Ferling observed, "the Republicans had carried four of the five states in which electors were chosen by popular vote" (as opposed to state legislatures).[24] Historian Bruce Ackerman rightly notes that his election established the "plebiscitary presidency." No longer was the president just a gentleman reluctantly serving when called to duty. He was now the product of "presidential democracy" and this legitimized both his role and his crafting of a positive platform on which to lead.[25]

Though Federalists might well disagree that Jefferson's election was the true "voice of the nation," they could hardly maintain that he was not constitutionally selected. Jefferson was careful, of course, to acknowledge the need for the Republican majority to be "reasonable," continuing the effort at reconciliation. Since he believed that the minority's "equal rights" were in fact the very rights that Republicans cherished anyway, this was not conceding much.

A Republican Vision for America

Reconciliation and legitimacy were themes, but the main focus was a reaffirmation of Republican (which for him were the same as republican) principles. He wished to build bridges, but he was more concerned with the solid ground on which they stood. For Jefferson, the election heralded the triumph of American republicanism, as he noted to scientist and friend Joseph Priestley two weeks after the inaugural:

> Our countrymen have recovered from the storm into which art & industry had thrown them...we can no longer say that there is nothing new under the sun, for this whole chapter in the history of man is new. The great extent of our republic is new. It's [sic] sparse habitation is new. The mighty wave of public opinion which has rolled over us is new...the order & good sense displayed in this recovery from delusion...bespeak a strength of character in our nation.[26]

Jefferson was an irrepressible optimist. Later in life, he would tell John Adams that: "I steer my bark with Hope in the Head, leaving Fear astern."[27] Not surprisingly, he could not even leave the opening paragraph without foreshadowing his vision of:

> [A] rising nation, spread over a wide and fruitful land, traversing all the seas with the rich productions of their industry, engaged in commerce with nations...advancing rapidly to destinies beyond the reach of mortal eye.

While true enough, Jefferson went further, reflecting that this government was "the world's best hope," echoing the founders' belief in

America as a beacon of freedom for the world. He also proclaimed that "I believe this...the strongest Government on earth." The fact that it lacked a respectable army, had a fledgling navy, owed millions in war debts and was essentially ignored as a force in world affairs by England and France seemed what might today be called "inconvenient truths."

Thus far, Jefferson had echoed sentiments common in presidential rhetoric. He was about to become uncommon—to lay the groundwork for an activist presidency. Whether he planned to be as active as he would become is less clear.

He no doubt recalled the weak executive role in which he found himself in his two one-year terms as Virginia's governor, from June 1779 to June 1781. The state that began the revolution against executive power with the motion for independence ended it with the defeat of Cornwallis, and its constitution took a dim view of executive authority. As governor, he could not act without the approval of a Council of State, which did not always agree with him. Indeed, his inability to secure men for the militia, provisions to enable them to fight, and a standing army to defend against the British invasion of the state in 1780 resulted in a painful rebuke by his own legislature, who resolved that "an inquiry be made into the conduct of the Executive of this state." Mercifully, the investigation was dropped after the victory at Yorktown, but the experience no doubt left a bad aftertaste. Jefferson was not anxious to repeat it.

His desire to lead thus met the opportunity inherent in the ill-defined institution of the presidency. As historians Horn, Lewis, and Onuf observed of Washington: "The presidency was the one office in the new government least amenable to prognostication, and its imminent occupation by the one living American whose unique political advantages history could never replicate meant that early precedents might not provide a reliable guide for the future."[28] And they did not.

Jefferson articulated the Republican vision carefully—and craftily. He laid out a set of principles anchored in his political philosophy. On first reading, they appear familiar and noncontroversial. Indeed, as historian Stephen Howard Browne noted, his writing here reminds us of his later description of the task he had set himself in drafting the Declaration of Independence in 1776: "not to find out new principles...never before thought of...but to place before mankind the common sense of the subject, in terms so plain and firm as to command their assent."[29]

In the third paragraph, Jefferson prefaced the list of principles to follow in the fourth:

> Let us, then, with courage and confidence pursue our own federal and republican principles, our attachment to union and representative government.

For Jefferson, the "and" was key: Republican government would be federal *and* republican, cherishing national union but always and only through elective representation. After recalling that Americans possessed a "chosen country, with room enough for our descendents to the thousandth and thousandth generation," he stated that only "one thing more" was necessary:

> [A] wise and frugal Government, which shall restrain men from injuring one another, shall leave them otherwise free to regulate their own pursuits of industry and improvement, and shall not take from the mouth of labor the bread it has earned. This is the sum of good government.

This classical statement about limited government was followed by a significant departure from his predecessors as Jefferson launched into a strong delineation of "the essential principles of our Government, and consequently those which ought to shape its Administration." As the first president to articulate a "platform," he listed 16 principles, abbreviated slightly here:

1. "Equal and exact justice to all men"
2. "peace, commerce, and honest friendship with all nations, entangling alliances with none"
3. "...State governments...as the most competent administrations for our domestic concerns and the surest bulwarks against antirepublican tendencies"
4. "the preservation of the General Government in its whole constitutional vigor;"
5. "the right of election by the people"
6. "absolute acquiescence in the decisions of the majority"
7. "a well disciplined militia, our best reliance in peace and for the first moments of war, till regulars may relieve them"
8. "the supremacy of the civil over the military authority"
9. "economy in the public expense"
10. "the honest payment of our debts"

11. "encouragement of agriculture, and of commerce as its handmaid"
12. "the diffusion of information and arraignment of all abuses at the bar of public reason"
13. "freedom of religion"
14. "freedom of the press"
15. "freedom of person under the protection of habeas corpus "
16. "trial by juries impartially selected."

They suggested no radical departure as Federalists may have feared, and in this sense fit the reconciliation theme. Indeed, Jefferson was stating principles that had long been the core of his political creed. They were not a departure from his (mostly private) record. In January 1799, he had written to Elbridge Gerry, a Massachusetts signer of the Declaration:

> I shall make to you a profession of my political faith...I am for preserving to the states the powers not yielded by them to the Union...I am for a government rigorously frugal and simple, applying all the possible savings of the public revenue to the discharge of the national debt...I am for relying, for internal defence [sic], on our militia solely till actual invasion...and not for a standing army in time of peace...I am for free commerce with all nations, political connection with none...I am for freedom of religion...for freedom of the press...I am for encouraging the progress of science.[30]

Yet upon closer inspection, there are hints of change, buried carefully in acceptable prose. The admonition against "entangling alliances," for example, echoed Washington's call for no "permanent alliances" but certainly supported an arm's length relationship with the British that would give Federalists pause. His call for strong state governments as a bulwark against antirepublican tendencies no doubt signaled a desire to restrain what he viewed as the national government's (monarchical) excesses, lately experienced under Adams (though, as we shall see, Jefferson would exert far more executive authority than he here permits).

Recommitment to the "right of election by the people" and the "absolute acquiescence" in majority rule buttressed the right to govern by the Republican majority and the spread of more direct democracy, which Jefferson had long championed. Indeed, he viewed those who governed more suspiciously the less often they had to be elected, so not surprisingly approved of the two-year cycle for members of the House more than the six-year cycle for members of the Senate—and detested most of all the judiciary, who were selected (not elected) for life.

The reliance on the militia was a direct attack on the Provisional Army that Adams had nearly put in the field in the quasi-war with France as well as Federalist willingness to accept a larger standing army. Honest payment of debts was a signal that amassing debt as a way to strengthen the national government may have been a Federalist but would not be a Republican policy, and "encouragement of agriculture, and of commerce as its handmaid" signaled universal agreement that both are needed, though a Federalist administration (under Hamilton's influence) might well have reversed the order. "Freedom of the press" was a signal that the abuses of the Sedition Act would no longer be tolerated.

From a leadership standpoint, Jefferson is seeking to find common ground while signaling his Republican base that they have, in fact, achieved the right to rule. It is a partisan statement clothed in nonpartisanship. It is a declaration of broad principles leaving the details of policy and administration to another time. It seeks agreement on ends leaving flexibility on means. After all, he is *not* seeking to alienate moderate Federalists but to bring them under the Republican banner. He is *not* trying to strengthen the Republican party as much as to eliminate the need for it.

Isolating the Opposition

For nearly a decade, Jefferson's political world had been divided between Federalists and Republicans. Yet he preferred harmony. If his inaugural softened divisions, it is in part because he wished to see the world that way. And seeing it that way, his words—and later actions—would try to realize it. This may have been "rose-colored-glasses" politics, but it was astute politics as well.

Part of this view of the political world may have reflected the lack of party animosity in his home state, "how little of party Spirit there is in Virginia," he wrote John Wise in 1798.[31] Part of it may have been due to his view that an extreme group had swayed the mass of reasonable Americans. As he wrote John Taylor that same year, "the body of our countrymen is substantially republican through every part of the union. It was the irresistible influence & popularity of Genl. Washington played off by the cunning of Hamilton which turned the government over to antirepublican hands...this is not the natural state."[32]

This view persisted into the early days of his administration. On March 27, he would write Henry Knox, Washington's secretary of war:

> I was always satisfied that the great body of those called Federalists were real Republicans as well as federalists. I know indeed there are Monarchists among us. One character of these is in theory only, & perfectly acquiescent in our form of government as is...a second class, at the head of which is our quondam colleague [Hamilton], are ardent for the introduction of monarchy."[33]

For Jefferson, the true number of enemies was small. Everyone else shared common principles and healing could thus proceed. Indeed, Jefferson's interpretation of the weeks leading to his election by the House was that such healing was nearly completed. Writing James Monroe on March 7, he would note:

> We may say that the whole of that portion of the people which was called federalist, was made to desire anxiously the very event they had just before opposed with all their energies, and to receive the election, which was made, as an object of their earnest wishes, a child of their own. These people (I always include their leaders) are now aggregated with us.[34]

Thus, we can see in Jefferson's enunciation of what will guide his Administration the assumption that all share common principles. The terms "us" and "our" pervade the language. Jefferson assumes the desirable and thus places those he calls the "incurables" outside "the bright constellation which has gone before us and guided our steps through an age of revolution and reformation." This is well-crafted rhetoric, but is it naive or astute politics?

The mastery of Jefferson's literary craftsmanship means that we will never know. Jefferson scholars Peter Onuf and Leonard Sadosky emphasize "the mythic quality of this harmonious 'imagined community,' and the selective forgetting it entailed."[35] Jefferson's election, they argue, was made possible not by the solidarity of Republicans but by the fact that Republicanism "could be so many different things to its growing legion of followers."[36]

Stephen Browne suggests that there may have been more calculation than wishful thinking in Jefferson's approach: "The conciliatory function of the address is thus more strategic, more ideologically cunning than is frequently acknowledged...he proposed to win over the major part of the amenable Federalists, leaving the intractable an impotent minority faction."[37] It is perhaps for this reason that Jefferson could write earlier in the address that dissent was tolerable because it would hasten consolidation:

> If there be any among us who would wish to dissolve this Union or to change its republican form, let them stand undisturbed as monuments of the safety with which error of opinion may be tolerated where reason is left free to combat it.

Implied, of course, was that those who disagreed were in "error," correctable through the application of (Republican) reason.

"The Circle of Our Felicities"

We also need to acknowledge Jefferson's use of imagery as a leadership tool. He was a storyteller. His stories are often archetypal contests between good and evil, for he tended to see the world in moral absolutes. As biographer Joseph Ellis noted: "The essence of that mind was a capacity for rendering the world into two competing narratives and inscribing himself indelibly into the preferred story...It always came down to the forces of light against the forces of darkness, with no room for anything in between."[38]

In the inaugural address, the forces of darkness are sometimes foreign ("the throes and convulsions of the ancient world," "the exterminating havoc of one quarter of the globe"), contrasted with the forces of American light ("the world's best hope"). They are also domestic, where the darkness assumes the mantle of "a political intolerance as despotic, as wicked, and capable of bitter and bloody persecutions" contrasted to the light of "harmony and affection" in social intercourse. But the end of the story is always to look forward. The new century opened with America advancing west, following the sun. Born on the edge of the Virginia frontier, having built the parlor of his beloved Monticello facing west, Jefferson was in this sense the perfect spokesman for "a rising nation."[39]

The effect of the narrative is enhanced with spatial metaphors familiar to his audience. Many follow a typically Jeffersonian nautical theme. He invites the reader to "steer with safety the vessel in which we are all embarked" in "the full tide of successful experiment," in which republican government is the "sheet anchor of our peace at home and safety abroad." Others invoke more geometric and astronomical metaphors, typical to the founding generation—good government will "close the circle of our felicities" and its principles will "form the bright constellation which has gone before us and guided our steps."

Jefferson, viewed by most as an apostle of reason, had developed a rich, emotional interior early in life. His heart had learned as well as his head. He lost his father when he was 14, and his older sister, Jane, when he was 22. He lost his best friend, Dabney Carr, when both were 30 and his wife when he was only 39. In his *Literary Commonplace Book*, passages on death were common, as when he quoted from Cicero: "What satisfaction can there be in living, when day and night we have to reflect that at this or that moment we must die?"[40]

He also appreciated poetry and music (early in life, he had practiced the violin for hours at a time). He found the "entertainments of fiction are useful as well as pleasant."[41] Indeed, more than three-fourths of the selections in his *Literary Commonplace Book*, mostly completed before he turned 30, are poems.[42] They doubtlessly contributed to his feel for language and felicity of expression as well as his moral sensitivities.

While his rhetoric may not be essential to the core of his message, it embosses that core in a soft sheen that raises hopes at best and cloaks the inevitable, coming use of more naked power.

Mentoring America

Throughout his early life, Jefferson had mentors. The most influential were the trio of Dr. William Small, his professor at the College of William and Mary, Royal Governor Frances Fauquier, and George Wythe, his law mentor in Williamsburg. Dumas Malone, Jefferson's biographer, dubbed that colonial capital, "a school for statesmen."[43] From the trio, at frequent palace dinners, Jefferson would later say that he heard "more good sense, more rational and philosophical conversations" than at any other time of his life.[44]

He returned the favor by mentoring others. Just 28, in a letter to a friend, Robert Skipwith, who had asked for a list of books for his private library, Jefferson suggested 148 works, spanning fine arts, politics, religion, law, modern and ancient history, and natural philosophy. (The Bible was listed under ancient history, not religion.)[45]

His inaugural is yet another effort to teach. Indeed, historian Jeremy Bailey noted that "Central to his transformation of executive power was changing the form of the inaugural address in order to meet the educative requirement of democratic leadership. Although democratic government is government by the majority will, majorities are comprised of citizens who need to have those very principles explained to them."[46]

Years later, Jefferson would state his belief in the good sense of the common man under the transforming power of education, in a letter to William Jarvis:

> I know no safe depositary of the ultimate powers of the society but the people themselves; and if we think them not enlightened enough to exercise their control with a wholesome discretion, the remedy is not to take it from them, but to inform their discretion by education.[47]

In the address, Jefferson subtly casts himself in the role of teacher. In fact, we can view the address as a dialogue between a president and the people, in which he clarifies his role and the requirements of the people for enlightened citizenship. He does so in part through acknowledging the need for debate—that the "contest of opinion" is a natural condition in republican society. Yet, that contest must be guided by reason, the sine qua non of all education.

He educates as well through the use of questions, though they are rhetorical:

> would the honest patriot...abandon a government which has so far kept us free and firm on the theoretic and visionary fear that this Government, the world's best hope, may by possibility want energy to preserve itself?

At other times, the teaching is declarative, such as his enunciation of republican philosophy, prefaced by noting that "it is proper you should understand what I deem essential principles of our Government." Indeed, after listing them, he claims that "They should be the creed of our political faith, the text of civic instruction."

Yet where there is a teacher, there is a pupil, and for Jefferson that pupil may lack full understanding. In his last paragraph, he states:

> When right, I shall often be thought wrong by those whose positions will not command a view of the whole ground. I ask your indulgence for my own errors, which will never be intentional, and your support against the errors of others, who may condemn what they would not if seen in all its parts.

Thus acknowledging he may err, he also claims to be the one who sees the "whole ground." It is hard to imagine Washington (or Adams) publicly claiming such powers of foresight and synthesis. Would history make hubris his natural companion?

The Nation Responds

After his address, Jefferson took the oath.[48] Artillery salutes concluded the ceremonies, and he returned to Conrad and McMunn's, dining with 24–30 others at the common table.[49]

His address was published that same day in Washington's *National Intelligencer*. By March 5, it had reached Baltimore and, within a week, Boston. It reached Charleston by March 17 and London on April 14.[50] Reactions mostly followed partisan divisions, though some Federalists took a wait and see attitude. James Bayard, whose abstention made Jefferson president, said the speech was "in political substance better than expected." John Marshall, not inclined to give Jefferson the benefit of the doubt, wrote to Pinckney on March 4 that: "It is in general well judged and conciliatory. It is in direct terms giving the lie to the violent party declamation which has elected him; but it is strongly characteristic of the general cast of his political theory." Even Hamilton seemed to accord Jefferson some leeway, telling the electors of New York State on March 21 that "we view it as virtually a candid retraction of past misapprehensions, and a pledge to the community that the new President will not lend himself to dangerous innovations."[51]

Other Federalists were more suspicious. Fisher Ames from Massachusetts dismissed it as "smooth promises, and a tinsel called conciliation," complaining that the country was now "too democratic for liberty."[52]

Words to Deeds: Executive Boldness from the Apostle of Executive Restraint

Jefferson's initial moves focused on style and staff. He continued to signal his distaste for monarchical forms by choosing to ride on horseback rather than liveried carriage. He dispensed with stiff, weekly formal levees—gatherings Washington used for those wishing to see him. For Jefferson, they were too similar to a king greeting his subjects. Preferring informal, small groups, he chose instead the dinner party, at which members of Congress, his administration, and foreign ambassadors, were the only invitees. In such a setting, he could cultivate relationships as he plied guests with French cooking, fine wine, and conversation about art, science, and nearly every topic except the one banned subject—politics.

In personnel choices, he assembled one of the most effective cabinets of any president. Unlike Washington, who sought intellect with scant attention to politics, and Adams, who chose continuity over loyalty, Jefferson insisted on smart, loyal, politically astute senior staff. He chose Madison, his Virginia protégé and architect of the Constitution, as Secretary of State and Albert Gallatin, a Pennsylvanian and one of the few who was a match for the financial wizardry of Hamilton, as Secretary of the Treasury. He appointed Henry Dearborn, a colonel under Washington, as Secretary of War, and Levi Lincoln, a Harvard graduate and eminent lawyer as Attorney General. Both Dearborn and Lincoln were from Massachusetts, and all four had been members, in some cases leaders, in Congress. The remaining cabinet spot was the weakest—Marylander Robert Smith as Secretary of the Navy. Smart enough (he later became Madison's Secretary of State), Smith got the post when Jefferson had trouble filling it because of his plan to downsize the navy.

Jefferson wished to be seen as nonpartisan, avoiding encroachment on the legislative branch. Indeed, he abandoned the practice of delivering the State of the Union address in front of Congress, which he likened to the king addressing the parliament, preferring to send a written statement—a precedent that stood until Woodrow Wilson. Yet, as historian Forrest McDonald notes, Jefferson pulled strings behind the scenes: "Officially, he stood aloof from them, maintaining a wall of separation."[53] But that was for appearances. Gallatin, a former floor leader in the House, led a strong, working coalition across the two branches, aided by Republican caucuses in both houses.

Looking at Jefferson's first term, his revolutionary wariness of executive power was easily overcome as president. In May 1801, he sent warships to the Mediterranean to fight the Barbary pirates, and in 1802 he established an engineering school on the Hudson River in New York, which in time became West Point—both from one who eschewed an adventurous navy and a standing army. In 1803, with the purchase of Louisiana, he doubled the size of the United States and ensured cheap land for the spread of yeoman farmers, even though he doubted the Constitution allowed him such power. A proponent of a free press, he nevertheless urged Pennsylvania's Republican governor,

Thomas McKean, to engage in "a few prosecutions of the most prominent [press] offenders."[54] Despite his admiration for Native Americans, he pursued a policy in which they were given the choice of assimilating into American agricultural society or being forcibly removed to the West. And, despite his concerns about encroachment on the legislature, he worked with Republicans in Congress to push through the Twelfth Amendment, which required presidential electors to cast separate votes for president and vice president, a move needed to prevent a repeat of 1801 but that also ensured Federalists could not sneak their own man into the vice presidency in 1804.[55]

In March 1801, of course, these steps were in the future. Initially Jefferson was careful to honor the electoral "deal" he claimed he had not made. He never moved against Hamilton's Bank and worked to discharge the nation's debt, putting it on a course that would cut it in half in ten years, though this was also in keeping with Republican principles.[56] He did not abolish the navy, but he did cut its appropriation, preferring gunboats for coastal defense rather than frigates that might be drawn into overseas adventures.

It was in the area of appointments that Jefferson moved most carefully, for it was here that reconciliation—or the lack of it—would be easily visible. He had two constraints. As a matter of principle, he believed the executive branch should remain small, and the number of office holders was itself small—fewer than 3,000 federal civil servants. Of those, he could directly appoint only 316.[57] Over the course of his administration, he would change fewer than half of those reporting to him, replacing them with capable, political loyalists.[58] While miniscule by modern standards, he nevertheless inaugurated the first "housecleaning" in presidential history, presaging the "spoils system" that Andrew Jackson would perfect.

Political savvy would confront philosophical purity, however, when Jefferson took on the courts. As the only branch not subject to the "elective principle," it was, for him, suspect from the start. Just five days before the end of Adams's term, the Federalist-led Congress had passed the Judiciary Act of 1801, which created six new circuit courts and sixteen judgeships. Adams promptly packed them with Federalists, and Jefferson wished to remove them just as quickly.

He could do nothing until the Republican-led Congress convened in December, and they promptly repealed the Act early in 1802. The court, in 1803, upheld the repeal, but Jefferson had by then earned the deft opposition of Chief Justice Marshall, who in *Marbury vs. Madison* that same year managed to establish the precedent that the court could rule an act of Congress unconstitutional. The battle would go on, with the Republicans impeaching Supreme Court justice Samuel Chase in the House in 1804, though failing to convict him in the Senate in 1805. By 1812, however, the Court had been "reformed" through Jefferson's appointments, with only three of seven justices on the bench having been appointed by Federalist presidents.

The First Inaugural and Presidential Democracy

The Federalists grew weaker with time. In 1804, Jefferson carried all but Delaware and Connecticut, with a 162–14 electoral vote defeat of Federalist Charles Cotesworth Pinckney. The House (116–25) and Senate (27–7) became even more solidly Republican as the Federalists faded into insignificance.[59] As John Adams would later write: "[T]he party committed suicide and indicted me for the murder."[60] The Republicans would hold the presidency until 1829, with the coup de grace for Federalists coming first in 1820 when they did not even field a candidate and finally in 1824, when Adams's son, John Quincy, was elected as a Republican. Indeed, all four candidates that year were "Democratic-Republican." Judged from the standpoint of electoral success, the political strategy embedded in the First Inaugural—absorbing moderate Federalists into the Republican ranks and isolating the "incurables"—worked perhaps even beyond Jefferson's own expectations, not that he doubted himself.

The record of the governing strategy articulated in the First Inaugural was more mixed. The first term had considerable success, even if Jefferson departed from bedrock principles when faced with the task of acting in the real as opposed to his imagined republic.

Yet, as with Washington, his second term foundered. In December 1807, he forced the passage of an Embargo Act to prohibit US vessels from trading with foreign governments. An attempt through commerce to keep the nation out of the Napoleonic Wars, the act was ignored by American seamen. Undaunted—and perhaps blinded by moral rigidity and his strong Republican majority in Congress—he pushed through more laws to plug loopholes and increase enforcement. Forsaking his principles, he asked for (but did not get) a major increase in the standing army. The chief outcome was a plunging economy, especially in New England, which eventually forced Jefferson to end the embargo three days before he left the presidency.

His second term, as well, did nothing to set slavery on a course to extinction. While as a young man hopeful that a way could be found to end what he termed an "abominable crime," he grew less hopeful, in both his personal and public lives, as he aged. He supported an 1808 bill outlawing the foreign slave trade, a ban permitted by the Constitution no earlier than 1809, but he left the domestic institution intact. In this, like his predecessors and 12 presidents to follow, he struck a bargain that sacrificed the nation's values and raised the price that would ultimately be paid.

The Legacy of the First Inaugural

Viewed from the higher plane on which Jefferson preferred to live, however, he continued to believe that the First Inaugural lit a republican beacon for the world. As he would say to Republican publisher William Duane in 1811: "The last hope of human liberty in the world rests with us."[61]

Ten years after leaving the presidency, he would tell Spencer Roane that the Republican victory celebrated in the First Inaugural had ignited a second American Revolution: the "revolution of 1800, for that was as real a revolution in the principles of our government as that of 1776 was in its form."[62]

In this conclusion, Jefferson was perhaps half right, for he changed the *form* of the presidency as much as he championed the principles of republican government. As Dumas Malone would note:

> His manners were conciliatory and his preferred methods those of gradualism and patience, but within a year he had manifested a degree of presidential leadership which he himself probably did not anticipate and actually tried to keep out of sight. Thus it came about that the herald of freedom...established his historic claim to the title of father of American political democracy.[63]

In claiming a mandate by the "suffrage of the people," he hastened the development of the modern presidency. If, in doing so, he was not always consistent with his own principles, this was a price he was willing to pay. Jefferson preferred to act based on present understandings not past traditions. As he wrote to John Colvin in 1810, reflecting on the circumstances under which a president might go beyond the written law to address national security:

> The question you propose, whether circumstances do not sometimes occur, which make it a duty in officers of high trust, to assume authorities

beyond the law, is easy of solution in principle, but sometimes embarrassing in practice. A strict observance of the written laws is doubtless one of the high duties of a good citizen, but it is not the highest. The laws of necessity, of self-preservation, of saving our country when in danger, are of higher obligation.[64]

Thus did a philosophical opponent of executive overreaching enhance the strength of the presidency as an independent source of political power, enabling American government to develop the activist executive needed in a dangerous world. Though eschewing political parties, he created the first modern version of party discipline and party control of the legislative and executive branches of government, moving America along the road to where party "contests of opinion" were actually welcomed as a means of propelling progress toward the aims of the Constitution's Preamble.

Though no lover of permanent constitutions, Jefferson's inaugural and presidency, as the first by a leader of the opposition, did much to establish fidelity to the American Constitution, at a time when the existence of the United States as a constitutional republic could not be taken for granted. Even his fight with the Supreme Court led, despite his intentions, to defining and strengthening the third branch of government.

The apostle of revolution strengthened the forms of government itself. The duality that was Thomas Jefferson thus found him to be an advocate of both change and stability. In perhaps an ironic turn of fate for a "natural aristocrat" who believed in rule by the educated and enlightened, Jefferson's advocacy of the elective principle and hence of broader democratic participation in government lent force to the growing democratic spirit in America that hastened the end of rule by philosopher-kings such as himself.[65]

The First Inaugural's strands are woven into the fabric of American democracy. We may not always recognize them as we drink the daily milk of our political discourse. Yet his words still have power. On the night before he was inaugurated in January 1961, John Kennedy attended a concert in Constitution Hall. As his biographer, Arthur Schlesinger Jr. tells it:

> An hour later they [Kennedy and his wife] left at the intermission to go on to the Inaugural Gala at the Armory... With the light on inside the car, he settled back to read Jefferson's First Inaugural, which had been printed in the concert program. When he finished, he shook his head and said wryly: "Better than mine."[66]

Healing the Wounds of Civil War: Lincoln's Second Inaugural

"The morning was dark and rainy, and the streets were very muddy," John Nicolay, Lincoln's secretary, recalled. A two-day downpour had left up to ten inches of mud on Washington's streets, and gale force winds had uprooted trees earlier in the day. At mid-morning, the rains that had briefly stopped came again. The temperature, barely in the 40s, and the bud-swelled trees, signaled that March 4, 1865, was one of those not-quite-winter, not-quite-spring days.[1]

As crowds began to gather, and as the inaugural parade (which in Lincoln's time came before the swearing-in) moved along Pennsylvania Avenue, the president was already at the Capitol. He had left, alone, earlier to sign legislation passed by the 38th Congress at the end of its term the day before.

In many ways, the day stood in stark contrast to his First Inaugural. His speech today would take no more than 6 minutes, compared to 35 in 1861. On that day, Lincoln felt he needed an extended argument that his constitutional duty obligated him to preserve the Union. On that occasion, war loomed, with the survival of the nation in grave doubt. On that day, Lincoln offered to enshrine slavery in the Constitution in the Southern states where it already existed, if that would hold the nation together. But on this day, the Union's survival seemed assured. Victory seemed inevitable, if still elusive. On this day, four companies of black soldiers of the 45th Regiment, United States Colored Troops, marched in the parade, and Lincoln's pen would enact into law the Freedmen's Bureau, passed the day before to aid the transition from slavery.[2]

Abraham Lincoln had reason to celebrate. His success had con-founded his critics, who had hounded him throughout the war as either too hard or too soft on the South, as inept, inflexible, and dictatorial. He had preserved the Union, and the Thirteenth Amendment that abolished slavery had passed Congress in late January. Eighteen states had already ratified it.

Yet Lincoln was not in a celebratory mood. At 56, he was weary, and the lines in his features seemed to have deepened, as if war had etched its losses directly into him. He knew, even if the crowd had forgotten, that his inauguration had been improbable as recently as the summer before.

On August 23, 1864, he had written a ten-line "blind memorandum," enclosed it in an envelope, and asked each of his cabinet officers to sign it, unseen. The text acknowledged that "it seems exceedingly probable that this Administration will not be re-elected."[3] He was right to be skeptical. After three years of a war that would ultimately claim 620,000 lives and more than 1 million casualties on both sides, victory still seemed out of reach. While he had finally found a fighting general in Ulysses S. Grant, and had promoted him to Lt. General (the first since George Washington) in charge of all Union armies and strategy, Grant had pursued Robert E. Lee south through Virginia from May till mid-June, without a crushing blow. In those seven weeks, the army of the Potomac lost 65,000 men, as many as in three previous years of war. The resulting slow advance led to an entrenchment against Lee at Petersburg. To the west, General William Tecumseh Sherman seemed to have had no more success pursuing Joseph Johnston in the battle to take Atlanta, losing nearly 17,000 men while still 20 miles from the city.[4] Though renominated by the Republican National Convention earlier in the summer, Lincoln had since faced panicked calls to replace him on the ticket.

Those calls ended when Atlanta fell on September 2. Sherman turned next to a gutsy (some said reckless) yet successful march to Savannah, which fell on December 21. He then headed north to the heart and origin of the rebellion, taking Columbia, South Carolina, and retaking Fort Sumter in mid-February. Back in Virginia, Phil Sheridan had driven Jubal Early out of the Shenandoah Valley in mid-October, and by election day, November 8, Lincoln's second term was assured. Perhaps he took satisfaction in his 212–21 electoral vote drubbing of George McClellan, the war Democrats' candidate and former general of the Army of the Potomac—who Lincoln had finally removed in 1862 after his consistent reluctance to fight. Perhaps he was pleased that he won 55 percent of the popular vote and that, unlike the 39.8 percent he managed in 1860, could now claim a popular mandate. But Lincoln seemed to take little outward comfort in military or electoral success. For him, both seemed infused with a deep sadness that seemed to hang on the sixteenth president like the awkwardly-fitting clothes that draped his lanky, six feet, four inch frame.

According to custom, Vice President–elect Andrew Johnson spoke and was sworn in first. Given the weather, this took place in the Senate chamber beginning precisely at noon. Johnson, former governor of Tennessee and the rare Southern politician to remain loyal to the Union, had been chosen by the convention as Lincoln's running mate, the president having decided to exercise no choice of his own. Ill and just back from Nashville, Johnson took a drink of whiskey to fortify himself, and then a second, and a third. "It is needless to say here that the unfortunate gentleman, who had been very ill, was not altogether sober at this important moment of his life," correspondent Noah Brooks recalled.[5] Johnson gave a rambling, 20-minute oration before finally being sworn in. Lincoln quipped to Missouri Senator John Henderson, a marshal for the ceremonies, "Do not let Johnson speak outside."[6]

Outside is where the ceremonies moved, when word was passed that the rain had safely stopped. The crowd, which had been forming for hours, was soaked and muddied, provoking Brooks to remark that "the greatest test of feminine heroism—the spoiling of their clothes— redounded amply to the credit of the women who were so bedraggled and drenched."[7] Brooks also described "a sea of heads in the great plaza in front of the Capitol, as far as the eye could reach, and breaking in waves along its outer edge."[8] At least one press account put the size of the crowd at thirty to forty thousand.[9]

Among the president's friends, Union troops, notables, and ordinary citizens stood John Wilkes Booth, hatless and behind an iron railing on a balcony above and behind the president. Booth had earlier tried to force his way into the procession that included the president as it moved through the Capitol and out to the East Front.[10]

At Lincoln's place stood a table with a tumbler of water. The table had been fashioned by B. B. French, Commissioner of Public Buildings, using three pieces left from the construction of the dome of the Capitol, which was unfinished at Lincoln's First Inaugural but now stood completed as silent testimony that the Union had endured.

Lincoln had prepared his address with care. Contrary to myth, he wrote his important speeches well in advance. A student of language and rhetoric, his texts showed increasing attention to artful expression as he grew in his presidency. He labored over words, crafting the Emancipation Proclamation, for example, a few sentences a day, putting it in a drawer and then returning to it the next day. He was done with the Second Inaugural at least by February 26, so he no doubt began it some time before that.[11]

What Lincoln looked and sounded like when he spoke can be approximated from contemporary accounts. He did not pay great attention to his appearance. The description at his Cooper Union address in February 1860 gives a clue: "The long, ungainly figure, upon which hung clothes that, while new for the trip, were evidently the work of an unskilled tailor; the large feet; the clumsy hands, of which...the orator seemed to be unduly conscious; the long, gaunt head capped by a shock of hair that seemed not to have been thoroughly brushed out."[12] Yet the New York *Herald* suggested that his manner of dress, at least, had improved, reporting on March 5, 1865 that "He has greatly improved in personal appearance lately, and dresses in good taste."[13] His voice was most often described as high and piercing in tone. Noah Brooks would describe it on this occasion by saying that "Every word was clear and audible" and that the address was delivered in "ringing and somewhat shrill tones."[14]

After the Senate's sergeant-at-arms bowed, hat in hand, to quiet and signal the crowd, Lincoln "advanced from his seat, a roar of applause shook the air, and, again and again repeated, finally died away on the outer fringe of the throng, like a sweeping wave upon the shore." And, "(J)ust at that moment the sun, which had been obscured all day, burst forth in its unclouded meridian splendor, and flooded the spectacle with glory and light."[15]

In his right hand, Lincoln held his speech, printed in two columns upon a half-sheet of foolscap. He would speak carefully. The address contained punctuation aimed at ensuring attention to the ears not just the minds of his audience. Lincoln understood the importance of how a message sounds and, like so much else about him, his growing gifts as a speaker had come from demanding work and practice. With friends in Springfield, where he had moved in 1837, he had been part of an informal group that included reading each other's work and practicing debates. His law work taught him the importance of careful writing coupled with the ability to speak simply. "Billy, don't shoot too high," he told his law partner Bill Herndon, "aim lower and the common people will understand you,"[16] He would use but four paragraphs and 703 words, of which 505 would be one syllable, to respond to the daunting leadership challenge he faced.

Gaining Followers for Peace

You're not a leader if no one follows, and Lincoln had struggled throughout the war to gain followers. Soon he would need them in peacetime, perhaps a more daunting task since the unity forged in battle seldom survives the silent cannon. His audience certainly included followers (though the presence of Booth attests that it contained angry Southerners as well), perhaps none more supportive than the blacks who owed their freedom to the sixteenth president. That Lincoln's followers differed dramatically in their support and expectations of him, he certainly knew. That his audience included distant millions in cities and towns throughout the North and South, as well as governments overseas, he also knew.[17] He would have to reach them all. As noted Lincoln scholar Douglas Wilson observed, the president was prepared to take a big risk in his address—not only in seeking common ground amid the conflicting expectations of his audience but in taking both a religious and prophetic view of the nation's past, present, and future.[18]

His opening salutation, "Fellow Countrymen," offers the first clue on his approach to gaining followers. His First Inaugural began with "Fellow Citizens of the United States," perhaps meant to emphasize the obligations of citizens under a Constitution and a Union at a time when both seemed to be falling apart. "Fellow Countrymen" suggests a more intimate connection, as well as a conclusion that the war had answered the question about whether we were still a nation.

What his audience expected is a matter of conjecture. As historian Ronald C. White, Jr. has noted, previous second inaugurals, as well as those to come, tended to focus on the president's achievements in his first term and plans for his second. They also traditionally offered some overt, or more likely subtle, self-congratulations.[19] Lincoln's audience may at least have expected details on his plans for reconstruction—a statement of policies if not also programmatic details.

Lincoln's Challenge to His Followers— The Closing Paragraph

They would not get what they expected. Effective leaders challenge followers with goals that are hard to reach.[20] A key to understanding Lincoln's leadership in the Second Inaugural is to begin at the end, where he issued such a challenge, in the fourth and final paragraph:[21]

> With malice toward none; with charity for all; with firmness in the right, as God gives us to see the right, let us strive on to finish the work we are in; to bind up the nation's wounds; to care for him who shall have borne the battle, and for his widow, and his orphan—to do all which may achieve and cherish a just and a lasting peace among ourselves, and with all nations.

Lincoln's message of forgiveness asks a great deal, but no more than he had already exhibited during the war. He was often criticized for his willingness to pardon civilians and soldiers. It was said of him that if the condemned could get an audience, preferably via wife or mother, a pardon was ensured. Lincoln was able to hold the need for toughness and forgiveness in the same mental framework without internal inconsistency. His driving principle was victory without malice, a managed complexity rare in any war. "I shall do nothing in malice. What I deal with is too vast for malicious dealing," he said in a letter to Louisiana Unionist Cuthbert Bullitt on July 28, 1862.[22]

The paragraph's single, 75-word sentence has all the elements of an effective challenge. Given the losses and anger on both sides in the Civil War, it *asks the near-impossible*—not just peace but an absence of malice and an offer of charity (which in Lincoln's time, as White has noted, was more akin to love than just support).[23] It is *inclusive*, asking equally of North and South, as the use of "us," "we," "all," and "ourselves" demonstrates. It offers a long-term *vision* ("a just and lasting peace") not simply a short-term goal ("bind up the nation's wounds"). It is a *message of hope* based on belief in the forgiving power of human nature. As Napoleon once said, "A leader is a dealer in hope," and Lincoln offered hope when it seemed most needed. The final paragraph is also a *call to action*: Lincoln asks, and expects, that his audience will see in his words something they can and should do.

Lincoln cannot have been under too many illusions about how receptive the audience would be. Northerners who wanted revenge might be too angry to hear it. The South would probably discount his call for charity, seeing in it a devious way to end the war, if they even read the speech. In commenting on his address in a March 15, 1865, letter to New York political leader Thurlow Weed, Lincoln acknowledged as much in saying that "I believe it is not immediately popular."

This may well be why Lincoln ended with his challenge, rather than using it as the first paragraph—to be followed by details of reconstruction policies. He knew it was asking a lot, that saying anything more specific could push the audience too far, too fast. He would need the first three paragraphs to get them ready for what he was asking.

Shaping Expectations—The Opening Paragraph

Of course his audience did not know what was coming, so the first paragraph was their only introduction to what would follow. It must have been heard as a rather strange introduction indeed. If you say the words aloud, and slowly ("I am compelled by nature to speak slowly," Lincoln once said.[24]), the tone appears heavy and somber. As White has observed, the words evoke such a mood: "there is *less occasion* for an extended address," "declarations have been *constantly called forth*," "contest which still *absorbs the attention and engrosses the energies*," "*little* that is new could be presented" (emphasis added).[25]

In addition, as White has also noted, Lincoln spends most of the paragraph saying what he will *not* talk about. He will *not* give an extended address. He will *not* talk about the course to be pursued. He will *not* offer a public declaration. He will *not* discuss the progress of arms. He will *not* even make a prediction about the war's outcome. This reinforces the subdued tone and must have confused an audience expecting a celebration of Union success.

From a leadership standpoint, the opening paragraph makes sense. Given where he wants to lead, Lincoln had to do two things at the outset. He needed to calm down the self-righteous and vengeful emotions of Northerners, and he needed to prepare them for hearing something they did not expect. His language thus seeks to lower their emotions by giving them nothing for which to cheer (and press accounts indicate that they did not cheer during his opening paragraph). Saying what he would not talk about, at the very least, must have raised a question in the minds of the audience: what *is* the president going to say? Questions open minds, and Lincoln's audience needed an open mind for the challenge he had prepared.

One also cannot escape Lincoln's sense of humility in the first paragraph. It was embedded in his character. Born in backwoods Kentucky, Lincoln spent his youth there and in Indiana in poverty and without access to good schooling. For his 1860 campaign biography, written by John Locke Scripps of the *Chicago Tribune,* Lincoln had shared that "the aggregate of all his schooling did not amount to one year."[26] He also told Scripps that his early life could be summed up in the single sentence from Gray's *Elegy*—"The short and simple annals of the poor."[27]

Humility also came with personal misfortune. No stranger to loss, Lincoln's mother had died when he was 9 and his older sister and younger brother had passed away before he reached 21. He lost his first sweetheart, Ann Rutledge when he was 26, a death so heart-wrenching that it provoked thoughts of suicide. He had lost two of four sons, Edward before age 4 and most recently, Willie, who died of typhoid in 1862, at age 12. Herndon wrote that Lincoln "was a sad-looking man; his melancholy dripped from him as he walked."[28]

Neither was he a stranger to political loss. His first election in 1832 ended in defeat. He served eight years in the Illinois state legislature, but his efforts for higher office were frustrated frequently. He served only one term in the federal House of Representatives and failed twice (1855, 1858) in bids for a Senate seat before his election to the presidency. His 1860 success, of course, was met immediately with the secession of Southern states, the firing on Fort Sumter, and years of lost battles and failed generals.

Lincoln's humility was not just a character trait; in his hands it became a leadership tool. Traveling to the Lincoln-Douglas debates in his 1858 run for the Senate, Lincoln rode in the regular passenger car in his everyday clothes (Douglas did not), to identify with the common man. (This also gave Lincoln invaluable access to voters and their concerns.) In his early years in the White House, he insisted on speaking with each petitioner in the hordes that lined the stairways and halls. As the pressures on him escalated, Lincoln still maintained a cordial and dutiful accessibility, including to black leaders whose access to the White House did not exist before his presidency. In October 1864, he met with the escaped slave, turned abolitionist, Sojourner Truth, who reported that she "never was treated by any one with more kindness and cordiality."[29]

So it is little surprise that he uses the personal pronoun "I" just once in the opening paragraph, and he takes credit for nothing. His reluctance to predict Union victory suggests that the course of the war has humbled even this already humble man. Demonstrating his humility, whether consciously or just as part of his way of being, also has the effect of subtly conveying that it is time for his audience to be humble as well. As a leadership strategy, this also lowers emotions and prepares them for what follows.

The Coming of War—The Second Paragraph

Having prepared them for something unexpected, Lincoln begins an important leadership tactic in the second paragraph. If "we" (North and South) must both practice "malice toward none" and "charity for all," then we must see ourselves as allies not opponents, as friends not enemies, as extending, open hands not opposing fists. This is a huge chasm to bridge, and Lincoln has two paragraphs to do it.

The most telling signal in the second paragraph is his use of collective nouns: "all" and "both." "All thoughts" were focused on the impending war. "All dreaded it—all sought to avert it." "Both parties deprecated war." Yet even as all hoped to prevent war, Lincoln's last sentence signals that "the war came." This has an air of inevitability, perhaps aimed at stopping North and South from blaming each other.

The second paragraph is also trying to thread a political needle. Having disappointed the North in the first paragraph, Lincoln must be careful not to lose them in the second. His reference to "saving the Union without war," "insurgent agents...seeking to dissolve the Union" and the fact that the South would "make war rather than let the nation survive" clearly take on a partisan air, perhaps calculated to keep the Northern audience engaged in the dialogue of the Second Inaugural. Indeed, this second to last sentence was, by contemporary accounts, the only one that received loud applause from the whole crowd.

Having thrown a partisan crumb to the North, Lincoln also uses words that allow the South to stay engaged. As president, he had to muster the political savvy to hold the North together and to offer the South a reason to lay down its arms. His political acumen is on display here. His reference to "insurgent agents" rather then "rebels" or "the South," may have been calculated to maintain his position that the Southern states never left the Union, to suggest that most southerners were different from and more allied with the North than a smaller number of "insurgent agents," and to keep the impact of harsher and more emotion-laden language from inflaming the South. In short, the paragraph seems calculated to allow everyone to see a reason to continue to listen, to feel that war was the result of historical forces, something almost outside the control of either party. That something is what Lincoln turns to next.

In leadership terms, Lincoln has lowered the emotional level of the audience and prepared it to hear something unexpected (first paragraph). He has given them reason to believe that the war was somehow inevitable and that while they may bear responsibility for it, that responsibility is shared (second paragraph). He has engaged them in a dialogue about the war. They must be active not passive in this ongoing dialogue, whose most important words will come after the war ends. So he ends the second paragraph by placing another question in their minds: why then did the (inevitable) war come? Lincoln's skillful use of questions to demand the audience engage in their own learning is a strategy to place the responsibility where the solution must be: among both North and South. It is they who must decide the meaning of the war if they are to fashion the peace. But Lincoln will give them some help.

Crafting Meaning through Story—The Third Paragraph

The third and longest paragraph, comprising nearly 60 percent of the address, presents Lincoln as a storyteller. Effective leaders tell, and engage followers in seeing themselves as part of, stories.[30] Our nation's most compelling story, the Declaration of Independence, begins with something as close to "once upon a time" as American history gets: "When in the course of human events." Like the best stories, it actively engages the listener in the quest for a satisfying ending. Indeed, Lincoln's Second Inaugural, like his Gettysburg Address, is yet another chapter in that founding story of freedom and nationhood.

Lincoln's story is about slavery, which "All knew . . . was somehow the cause of the war." This is a dramatic turn, a different story line for most of the nation, who thought the cause of the war was to preserve the Union. Lincoln knows it.

Adherence to the Constitution, including its limits on presidential action (regardless of his personal morality), had constituted Lincoln's North Star. He took his oath with gravity and determination. As he said to the South in his First Inaugural, "*You* have no oath registered in heaven to destroy the Government, while I shall have the most solemn one to 'preserve, protect, and defend it.' " This explains why, in that same address, he stated that "I have no purpose, directly or indirectly, to interfere with the institution of slavery in the States where it exists. I believe I have no lawful right to do so, and I have no inclination to do so." It explains why he pledged to uphold the 1850 Fugitive Slave Law, which required the North to return those who had escaped to freedom. It explains why he reversed two generals early in the war who freed slaves in captured Southern territory. It explains why his Preliminary Emancipation Proclamation in September 1862 permitted Southern states that ceased their rebellion to keep their slaves, as long as they rejoined the Union before January 1, 1863.

But once, as Commander in Chief, he freed the slaves in areas still in rebellion—a war measure calculated to swell the ranks of the Union army and turn Southern blacks against their masters—the same sense of obligation moved abolition throughout the United States into a core principle in his thinking. Once he began to put blacks into the manpower-starved Union army, where their numbers grew close to 200,000 by 1865, there was no turning back. The war that began to save the Union was transformed for Lincoln into a war to end slavery as well.[31]

This invited criticism from almost everyone. Abolitionists, who demanded social equality as well as emancipation, never felt Lincoln went far enough. War Democrats who were willing to continue the fight to preserve the Union were not willing to do so to free the slaves, and Peace Democrats wanted an armistice and a return to the status quo ante with slavery intact. Western Free Soilers hated Lincoln for emancipating any slaves, whom they believed would move west and "despoil" white territory. Freed slaves, like Frederick Douglass, criticized Lincoln because abolition in the 1863 Proclamation seemed too narrow and too slow. All of this was among Lincoln's Northern war coalition!

It was amid these passionate and seemingly incompatible positions that Lincoln was now seeking to lead. His approach was to explain his new understanding of the meaning of the war.

That justification is perhaps the most powerful attempt at presidential leadership in American inaugural history: the war is God's punishment for the institution of slavery. The inevitability at the end of paragraph two ("And the war came.") is explained:

> If we shall suppose that American slavery is one of those offenses which, in the providence of God, must needs come, but which, having continued through His appointed time, He now wills to remove, and

that He gives to both North and South this terrible war, as the woe
due to those by whom the offense came, shall we discern therein any
departure from those divine attributes which the believers in a living
God always ascribe to Him?

This is leadership heavy lifting, especially for the North who
would rather feel revenge than guilt. But Lincoln, since he must
engender equal responsibility for the war to gain equal responsibility for the peace, does not choose sides, as God does not: "Neither
party expected," "Neither anticipated," "Both read the same Bible
and pray to the same God, and each invokes his aid against the
other."

His reference to "American slavery," not "Southern slavery" is a
subtle yet unmistakable signal of joint culpability. For Lincoln, the
explanation for unending war seems clear:

Yet, if God wills that it continue, until all the wealth piled by the
bondsman's two hundred and fifty years of unrequited toil shall be
sunk, and until every drop of blood drawn with the lash, shall be paid
by another drawn with the sword, as was said three thousand years
ago, so still it must be said 'the judgments of the Lord, are true and
righteous altogether.'"

Clearly, the audience might see this as leadership slight-of-hand, as
Lincoln evading responsibility for the costs of war. Yet Lincoln does
not exclude himself from culpability. In the second paragraph, he
acknowledges that he "accepted war" just as in the first paragraph
he acknowledged his obvious responsibility for pursuing it. Lincoln's
meditation on the war in the third paragraph was the result of his
own struggle to answer the same question he asked of his followers:
why did the war come and why does it continue? As White notes, as
early as September 1862, shortly after the Union defeat at the Second
Battle of Bull Run, Lincoln had written his own thoughts on the war,
on a paper discovered by his secretary, John Hay, after his death. Hay
titled it "Meditation on the Divine Will":

The will of God prevails...In the present civil war it is quite possible
that God's purpose is something different from the purpose of either
party...I am almost ready to say this is probably true that God wills
this contest, and wills that it shall not end yet."[32]

Lincoln continued to think this way, as we know from two letters he
wrote in 1864. The first, dated April 4, to Albert Hodges, editor of
the Frankfort, Kentucky *Commonwealth*, summarized a conversation

Lincoln had had with Hodges and two other Kentuckians in the White House. At the letter's end, Lincoln said:

> I claim not to have controlled events, but confess plainly that events have controlled me...If God now wills the removal of a great wrong, and wills also that we of the North as well as you of the South, shall pay fairly for our complicity in that wrong, impartial history will find therein new cause to attest and revere the justice and goodness of God.

In a letter dated September 4, to Eliza Gurney, the widow of an English Quaker, who had visited him in the White House in 1862, a visit Lincoln still recalled, he wrote:

> The purposes of the Almighty are perfect, and must prevail, though we erring mortals may fail to accurately perceive them in advance. We hoped for a happy termination of this terrible war long before this; but God knows best, and has ruled otherwise...Surely He intends some great good to follow this mighty convulsion, which no mortal could make, and no mortal could stay.

Leadership as Learning and Teaching

From a leadership standpoint, Lincoln is doing three connected and mutually reinforcing things in the third paragraph. First, he is seeking to learn, and inviting his audience to learn. Rather than the self-assurance and confidence common in inaugurals, Lincoln is presenting questions, doubts, and the possibility of personal growth through the search for answers.[33]

Lincoln was nothing if not a constant learner. Though he would declare his "Education defective" in a request for a brief sketch for a compilation of biographies of members of Congress,[34] his cousin, John Hanks, described him as "a Constant and voracious reader."[35] His stepmother, Sarah Bush Johnston Lincoln, recalled that "Abe read all the books he could lay his hands on."[36] Too poor to own most of them, he would commit passages from borrowed books to writing in a commonplace book to learn them better and draw on them later. He was a child of the Enlightenment without the trappings of position or property that graced the founders he most admired—Washington and Jefferson.

Learning also required Lincoln to struggle with his views about slavery, which were more complex than traditional hagiographies suggest. Though in 1864 he said he was "naturally anti-slavery" and that "I cannot remember when I did not so think and feel,"[37] he was willing to take both sides of the issue as a young lawyer. In 1841 he defended a slave and won her freedom, yet in 1847, he argued on behalf of a slaveholder trying to recover runaway slaves. In 1837, he told the Illinois state legislature that "the institution of slavery is founded on both injustice and bad policy,"[38] yet he refused to support measures to end slavery where it existed because he felt that the Constitution did not permit such a step.

On one point, however, Lincoln was always firm. In a speech in Peoria, Illinois in 1854, when passage of the Kansas-Nebraska Act, with its repudiation of the Missouri Compromise, propelled Lincoln back into national politics, he said he hated the spread of slavery: "I hate it because of the monstrous injustice of slavery itself. I hate it because it deprives our republican example of its just influence in the world."[39] The nonextension of slavery became a principle on which Lincoln staked his politics. When he took a stand, he was usually immovable. As his wife, Mary, said: "He was a terribly firm man when he set his foot down...no man nor woman could rule him after he had made up his mind."[40]

His opposition to extension, however, has itself been misinterpreted. Before the Emancipation Proclamation, Lincoln wished to see slavery end, yet he was concerned as well about preserving the West for white Americans. He had believed that freed slaves should live outside the United States and thus supported compensated emancipation and colonization all the way through 1862. It was not until free blacks fought for the Union that he acknowledged that former slaves wanted and must be allowed to become part of America's future.[41] In short, a devastating war and continuous reflection helped him see anew. With this learning, and on this ground, he would indeed stand firmly.

The Second Inaugural can thus be understood as a series of complex questions that Lincoln used to propel the audience on a learning journey, one he had followed through four years of conflict. While he may not have intended to use the speech as a teaching device, it served that purpose. Consider the questions offered or implied in the first three paragraphs:

First paragraph:
- What is it "fitting and proper" to talk about today?
- If the president is not going to talk about the progress of the war, what is he going to talk about?

Second paragraph:
- Why was war inevitable?

Third paragraph:
- How was the slave interest the cause of the war?
- Why has war lasted so long? Why did God not take "our" side?
- What is God's purpose?
- Why would God will the war to continue? When will it end?
- What is God's righteous judgment?
- (Implied) What are we required to do now?[42]

But in asking his audience to consider these questions, Lincoln seeks nothing more than he is willing to do. In his State of the Union address in December 1862, he said:

> The dogmas of the quiet past, are inadequate to the stormy present... The occasion is piled high with difficulty and we must rise to the occasion. As our case is new, so must we think anew, and act anew. We must disenthrall ourselves, and then we shall save our country.

Leadership as Meaning Making

Second, Lincoln is practicing leadership as "meaning making." The facts of the war are not in doubt. What those facts mean had been contested by both sides and within multiple parties in the North. Leaders gain followers when the meaning they make of the facts is persuasive, enabling followers to see that meaning as part of a broader story and to see how to act within it. The meaning is in this third paragraph. The required action is in the fourth.

For Lincoln, the meaning of the war shifted from what he gave it in the First Inaugural, preservation of the Union. The abolition of slavery had now taken center stage. An argument that he could not make, politically and perhaps even personally, at the start of the war is acceptable, indeed imperative now.

Leadership as Fostering Responsibility

Third, Lincoln is asking the audience to accept responsibility for the war and its aftermath—the "great good" to follow *cannot* come until God wills the war to end—and it *will not* come unless human agents do the work.[43] Men began the war. God will end it. And then men must assume responsibility for fashioning "a just and lasting peace." Lincoln has finally prepared the audience for the message in his concluding paragraph.

Diagnosis complete, he is ready for prescription. Before returning to his soaring conclusion, however, we should look behind the text of the first three paragraphs at two additional leadership challenges Lincoln met. First, while on the surface he told a fairly simple story about the war, the underlying thinking is morally and politically complex. Indeed, this is one of the signal achievements of his leadership—the ability to put complex thoughts into words for a general audience.

The moral complexity emerges from his understanding of human nature. As early as October 4, 1854, in attacking Douglas's Kansas-Nebraska Act for allowing slavery to be opened to any new state if its voters so chose, Lincoln refused to cast the South or even slaveholders as evil against a virtuous North. In that speech, he said that "[t]hey are just what we would be in their situation. If slavery did not now exist amongst them, they would not introduce it. If it did exist among us, we should not instantly give it up."[44] Lincoln returns to that theme in the third paragraph of the Second Inaugural. We are all responsible for the evil of slavery. Despite the wishes of his Northern audience, Lincoln would not compromise on the proposition that slavery was a national crime. While the South held slaves, the North had largely acquiesced even while signing the Declaration of Independence.

The political complexity comes from the careful way Lincoln keeps stakeholders engaged. His analysis offers a rationale in which each can find some agreement. His use of religion both to deny them the "cover" of being on "God's side" and to help them see that they have defied God's will, provides a source of power behind his argument when his own power is, in the end, weak indeed. Lincoln thus positions his audience to rise to the challenge he is ready to give them.

"The Work We Are In"—Flexibility and the Fourth Paragraph

That Lincoln intends North and South to take responsibility for the peace is clear. He argues that this is not just a practical aim but a moral obligation. After four years of war, he can finally tell the nation that they have not only a duty to repair the Union but a moral obligation to end slavery. At last, such a peace can be their responsibility as well as his.

He is more elusive on what that peace will contain. Lincoln is at his rhetorical and perhaps leadership best in the final paragraph. Core values that matter to followers are a key source of leadership power. The paragraph is driven by four of them: forgiveness, love, caring, and justice. They provide the only specifics Lincoln offers. The goal these values serve is twofold: "finish the work we are in" and "achieve and cherish a just and lasting peace."

This is what James McGregor Burns has termed "transformational leadership."[45] Lincoln is asking his followers to rise to a set of moral values. He cannot lead by what Burns calls coercion; the reliance on raw power diminishes with the war's end. Neither can he lead through what Burns calls "transactional leadership," making promises to engender desired behavior. While a promise of fair and empathetic treatment may help, it alone will not rebuild a country and "countrymen" given what both sides have suffered.

Lincoln will say nothing further. This is a deliberate choice. From a leadership perspective, it is the right choice. The best leadership challenges provide the values and the goal or purpose, and leave the details to followers. Adding their own details builds follower commitment. Still further, Lincoln could not possibly know all the programs and policies that would be needed. That is the work of what Harvard professor Ron Heifetz calls "adaptive leadership."[46] Followers need to craft their own best solutions. Leaders cannot know enough, and should not even try, to make all the right calls.

Politically, he would not have been wise to be specific. Specifics would invite opposition. Historian Gary Wills has made the excellent point that the power of Lincoln's Second Inaugural is its flexibility.[47] There were so many questions to answer as the war neared an end, and Lincoln needed flexibility to answer them as conditions "on the ground" warranted. He had consistently refused attempts by Congressional radicals to impose harsh and precise terms on the South, and his own initial thoughts on reconstruction suggested only simple ones— reintegration with the Union, a prospective loyalty oath, and the abolishment of slavery.

Lincoln may be at his most flexible in his intriguing phrase "the work we are in." What, exactly, that "work" is can be answered in many ways. It may be the war. It may be the abolishment of slavery. It may be caring for the wounded and the survivors—on both sides of the conflict. It may be balancing the need to bring the South back into its "practical relation with the Union" while at the same time ensuring the security and livelihood of the newly-freed slaves. It may be the "just and lasting peace" to follow the war.

It may also be nationhood. Lincoln went to war to save the Union. But Union for him was not just a political arrangement. It represented a sentimental attachment to each other and to the idea of republican government. Washington, in his Farewell Address, had reminded a nation whose attachment to union was paramount in his mind, that they had "every inducement of sympathy and interest" to maintain the "sacred ties" that held the nation together. Lincoln had ended his First Inaugural with the following paragraph in which we can hear his plaintive plea to keep the "inducement of sympathy" alive:

> Though passion may have strained it must not break our bonds of affection. The mystic chords of memory, stretching from every battlefield and patriot grave to every living heart and hearthstone all over this broad land, will yet swell the chorus of the Union, when touched, as they surely will be, by the better angels of our nature.

Perhaps, in Lincoln's view, the time had finally come when "the better angels of our nature" would indeed swell the chorus of Union again.

Lincoln referred to "unfinished work" in his Gettysburg Address as well. That he clearly meant more than the work of war was evident, "the great task remaining before us" was the cause "that this nation...shall have a new birth of freedom—and that government of the people, by the people, for the people shall not perish from the earth." For Lincoln, the war would continue until atonement for slavery was complete, but it was also a war to preserve the republican idea. In his message to Congress on July 4, 1861, his first such statement since the firing on Fort Sumter, he had said:

> And this issue...presents to the whole family of man, the question, whether a constitutional republic, or a democracy—a government of the people, by the same people—can, or cannot, maintain its territorial integrity, against its own domestic foes...On the side of the Union, it is a struggle for maintaining in the world, that form, and substance of government, whose leading object is, to elevate the condition of men.[48]

So, in a sense, the Second Inaugural ends where the First Inaugural also ended, with a plea for a union built on sympathy and the power of nationhood to preserve liberty.

The Impact of Lincoln's Leadership

Upon concluding, Lincoln turned toward Chief Justice Salmon Chase, held up his right hand, placed his left hand on the Bible held by the Clerk of the Supreme Court, and took the oath. He then bent forward and kissed the Bible. "A salvo of artillery boomed upon the air, cheer upon cheer arose below, and, after bowing to the assembled host, the President retired within, resumed his carriage, and the procession escorted him back to the White House."[49] His son, Tad, sat by him.

Lincoln, by his admission, was satisfied with what he said. Though acknowledging to Thurlow Weed that he doubted it would be immediately popular, he said in the same letter that "I expect the latter [his inaugural] to wear as well as—perhaps better than—anything I have produced." He acknowledged that "Men are not flattered by being shown that there has been a difference of purpose between the Almighty and them." But, he concluded, "It is a truth that I thought needed to be told."[50]

At the White House, Lincoln received guests, and in those days that meant just about anyone who wanted to come—though according to at least one account, orders had been issued by someone not to admit blacks. Lincoln, quite naturally, was interested in the reaction to his address.[51]

The reaction at the Capitol was muted, except for blacks who frequently applauded. Noah Brooks recorded that "[t]he inaugural address was received in most profound silence" with applause primarily at the line in the second paragraph noted above and "occasional spurts of applause, too, at other points."[52]

In the White House, Lincoln insisted on shaking everyone's hand until, as the New York *Herald* reported, "his glove was half tore off."[53] He was especially eager to hear from Frederick Douglass, the former slave now renowned abolitionist, a man whose respect for the president grew only after the Emancipation Proclamation. After insisting Douglass be admitted when guards tried to prevent his entry, Lincoln said: "Douglass, I saw you in the crowd today listening to my inaugural address. There is no man's opinion that I value more than yours; what do you think of it?" "Mr. Lincoln, it was a sacred effort," Douglass replied, and he would later say that "the address sounded more like a sermon than a state paper," a wholly accurate observation.[54]

Beyond these initial judgments, Lincoln's assassination by John Wilkes Booth just six weeks later on April 14 makes a fair appraisal of the impact of his leadership in the Second Inaugural nearly impossible.[55] We can look at immediate reactions, as captured in newspapers in the North and South. We can assess Lincoln's actions in the remaining days of his life, and we can examine actions by others in the weeks before and months following his assassination. But how much impact the leadership in the Second Inaugural *could* have had is a question that became unanswerable when Lincoln's voice died on April 15.

Northern papers were mixed. *Harper's Weekly* said that it was "characteristically simple and solemn," and cited its "grand and quaint vigor."[56] The *Boston Daily Evening Transcript* cited Lincoln's closing as presaging "a new and blessed era alike for the victors and the vanquished."[57] The New York *Tribune* felt the address should have issued an appeal to the rebels for a cessation of hostilities.[58] The New York *Herald* correctly gathered that "Mr. Lincoln accepts the war as a national punishment from the Almighty for the 'offence' of slavery" but it castigated him for this approach saying, "Now this may be a strictly orthodox declaration...but is it calculated to do any good? We think not." The *Herald's* concern was that it would inflame "last ditch" Southern leaders and wondered how "the additional bloodshed and destruction of Southern white manhood and property could be considered the 'charity for all' which Mr. Lincoln recommends."[59] The *Herald* and the *New York Evening Post* both thought Lincoln should have addressed policy questions facing the nation.[60] The abolitionist *Liberator* thought he should have said more about how the needs of freedmen would be provided for in the postwar period.[61]

Southern papers were uniformly negative, if they reported on the speech at all. At least three reprinted the whole address; others just included excerpts. The *Richmond Dispatch* reprinted the speech and, on the next day, commented on it, making mention neither of Lincoln's statement that the war was a punishment for both the North and South nor his call for "malice toward none" and "charity for all." The *Lynchburg Virginian* included excerpts but took a similar approach in finding nothing positive to say.[62]

Lincoln had begun to live his own call for charity long before the war ended. As biographer William Lee Miller observed, "Lincoln was quite explicit in disavowing vengeance." In the draft of a letter to Secretary of War Stanton in March 1864, the president said, "(The government) can properly have no motive of revenge, no purpose to punish merely for punishment's sake."[63]

In his State of the Union address in December 1863, he had announced a proclamation for amnesty and reconstruction that offered a "full pardon...with the restoration of all rights of property, except as to slaves" for all but high-ranking Confederate officials, and he said he would recognize Southern states as reintegrated with the Union when they formed new governments supported by a future promise of loyalty, via oath, from as little as 10 percent of those who voted in 1860. For this reason, he used a pocket veto on July 2, 1864, to kill the Wade-Davis Bill for reconstruction, engineered by Radical Republicans and containing the requirement for an "iron-clad" loyalty oath whose signers, a required 50 percent of those who voted in 1860, had to state that they had never voluntarily fought against the Union or aided in the rebellion.

"Charity for all" included enslaved Americans as well. At the end of January, Lincoln saw Congress pass the Thirteenth Amendment and send it to the states, and he could take some comfort in the fact that he had pushed for this result without waiting until the safer Republican numbers of the recently elected Congress could have assured him an easier victory. It may serve as a mark of Lincoln's own transformation that he entered the presidency willing to accept a Congressionally passed Thirteenth Amendment that would enshrine slavery in the states where it existed and ended his presidency with a Thirteenth Amendment that abolished it everywhere.[64]

On February 13, 1865, Lincoln issued an Executive Order to the military officers in West Tennessee commanding that they "relieve the people from all burdens, harassments and oppressions so far as is possible...the object of the war being to restore and maintain the blessings of peace and good government."[65] In late March 1865, when Lincoln met Grant at City Point on the Potomac in the southern peninsula of Virginia, he spent five hours visiting soldiers in field hospitals and personally shook hands with hospitalized Confederates.[66] On March 28, when he met with Grant, Sherman, and Admiral David Porter aboard the presidential steamer, *River Queen*, he said of the Confederates: "Let them surrender and reach their homes...Let them all go, officers and all, I want submission, and no more bloodshed. I want no one punished; treat them liberally all round."[67]

Grant complied. In offering generous surrender terms at Appomattox on April 9, he also set the precedent for other Confederate units that laid down their arms. Officers could keep their side arms and personal possessions. Those who owned their horses could keep them, and all could go home, to begin their lives anew. Grant also provided

25,000 food rations for Lee's starving army. Even further, when Union troops began to cheer and fire artillery in celebration, Grant stopped them. As he remembered it later, he said: "The war was over. The rebels were our countrymen again."[68]

Lincoln's last speech, on April 11, to a cheering crowd outside the White House, also gives an indication of how the Second Inaugural may have been carried into practice if he had lived. After acknowledging that "we, the loyal people, differ among ourselves as to the mode, manner, and means of reconstruction," he recalled the terms he had offered in his 1863 State of the Union message and the generous terms he had offered to Louisiana for its return to the Union. He urged flexibility and accommodation and acknowledged, the first time for an American president, that limited suffrage for "the very intelligent" and "those who served our cause as soldiers" be granted to blacks. John Wilkes Booth was in the crowd and vowed that "This is the last speech he will make."

On the morning of his assassination, Lincoln convened a cabinet meeting, whose major topic was reconstruction policy. Gideon Welles, Secretary of the Navy, recalled the president's instructions:

> He hoped there would be no persecution, no bloody work after the war was over. None need expect he would take any part in hanging or killing these men, even the very worst of them. Frighten them out of the country, let down the bars, scare them off, said he, throwing up his hands as if scaring sheep. Enough lives have been sacrificed. We must extinguish our resentment if we expect harmony and union. There was too much desire on the part of our very good friends to be masters, to interfere with and dictate to these States, to treat the people not as fellow-citizens; there was too little respect for their rights. He didn't sympathize in those feelings.[69]

Lincoln's hopes in the Second Inaugural persisted for at least a while after his death, as chronicled in historian Jay Winik's *April 1865*.[70] Without the Second Inaugural, it is at least plausible that some Southern officers may have taken their troops into the mountains to continue the war. Yet hopes were soon replaced with acts of revenge. President Johnson initially tried to honor the slain president's reconstruction wishes, pardoning many Confederate leaders, approving limited black suffrage, and forgoing trials for treason (Capt, Henry Wirz, commandant of the Confederate Prison Camp at Andersonville, Georgia, was the only Confederate tried, convicted, and executed for war crimes). The Thirteenth Amendment was ratified in late 1865.

But reconstruction then took a turn. Radical Republicans gained control of Congress in 1866 and began to extract more punitive terms, including military rule in Southern states and disenfranchisement of thousands of white men. The Radical Republicans overrode one Johnson veto after another and fell just one vote short of successfully removing him from office in a Senate trial. They also refused to readmit any Southern states into the Union until June 1868, when Arkansas, Florida, and Louisiana were the first to rejoin. While pensions for soldiers and sailors who were invalids and for widows and orphans in the North were already well established by 1864, the Radical Republicans denied any veterans' benefits to Confederate soldiers (a ban that lasted until Congress overturned it in 1958), and the national cemetery system they enacted accepted only Union war dead and veterans.

Johnson lacked Lincoln's humility and humanity. In his selection of a vice president, we find perhaps Lincoln's greatest leadership failing. In letting the Republican Convention choose his running mate, Lincoln surrendered the opportunity and obligation to attend to leadership succession. Lincoln's hopes in the Second Inaugural suffered an irretrievable blow for that mistake. As Gary Wills recounts, when Frederick Douglass made his first appearance at the White House to meet with President Johnson, he was lectured about how blacks had oppressed poor whites. After Douglass left, Johnson said to a sympathetic reporter, "Those damn sons of bitches thought they had me in a trap. I know that damned Douglass...and he would sooner cut a man's throat than not." As Wills observed, "It is clear that Lincoln's inaugural address did not reach the befuddled Vice President who sat behind him as he delivered it...The executive mansion was a darker place in every way when Lincoln was removed from it, and from us. The Second Inaugural is the towering measure of our loss."[71]

In a similar vein, Lincoln's leadership strength of maintaining great flexibility of *means* in the service of core war *ends* would only work in peacetime if Lincoln were present to select the programs and policies that would guide reconstruction. Without more attention to these details, his flexibility became a weakness when Lincoln was no longer on the scene. In modern leadership language, Lincoln got the strategy right but failed in its execution. He lacked a team that both understood and was passionately committed to the story of the Second Inaugural.

If Lincoln's leadership through the Second Inaugural was cut short as his life was cut down, his words live on. Emblazoned on the

North Wall of the Lincoln Memorial, they greet new generations of Americans. "To care for him who shall have borne the battle and for his widow, and his orphan" has become the motto of the Department of Veterans Affairs and graces its entrance in Washington, DC.

But the power of the address may lie, most of all, in the integrity of the man. Lincoln did not flinch from the truth, and he insisted that the nation face it with him. Lincoln held up both a mirror that forced it to look and a light to guide it on the way. He showed us that leaders can employ the truth, with humility and hope, and that is perhaps the greatest legacy Lincoln leaves for the turning points we face.

The Struggle for Woman Suffrage: The Trial of Susan B. Anthony

The case of *United States v. Susan B. Anthony* was called at 3 p.m. on Tuesday, June 17, 1873. The crowd inside the Greek-revival Canandaigua Courthouse included a former president, Millard Fillmore. Twelve men sat on the right to try one woman; women were not allowed to sit on juries. Supreme Court Associate Justice Ward Hunt sat on the bench, riding circuit, in what would be the most notable case of a rather indistinct, ten-year career in the federal judiciary. Hunt had taken his seat on the highest court in January, appointed by President Grant. It was voting to reelect Grant that had put Anthony on trial.

On a quick glance, one could be forgiven for thinking that the five feet, five inch, 53-year-old could possibly have generated the controversy that led to her arrest for voting "without a lawful right to vote." Yet her strong chin and angular features, her composure and the fastidiousness of her dress signaled that a quick glance would not capture the essence of this formidable woman. Detractors had described her as "lean, cadaverous...with the proportions of a file and the voice of a hurdy-gurdy" and as a "typical old maid." They were among many who underestimated her.[1]

A century after tea was thrown into Boston harbor, one-half of America was still governed without a voice at the ballot box. Only Wyoming Territory had granted women the franchise, and even that was something of a mistake.[2] Twenty-five years of petitions still provoked—when they provoked a reaction at all—derision and lopsided defeats in legislative chambers and public referenda. It was this frustration, in post–Civil War America where slaves had been freed and enfranchised (at least the males), that led Anthony and 14 other women in the Eighth Ward in Rochester, New York to vote on November 5, 1872. She would be the only one tried.

Her conviction was a foregone conclusion (unbeknownst to the defense, Judge Hunt had already written his statement finding her guilty). She would not be allowed to testify in her own defense.[3] Her case would never go to the jury. But, in the end, she would not be silenced. Canandaigua, the county seat, took its name from an Iroquois word meaning "chosen spot." It would become one for Anthony. In some ways, this was a foregone conclusion too, even if she was somewhat of a latecomer to the suffrage cause.

Not Present at the Creation

In July 1848, when the American movement for woman's rights was launched with the Declaration of Sentiments and Resolutions in Seneca Falls, New York, Anthony was a teacher in Canajoharie, 130 miles to the east.[4] She would not attend her first woman's rights convention until 1852. Still, most of the first three decades of her life were preparation for her role as an advocate for women.

Her "late" entry into the cause is understandable. Few women of her time contemplated improving their own condition; their involvement in social efforts to help others was more acceptable. The eighth resolution at Seneca Falls, "[T]hat it is the duty of women of this country to secure to themselves their sacred right to the elective franchise," almost did not pass in the predominantly female gathering, and some of the women who signed it later tried to remove their names under blistering criticism.[5] As a Quaker, voting was not even, initially, a pressing issue for Anthony: Quakers did not vote because the governments that voters chose supported war.

Though exposed to some of the severe limits on women in early nineteenth-century America, such as the fact that no college and most professions would not accept them, in 1848 these had not registered on her as shackles. Single, she did not suffer from laws that prohibited married women from owning property and denied them legal custody of their children. Her teaching salary (a fraction of that for men) was her own, which would not have been true if she had wed. Nor was she constrained by the prevailing English common law, which held that "[t]he husband and wife are one, and that one is the husband."[6]

Despite the crushing weight of law and tradition, the latter reinforced by (male) ministers who "found" in the Bible the justification for women's subjugation, Anthony grew up in an environment that cushioned such blows. Yet that environment was ideally suited to make her a reformer.

Education was central to Daniel and Lucy Anthony, for their daughters as well as sons, and Susan, born on February 15, 1820, near Adams, Massachusetts, began to read and spell at age three. Her father opened a private school in his store so he could choose the teachers for his children. As they grew, he expected them to teach as well, first in his own school and then for neighboring families. In Deborah Moulson's Female Seminary, where Susan was sent at 17, she learned algebra, philosophy, chemistry, physiology, and bookkeeping, subjects unavailable for most young women of her day.

Added to a sound education in mind was her parents' example in morals. Despite disapproval of the Society of Friends, her father had married a Baptist. As a Quaker, he had also rejected the Pauline precept that said, "Let your women keep silence in the churches." Indeed, Susan attended Quaker Sunday meetings where women participated actively in decision making, and her aunt was a Quaker preacher. Her parents and sister had even attended the second woman's rights convention, in Rochester, two weeks after Seneca Falls. They voted for all the resolutions, including the franchise for women.

When she was six, her family had moved to Battenville, New York, where her father entered cotton manufacturing. He became the first in the area to ban the sale of liquor in his company store and organized a temperance society. He refused any cotton produced by slave labor. When the family moved to a farm outside Rochester in 1845, he became a leader in the Underground Railroad and hosted abolitionists in his home—Sunday gatherings where Susan met men such as Frederick Douglass and William Lloyd Garrison and participated in their conversations.

A questioning mindset was thus the water in which the Anthony children swam. As a student in Moulson's Seminary, on her eighteenth birthday, Susan wrote home that "[a] Phrenologist gave us a short lecture this morning and examined a few heads, mine among them. He described only the good organs and said nothing of the bad. I should like to know the whole truth."[7]

"I had all the freedom I wanted from the time I was a child," Anthony said.[8] Out in the world, as well as in her father's business, that freedom exposed her to women in a range of roles that demanded strength. Piety, purity, domesticity, and submission to men, the bed-rock principles of the prevailing "cult of true womanhood" matched neither her observation of women nor her interests for herself. Though she received proposals, she never married. Late in life she explained: "When I was young if a girl married poor she became a housekeeper and a drudge. If she married wealthy, she became a pet and a doll. Just think, had I married at twenty, I would have been a drudge or a doll for 55 years. Think of it!"[9]

Not surprisingly, she tired of teaching in Canajoharie by 1849 and resolved to move on. The butterfly was struggling to escape the chrysalis. She briefly lamented that she could not join the California Gold Rush: "If I was a man wouldn't I be off," she said.[10] But social betterment drew her forward, and she would not lament for long.

First Cause, First Frustration: Temperance

Shortly after moving to Canajoharie in 1846, Anthony had joined the Daughters of Temperance, set up by the Sons of Temperance as the appropriate vehicle for women to aid the movement. Indeed, temperance was perhaps the only social reform in which women could acceptably engage. She took the post of secretary, but it would be three years before, in March, 1849, she made her first public speech. "Our motive," she said, is a "radical change in our Moral Atmosphere." "How is this great change to be wrought," she asked. "I answer, not by confining our influence to our own home circle."[11]

When she left Canajoharie, she spent time from 1850 to 1851 at her father's farm, chafing at the bit. Her temperance work continued with fund-raising suppers and festivals. Attending the Sons of Temperance convention in Albany in 1852, however, her credentials were accepted but not her voice. The presiding officer informed her that "the sisters were not invited here to speak but to listen and learn." Anthony stormed out.[12]

That same night, she helped organize a Woman's State Temperance Convention, which convened in April 1852. She spent the summer visiting 30 counties and gathering 28,000 signatures on petitions for a "Maine Law"—to mirror legislation enacted the previous year in that state to limit the sale of alcohol. The petitions, presented to the New York State legislature in January, were derisively received by one young member who said the women were "out of their sphere." "Who are these asking for a Maine Law?" he charged. "Nobody but women and children!" As Ida Husted Harper, Anthony's authorized biographer put it, "Miss Anthony then and there made a solemn resolve that it should be her life work to make a woman's name on a petition worth as much as a man's."[13]

Her resolve intensified when delegates from the Woman's State Temperance Society were invited to attend the World's Temperance Convention in New York in September 1853. At a preliminary meeting in Syracuse, however, their credentials were rejected by the men. As if this was not enough, more rejection came that same spring when the Woman's State Temperance Society, which allowed men to join but not hold office, changed its rules to give them equal opportunity to serve. The men, aided by conservative women who balked at some of the woman's issues that were making their way into the temperance agenda, promptly took over the group and ousted Elizabeth Cady Stanton, author of the Seneca Falls Declaration, from her role as president. Anthony, as secretary, resigned in protest from the organization she and Stanton had launched just a year before.

While she would remain supportive of the temperance movement, Anthony concluded that unless women gained economic and political independence, they would be forever subservient. The woman's rights movement thus emerged as an inevitable choice. But her commitment to that cause had some help.

The Powerful Partnership of Susan B. Anthony and Elizabeth Cady Stanton

Anthony's work in the Woman's State Temperance Society with Stanton had emerged from a chance street-corner encounter in Seneca Falls in May 1851. That meeting produced a partnership that would last 51 years and both define and propel the suffrage movement. As Geoffrey Ward and Ken Burns, creators of the PBS documentary, *Not for Ourselves Alone*, put it: "Stanton had failed to radicalize the temperance movement, but she had done something far more important...she had helped to radicalize Susan B. Anthony." "In turning the intense earnestness and religious enthusiasm of this great-souled woman into this challenge," Stanton would write, "I soon felt the power of my convert goading me toward a more untiring work."[14]

On the surface, the new friends were so different as to question the attraction. Stanton was the daughter of a wealthy judge, married, mother of four, and accustomed to material comfort. Anthony was the daughter of a struggling businessman, single, and dependent on her own earnings. Stanton was plump, gregarious, and tired more easily from the burdens of maintaining a busy home. Anthony was trim, restrained, needed to care only for herself, and had boundless energy. She even underlined words in her letters to add emphasis on an otherwise placid page.

Beneath the surface, the women were different too, but in ways that complemented their talents. Stanton was the writer and philosopher and took a panoramic view of woman's rights. She pushed almost every issue, including the "third rails" of divorce and the subjugation of women by religion. Anthony would become the manager of the movement, handling the details of organization, petitions, fundraising, conventions, and politics that were either not Stanton's interests or simply impossible given her growing family. In time, Anthony would decide to push only one issue—the franchise—convinced that everything else depended on it. Throughout this masterful "marriage," both would offer support when the other was tested and would, as in all marriages, test each other as well. They would not agree on everything, but they would stay together through everything.

If Stanton was the general in the tent, Anthony was the colonel in the field. "Miss Anthony was the connecting link between me and the outer world," Stanton would say, "the reform scout who went to see what was going on in the enemy's camp and returned with maps and observations to plan the mode of attack."[15] "I forged the thunderbolts, and she fired them."[16] Or, as Stanton's husband Henry put it to his wife: "You stir up Susan, and she stirs up the world."[17] In 1878, Theodore Tilton, abolitionist and woman's rights champion, captured the partnership well: "I know of no two more pertinacious incendiaries in the whole country...this noise-making twain are the two sticks of a drum keeping up what Daniel Webster called the 'rub-a-dub of agitation.'"[18]

Among their first successful agitations was a law enacted in New York dramatically extending property rights for women. But it took six years.

Anthony made a canvass of southern New York on behalf of this cause, finding that almost every woman's temperance group she helped organize the year before had failed for lack of funds. She returned to Rochester strengthened not only in her belief that women could not depend on men but with a plan for a state convention and a petition drive to confront the legislature. It would be unmoved until 1860, when it finally passed a landmark bill, but her work had already earned her the title "Napoleon of the movement" from Unitarian clergyman William Henry Channing.[19]

But "Napoleon" needed troops. She would work to gain and train them the rest of her life. It was slow going at first, partly because of the women themselves. Finally given permission to address the 1853 New York State teachers' convention, she made her first memorable speech, noting that men would continue to get low wages in the profession so long as they had to "compete with the cheap labor of women. Would you exalt your profession, exalt those who labor with you," she said. But many of the women felt that she should have remained silent. "I was actually ashamed of my sex," one commented.[20] At a state teachers' convention in 1857, Anthony introduced a resolution she and Stanton had written calling for equal educational opportunities for men and women in schools, colleges, and universities. Most of the women voted against it.

She would lose patience with such women, as she would when women left the movement for child rearing, becoming exasperated with Stanton who would have seven children. "Those of you who have talent to do honor to poor—oh!—how poor—womanhood have all given yourselves over to baby-making; and left poor brainless me to do battle alone," Anthony vented. Stanton had to remind her that "You need rest too, Susan. Let the world alone awhile. We cannot bring about a moral revolution in a day or year."[21]

The Civil War would force a respite whether Anthony wanted it or not. The nation would accept only one conflict for rights at a time.

Second Cause—and Disenchantment: Emancipation and Black Male Suffrage

Anthony always opposed slavery, so it was natural to support emancipation as the crisis peaked in the 1850s. When Samuel May, Jr., secretary of Garrison's American Anti-Slavery Society, asked her help to build support for abolition in western and central New York in 1855, she agreed. Her agreement came with a cost and a concern.

The cost was less time to focus on woman's rights. Annual woman's rights conventions, central to recruitment and momentum, would eventually prove impossible as energy and attention focused on slavery and war. The cost also included anger directed at Anthony by those who hated the Garrisonians, whom they blamed for the war.

In Syracuse in early 1861, her attempt to speak at an abolition meeting was met with rotten eggs and broken benches. She was burned in effigy later that night.[22]

The concern was that support for abolition would not be returned by men after the war. Stanton believed it would come; Anthony doubted it. The first indication that she was right came in April 1862 when the New York legislature took back some of the women's 1860 gains, leading Anthony to conclude that "while the old guard sleep the 'young devils' are wide awake, and we deserve to suffer for our confidence in 'man's sense of justice.'"[23]

Nevertheless, Anthony and Stanton never did things halfheartedly. When Lincoln's Emancipation Proclamation in January 1863 freed only slaves in states still in rebellion, abolitionists pressed for a constitutional amendment. In May, Anthony and Stanton formed the Women's Loyal National League to support it. Within a year they presented 400,000 signatures in support of legislation that would become the Thirteenth Amendment.[24] Though the League's initial resolutions also asked for equal political rights for women, that was ignored when the amendment passed—another sign that Anthony's prediction was accurate.

Anthony's sense of abandonment deepened after the war. One month after Appomattox, the American Anti-Slavery Society took up the cause of a Fourteenth Amendment to ensure freed black men got the vote. Wendell Phillips, its new president and a previously staunch advocate of woman suffrage, concluded that support for the amendment from Democrats and conservative Republicans required insertion of the word "male" in the section punishing any state with proportionate loss of representation for denying the franchise, the first time sex had ever been used as a distinction in the Constitution. Anthony fumed: "I would sooner cut off my right hand than ask the ballot for the black man and not the woman," she said. Despite ten thousand signatures pleading to include women, Congress passed the restrictive amendment in June 1866, and it was ratified two years later.[25]

In late 1866, a proposal to remove "male" from a Senate bill to extend the vote to Negroes in the District of Columbia also failed, 37–9. In June 1867, the chairman of the committee on suffrage at the New York State Constitution Convention, editor Horace Greeley, an early supporter of woman's rights, curtly dismissed the call for woman suffrage, lecturing Anthony and Stanton: "Ladies, you will please remember that the bullet and ballot go together. If you vote, are you ready to fight?" Anthony's reply: "Certainly, Mr. Greeley, just as you fought in the late war—at the point of a goose quill," made him furious. Confronting him soon after with a petition on behalf of woman suffrage that included the signature of his wife turned him into a lifelong enemy.[26]

That fall, Kansas became the first state to allow a popular vote on the enfranchisement of women along with a vote on enfranchising Negroes. The initially supportive Republican party changed its mind, opposing the former for fear of losing the latter. Despite Anthony's canvass of the state, woman suffrage failed, 3–1.[27] She was further stung by opposition from friends for allowing an antiblack, copperhead Democrat, George Francis Train, to campaign with her (in hopes of securing Democratic votes to offset Republican defections). The Kansas vote would be the first of 479 efforts to secure the ballot through state legislatures and the first of 56 statewide campaigns, almost all of which would prove fruitless over the next 50 years.[28]

Even one seeming bright spot turned dark. When Train first arrived in Kansas, he startled Anthony by announcing she was going to start a woman suffrage paper, with his financial backing: "Its name is to be *The Revolution*; its motto: 'Men, their rights and nothing more; women, their rights and nothing less.'" The first issue of the 16-page weekly came out on January 8, 1868, but it never got beyond a small—though national—readership. When Train could not live up to his financial promises, the paper failed two years later, leaving Anthony with a $10,000 debt that took six years to pay off.

Republican anger at Train also became a wedge in the American Equal Rights Association (AERA), a group of former abolitionists and suffragists Anthony and Stanton helped form in 1866 to advance the interests of blacks and women. By 1869, anger over Train's antiblack rants and Anthony and Stanton's embrace of a Democrat helped fuel a major clash over a proposed Fifteenth Amendment to ensure black male suffrage when the Fourteenth Amendment could not. The men told the women that it was "the Negro's hour" and that woman suffrage would have to wait. Anthony protested: "The question of precedence has no place on an equal rights platform...the business of this association is to demand for every man, black or white, and every woman, black or white, that they shall be enfranchised."[29]

When the AERA voted to endorse the amendment anyway, many women bolted and formed the National Woman Suffrage Association, led by Anthony and Stanton. Its focus was to be a sixteenth amendment granting woman suffrage. By November, however, a group of more conservative New England women formed the rival American

Suffrage Association, focused on a state-by-state approach and because they did not support some of Stanton's more far-reaching women's rights stances. This rift would weaken the movement for the next two decades.

Moses in the Wilderness

By the early 1870s, then, Anthony had lost every suffrage campaign, lost on the Fourteenth and Fifteenth Amendments, lost *The Revolution*, lost control of the AERA, lost the support of much of the Republican party leadership, lost a segment of the movement to the rival American Suffrage Association, and even lost active support from Stanton, who—wounded by the battles and with a family to support—retreated to the paid lecture circuit.

Writing to a friend, Lepha Canfield, Anthony said that "I suppose our movement, like all from the beginning must have its Forty years in the Wilderness."[30] She underestimated. From 1848, it would take 72 years before passage of the Nineteenth Amendment, but the analogy is apt. Like Moses, she had undergone a period of testing before emerging to help lead a movement. Like Moses, she gained a considerable set of skills for the task. She would need them in the jury trial to come and its aftermath.

Perhaps her principal talent was dogged determination. Once focused on the ballot, all else became secondary. "Woman and her disenfranchisement is all I know," she said. It's not that she didn't care about other issues, it's that these were effects not root cause. "I am as deeply and keenly interested in the many reforms... as any one can possibly be—but knowing that no right solution of any great question can be reached until the whole people have a voice in it—I give all of myself to getting the whole people inside the body politic," she would write in 1894.[31]

Intense focus was also associated with risk taking and its attendant disapproval:

> Cautious, careful people, always casting about to preserve their reputation and social standing, never can bring about a reform. Those who are really in earnest must be willing to be anything or nothing in the world's estimation... and bear the consequences.[32]

To this she committed energy even when age could have earned her a rest: "I don't want to die just as long as I can work," she said. "The minute I can't, I want to go."[33] At a party given her on her fiftieth birthday, she acknowledged that

> [i]f this were an assembled mob opposing the rights of women I should know what to say. I never made a speech except to rouse people to action…when the Secretary of State proclaims that this amendment has been ratified by twenty-eight States, then Susan B. Anthony will stop work—but not before.[34]

In later years, Stanton would write of Anthony that next to Theodore Roosevelt, she was "the nearest example of perpetual motion."[35] Biographer Lynn Sherr recalls Anthony's stay at Washington, DC's Shoreham Hotel at age 84, when the proprietor

> hesitated about inviting Anthony to see the view from the top floor because she had to take a flight of stairs to get there. When a colleague noted that the famed suffrage leader regularly ran up and down stairs, Anthony replied. "No, I do not do that any longer because I don't think it wise, but I never walked up stairs until I was eighty.[36]

Anthony's focus and energy were enhanced by her humility. She never took a salary from the associations she led and often donated from meager earnings to help women pay expenses to attend conventions. At the women's rights convention in 1903, she received a huge welcome from the raucous delegates. Baffled, she asked what was happening. "You happened, Aunt Susan," replied her close colleague, Anna Shaw.[37]

Her energy fed her optimism and vice versa. She would need such hope whenever she lost in court, yet losses were rarely interpreted as defeats. When suffrage failed in Kansas in 1867, her response was characteristic: "Never was so grand a success—never was *defeat* so glorious a victory. But depend on it," she wrote fellow suffragist Olympia Brown, "there is a wise *destiny* in our *delay*—it is not defeat."[38]

Anthony was, of course, also managing a movement. In the nineteenth century, this meant travel and speaking, resolutions, petitions, conventions, and mailing literature. She canvassed nearly every city or town where they would listen, and many where they would not. "Thus closes 1871," she would write in her diary, "a year full of hard work, six months east, six months west of the Rocky Mountains; 171 lectures, 13,000 miles of travel."[39] At 76, in the California campaign, she would spend eight months speaking three times a day.[40]

She orchestrated meetings with an artistry that foreshadowed the best "advance man" of the twentieth century. As Dorr describes her work in the 1867 Kansas campaign:

> she had to manage the entire campaign, see to the halls, the lighting...the advertising, the newspaper notices, tickets and ushers, and practically all the advance correspondence... it was her duty to rush to the hall, consult with committees, interview newspaper editors, look up absentee janitors, get everything in order for the meeting.[41]

And she raised money. As biographer Lynn Sherr notes, "it was she who passed the hat (or bonnet), begged for subscriptions to women's journals, identified potential contributors." She even auctioned off pieces of her seventy-eighth birthday cake to raise cash for the cause.[42]

While her wilderness wanderings may be viewed as fruitless in producing suffrage victories, they provided lessons in political management that women could gain no other way. As she taught what she learned to others, these lessons were instrumental in the movement's eventual success, especially in the years after her trial.

"Governments never do any great good things from mere principle, from mere love of justice," she would say in 1891.[43] Early in her career, she learned how to get the attention of politicians—and how to count votes. One of her scrapbooks contained a seating chart of members of Congress, and she knew the value of being in Washington. She insisted on holding annual women's rights conventions there, and preached the need for a "Watching Committee" that could do its own lobbying to match "all the great moneyed interests" who "keep hundreds of agents at the national Capitol" while "[W]e have no one here."[44] She also knew the power of the press: "Our movement depends greatly on the press. The worst mistake any woman can make is to get crosswise with the newspapers."[45]

These were all tools in a strategy that depended on educating and organizing women for political action. She called her efforts "subsoil plowing" and knew they would take years to bear the fruit of the franchise. Her initial approach, gaining suffrage state by state, had achieved very limited success by the late 1860s. Her hopes that Congress, through the postwar amendments, would enfranchise women were also fading. But she would make one last attempt, hoping the courts had the courage that politicians lacked. She would find that this was expecting too much as well.

Deciding to Vote

In the winter of 1869, Anthony joined the Lyceum lecture circuit, a relief since it provided payment for her speeches and handled logistics that otherwise required her attention. In St. Louis, she stayed with Francis and Virginia Minor, he a highly regarded lawyer and she a suffragist. Francis argued that the Fourteenth Amendment, ratified the previous July, could be interpreted as already granting women the vote. On October 14, he sent Susan a letter with six resolutions adopted by the Woman Suffrage Association of Missouri to that effect, based on the claim that women were citizens and that voting was one of the "privileges and immunities" that states could regulate but not "abridge."

This idea was picked up in January 1871 by editor and financier Victoria Woodhull, who burst onto the suffrage scene with testimony in front of the House Judiciary Committee in which she claimed that women had the right to vote under both the Fourteenth and Fifteenth Amendments.[46] Anthony immediately invited her to address the National Woman Suffrage Association's convention in Washington the next day. Jumping on both the Minor and Woodhull arguments, the convention adopted two resolutions, the first asking Congress to pass a declaratory act that the Fourteenth Amendment had granted all citizens the franchise and the second saying that "it is the duty of American women...to apply for registration" to vote and that if denied "to see that suits be instituted in the courts" to secure that right.[47] By the end of the month, the Judiciary Committee's majority report denied that Congress could intervene in state control over voting rights, but the minority report held that "the right of suffrage is a fundamental right of citizenship" protected under the Fourteenth Amendment.[48] A difference existed, and Anthony intended to exploit it. She desperately needed a victory.

She pushed the Minor-Woodhull interpretation in 1872 as the focus of the National's convention and testified before the Senate Judiciary Committee on January 12. As the House had done the year before, the Senate also refused a declaratory act.

In a last effort, Anthony attended both the Republican and Democratic national presidential nominating conventions that summer. The Republicans adopted a plank (which Stanton called a "splinter") saying the party "is mindful of its obligations to the loyal women of America for their noble devotion to the cause of freedom...and the honest demands of any class of citizens for equal rights should be treated with respectful consideration."[49] The Democrats would not grant even this much, so Anthony worked for Grant's reelection, not because she was a Republican but because that party offered at least a glimmer of hope.

That hope faded as Grant's prospects improved against his opponent (and Anthony's nemesis, Horace Greeley). The Republican "promise" to women receded into insignificance. Politicians would not act; working through the courts was the last available step.

Following the Minors' argument in 1869 and the strategy outlined in the 1871 resolutions, Anthony would try to register to vote. She expected to be turned away. As she wrote to Martha Coffin Right, former vice president of the AERA, in January 1873: "I never dreamed of the U.S. officers prosecuting me for voting—thought only that if I was refused—I should bring action against inspectors."[50] That action would have allowed her to appeal, if necessary, all the way to the Supreme Court for a ruling on the Fourteenth Amendment, but it was the first of the miscalculations and surprises on all sides to come. On Friday, November 1, 1872, she and 14 other women went to the registry office for the Eighth Ward, located in a barbershop, and asked to register. The three male inspectors refused, but Anthony persisted, reading them the Fourteenth Amendment and threatening to have them arrested. Two of three backed down, and the women's names were added to the rolls.[51] Anthony went promptly to a newspaper office to ensure coverage.

She then visited a number of lawyers to gain their advice on her right to vote. Only one would help her—Henry Selden, formerly judge of the court of appeals. With his offer to defend her, she returned to the barbershop on November 5. Sylvester Lewis, a poll watcher for the Democrats, challenged her, requiring her to swear an oath that she was qualified to vote. By law, the inspectors then had to accept her vote. The other 14 also voted, although about 30 other women who tried to register in other wards were prevented by registrars.[52] The Associated Press carried the news across the country, no doubt precisely what she hoped. "Well I have been & gone & done it!!" she wrote in a letter to Stanton that same day. "Positively *voted* the Republican ticket—straight—this AM at 7 o'clock and *swore my vote in at that*...So we are in for a fine agitation in Rochester."[53]

Arrest and Trial

Acting on a complaint from Lewis, U.S. Commissioner William C. Storrs issued an arrest warrant for Anthony, and on November 18, a U.S. deputy marshal showed up at her Rochester home. Anthony demanded to be handcuffed, but he refused. He took her in a horse-drawn cart (she insisted he pay her fare) to Storrs' office, which Anthony described as "the same dingy little room where, in the olden days, fugitive slaves were examined and returned to their masters." On arriving, she learned that not only had the 14 other women also been arrested, but the 3 inspectors as well.[54]

In a series of examinations ending on December 26, Storrs concluded that Anthony should be held pending action of the federal grand jury in January, since the charges against here were for voting for members of Congress, in violation of the Enforcement Act of 1870.[55] Anthony was ordered to post $500 bail. She refused but was not jailed. On January 2, Selden petitioned U.S. district judge Nathan Hall for a writ of habeas corpus arguing that Anthony should not be held in custody, but Hall would not agree (or jail her). On January 24, the federal grand jury in Albany indicted all 15 women, and Anthony was arraigned and ordered held on $1,000 bond. Selden posted her bond, a tactical mistake since it cut off any chance to appeal her incarceration through the courts. A May trial date in Rochester (Monroe County) was set.

Anthony spent March and April speaking in 29 villages and towns in Monroe County, asking each time, as the title of her speech put it, "Is It a Crime for a U.S. Citizen to Vote?" At the end of each speech, the audience voted and always concluded it was not. She counted on swaying the jury pool, writing to Congressman Benjamin Butler at the end of April that "I rather guess the U.S. District Attorney...will hardly find twelve men so ignorant...as to agree on a verdict of Guilty."[56] She calculated correctly but may not have anticipated what happened next. On May 22, U.S. Attorney Richard Crowley, convinced she had indeed tainted the jury pool, asked that the trial be moved to the circuit court in Ontario County, where it would be tried by Supreme Court Associate Justice Ward Hunt. Undeterred, Anthony began a canvass in Ontario County with the same speech, ending the night before the trial.

With Hunt on the bench, Anthony's approach had both worked and backfired. Woman suffrage would now get wide attention, since circuit court cases generally did, but it would be before a judge who was no friend to the cause. Though only on the Supreme Court a few months, Hunt had already voted with the majority in the *Slaughter-House* cases in April, ruling that the Fourteenth Amendment's "privileges and immunities" clause affected only the rights of United States not state citizenship, that it was intended to protect former slaves and thus should not be applied more broadly. Hunt voted with the majority again that same month in *Bradwell v. State of Illinois*, accepting the state's argument that Mary Bradwell could be denied membership in the state bar because she was a woman, denying protection of the Fourteenth Amendment. More ominous, Hunt decided to try Anthony's case himself, instead of allowing district court Judge Hall to sit with him, as was common in criminal cases. If he had, another avenue of appeal might have existed for Anthony if the two judges disagreed.

Selden's three hour argument at trial on June 17 argued that voting was a natural right or else "consent of the governed" had no meaning and other rights could not be protected. He further claimed she was not guilty because she voted believing she had a right to vote and thus lacked criminal intent. He called her to testify, but Crowley objected that she was "not competent as a witness in her own behalf," an objection that Hunt sustained. Crowley's two hour speech challenged Selden's premise, arguing that voting was not protected under the "privileges and immunities" clause of the Fourteenth Amendment and that suffrage was up to the states to regulate, citing both *Slaughter-House* and *Bradwell*.

After these arguments, Hunt, on the morning of June 18 , shocked the courtroom by directing a verdict of guilty, using the rationale that there existed only questions of law, not fact, and that a jury could only rule on the latter so was unneeded. Over Selden's objection, Hunt ordered the clerk to "[T]ake the verdict." When Selden asked that the jury be polled, Hunt discharged them (several later reported they would have acquitted her). That afternoon, in a separate trial, the three inspectors were found guilty—at least this time the case went to the jury, though Hunt kept them in the courtroom saying they had little to deliberate about.

On June 19, Selden appealed the directed verdict, an appeal that in circuit court had to be made to the same judge. Hunt denied the appeal and then made the mistake that would turn his carefully managed trial on its head. Ordering Anthony to stand up, he asked: "Has the prisoner anything to say why sentence shall not be pronounced?" A routine question asked of anything but a routine defendant.

At Last Anthony Speaks

"Yes, your honor, I have many things to say," Anthony replied as she rose.[57] She was addressing the court but speaking to the nation, if not beyond. Her goal for two decades had been to sway public opinion. Her legal guilt mattered less than moral vindication, which was now her principal leadership task. She was at a turning point. Executive, legislative, and judicial remedies had all failed. Whatever came next—and she knew this meant a constitutional amendment—would require moral weight to garner the broadest public support.

It is unlikely she had prepared her speech. She never felt comfortable with her writing skills; insecurity bred in part through hypercritical attacks by Deborah Moulson, her seminary teacher, who even edited Susan's letters to her family. "Whenever I take my pen in hand, I always seem to be mounted on stilts," she would say to her biographer.[58]

Neither did she consider herself a professional speaker, always feeling that Stanton was the master at that. Despite years of addressing audiences in settings from huge lecture halls to family parlors, her unease showed when she said, as late as 1895, that "I haven't gotten over it yet. It is always a little hard for me to face an audience. I have no natural gift for speaking."[59] In the early years, she wrote her speeches and tried to memorize them. She gave that up by 1857 and now talked using at most a few brief notes. There is no record that indicates she had notes in front of her now. What she did have was laser-like intensity. "Miss Anthony's style of speaking is rapid and vehement," Stanton once said. "In debate she is ready and keen, and she is always equal to an emergency."[60]

An emergency was at hand. Fueled by moral clarity, schooled through defeat in the politics of victory, Anthony managed her indignation. If she did not have a prepared speech, that did not mean she was unprepared.

Declared guilty in a court of law by a judge who claimed there were only questions of law, Anthony reached beyond the law. She had to lead her audience to justice. Ninety years later, Earl Warren, Chief Justice of the Supreme Court, would capture well the approach Anthony decided to take: "There is thus a law beyond the law, as binding on those of us who love our institutions as the law itself."[61]

She would make two broad arguments, to the head and to the heart. Both appeared in her opening:

(i)n your ordered verdict of guilty, you have trampled under foot every vital principle of our government. My natural rights, my civil rights, my political rights, my judicial rights, are all alike ignored.

Here was the rational attack, based not on the Enforcement Act of 1870 under which she was convicted but on the natural law beyond the law.

And then:

> Robbed of my fundamental privilege of citizenship, I am degraded from the status of a citizen to that of a subject; and not only myself individually, but all of my sex, are, by your honor's verdict, doomed to political subjection under this so-called form of government.

Here was the emotional appeal, woman as subject rather than citizen, connecting both to the recent history of slavery and the not so distant memory of subjection to the British Crown.

Judge Hunt quickly made the first of several failed attempts to silence her: "The Court cannot listen to a rehearsal of arguments the prisoner's counsel has already consumed three hours in presenting," he said. Anthony would make the first of several decisions to ignore him.

It was time to get more specific. She relied on the core values and founding documents that justified violating civil law:

> Your denial of my citizen's right to vote [civil law], is the denial of my right of consent as one of the governed, the denial of my right of representation as one of the taxed [Declaration of Independence], the denial of my right to a trial by jury of my peers as an offender against law [Constitution], therefore, the denial of my sacred rights to life, liberty and property [natural law].

In the order of the argument, Anthony reminded the courtroom that natural law stood above all else. Hunt tried, and failed, again: "The Court cannot allow the prisoner to go on."

It would seem, at this point, that Anthony had two choices. She could continue to make the rational case, detailed with facts, constitutional arguments, and efforts to draw on various recognized authorities, as she had done thoroughly in speeches during the months before her trail. This would have been easy—but it would have been wrong. It would have covered old ground that the audience had heard. It would have taken time—the judge at any point could have used the full authority of the court to compel her silence, and the longer she went on the more justified he would have seemed in doing so. Finally, it would have moved the argument into specifics, taxing the memory and diminishing the emotional thrust of her presence in the court. Her second choice was to ratchet up the emotional appeal to justice.

Physically, she had a lot going for her. She was a woman alone and isolated before men and the court. She had not been allowed to speak before, nor had any other woman been heard in the courtroom. Leaders know they are on stage, and she played the scene well:

> But your honor will not deny me this one and only poor privilege of protest against this high-handed outrage upon my citizen's rights...since the day of my arrest last November, this is the first time that either myself or any other person of my disenfranchised class has been allowed a word of defense before judge or jury.

"The prisoner must sit down—the Court cannot allow it." Anthony ignored him again.

If leaders are storytellers, Anthony had a story to tell. The best leadership stories are archetypal. Anthony was David against Goliath, subject against tyrannical king:

> All my prosecutors...Not one is my peer, but each and all are my political sovereigns; and had your honor submitted my case to the jury, as was clearly your duty, even then I should have had just cause of protest for not one of those men is my peer...a commoner of England, tried before a jury of Lords, would have far less cause to complain than should I, a woman, tried before a jury of men. Even my counsel...is my political sovereign.

Should the audience miss the comparison, Anthony told the story of slavery versus freedom, tying the subjection of woman to the subjection of slaves, who were now themselves free. Once more she brushed aside Hunt's latest attempt at reminding her that "the prisoner has been tried according to the established forms of law":

> Yes, your honor, but by forms of law all made by men, interpreted by men, administered by men, in favor of men,...and hence, your honor's ordered verdict of guilty...simply because that citizen was a woman and not a man. But yesterday, the same man-made forms of law, declared it a crime punishable with $1,000 fine and six month's imprisonment...to give a cup of cold water, a crust of bread, or a night's shelter to a panting fugitive as he was tracking his way to Canada.

Anthony sprinkled her story with strong images: "trampled under foot," "crust of bread," "panting fugitive." Since, in a leadership story, followers must be given a role to play, Anthony invited them to do so:

> And every man or woman in whose veins coursed a drop of human sympathy violated that wicked law, reckless of consequences, and was justified in doing so.

In the end, if she could not be David, she determined to do the next best thing, the only choice left the powerless—become a martyr. She would become Socrates and Thoreau:

> But failing to get this justice—failing, even, to get a trial by a jury not of my peers—I ask not leniency at your hands—but rather the full rigors of the law.

In what must have appeared somewhat comic, she then sat down only to hear Hunt, finally allowed by her to pass sentence, direct that "The prisoner will stand up." Her sentence: "a fine of one hundred dollars and the costs of prosecution."

Anthony would have the last word, connecting her action to God's law:

> I shall never pay a dollar of your unjust penalty. All the stock in trade I possess is a $10,000 debt, incurred by publishing my paper—The Revolution-...I shall work on with might and main to pay every dollar of that honest debt, but not a penny shall go to this unjust claim... "Resistance to tyranny is obedience to God."

Hunt would finally end the proceedings: "The Court will not order you committed until the fine is paid." This deft move, perhaps the final surprise for Anthony, prevented her filing a writ of habeas corpus to the Supreme Court since she was never incarcerated.[62]

From a legal standpoint, Anthony's conviction ended all strategies but a case that *could* reach the Supreme Court or a constitutional amendment. She had lost but, typically, reframed it as a victory. She thought of herself as Dred Scott, who was declared outside the political system by Supreme Court Justice Roger Taney in 1857, writing to Robert Williamson, a young Rochester clerk:

> Judge Hunt's opinion based on precedent and prejudice does not settle the question against the truth & right—that to be a citizen is to be a voter, any more than Judge Taney's decision...when he said that

a black man was not one of the people an[d] hence was not a citizen. A judicial opinion—unless based on evenhanded justice and truth—is not worth the paper it is written on.[63]

The Trial as Tactic

Since Anthony was allowed to register, she could not use refusal to register her as the basis for appealing the reigning interpretation of the Fourteenth and Fifteenth Amendments. She would have to use her conviction as a wedge to advance suffrage instead.[64] To make sure the world knew what had happened, she spent $700 to print 3,000 pamphlets containing a full report of the trial (and her version of her presentencing statement) and sent them to law journals in the United States and Canada and many newspapers to gain national coverage.[65]

One upstate New York paper concluded helpfully that "[i]f it is a mere question of who got the best of it, Miss Anthony is still ahead. She has voted and the American constitution has survived the shock. Fining her one hundred dollars does not rule out the fact that ... women voted, and went home, and the world jogged on as before."[66]

The greatest press attention was directed not at Anthony but at Hunt, who had contributed mightily to her martyrdom. The *Albany Law Journal* concluded rather unemotionally that "Miss Anthony had no trial by jury. She had only a trial by Judge Hunt. This is not what the constitution guarantees." The *Legal News* of Chicago opined with more distaste that "Judge Ward Hunt, of the Federal Bench, violated the Constitution of the United States more in convicting Miss Anthony of illegal voting than she did in voting."[67] The *New York Sun* was enraged, charging that Hunt "must be impeached and removed."[68]

Since she had been fined, she could petition Congress to remit the fine. If that worked, it would be an admission that she had been found guilty unjustly. Selden filed her appeal, but Congress dodged it. In May, the House Judiciary Committee said that "Congress cannot be converted into a national court of review," and the Senate Judiciary Committee lacked even that much gumption, claiming in June that they were not sure that Selden's petition was an accurate report of what took place at trial.[69]

Another effort to extract political advantage came in the attention her conviction directed to another case. Virginia Minor also tried to register in Missouri in the 1872 election. Since she was barred by the registrar, Reese Happersett, she filed an appeal, citing the Fourteenth Amendment. The case reached the Supreme Court in 1875, but the Court ruled unanimously against her. It found Mrs. Minor: "has always been a citizen from her birth, and entitled to all the privileges and immunities of citizenship." Yet, the Court held: "The Constitution does not define the privileges and immunities of citizens." The United States had no voters of its own creation; only the states confer that privilege. On this basis, it was the Court's "opinion that the Constitution of the United States does not confer the right of suffrage upon any one, and that the constitutions and laws of the several States which commit that important trust to men alone are not necessarily void."[70]

Campaign for an Amendment

Thirty-seven years after demanding the vote in the Declaration of Sentiments, women now had no choice but to seek amendments in state constitutions and/or the federal Constitution. The Anthony and Minor cases created clarity. All energy could now be concentrated on one strategy—that would take another 44 years to fully succeed. Anthony would not live to see it.

She had publicly called for a Sixteenth Amendment as early as 1870. It was not until January 16, 1878, however, that women got Sen. Aaron Sargent of California to introduce it: "The right of citizens to vote shall not be denied or abridged by the United States or by any State on account of sex." The amendment failed to clear committee and would not even be voted on by the full Senate until 1887, when it failed 34–16. It would be reintroduced in every session of Congress until it finally passed, with that exact wording, in June 1919.

In the long interim, Anthony and the suffragists would focus on state and national action. Each year, she would hold the National's convention in Washington so women could lobby Congress. Each year, she would travel to states where woman suffrage was on the ballot and had any hope of passage. In 1874, she canvassed Michigan, where a woman suffrage amendment lost by 5–1. Her response was to note that "The Michigan *40,000 votes* was really a wonderful success—a triumph."[71] In 1875, she gave 60 lectures in Iowa, only to see defeat in the legislature. She tried again in New York in 1894, when at 74 she spoke in all 60 counties on behalf of including suffrage in amendments to the constitution. But even with Horace Greeley gone (he died while running against Grant in 1872), the effort failed. In

1896, she spent eight months traveling in California in another effort that fell short.

There was some success, to be sure. Colorado granted woman suffrage in 1893, as did Utah and Idaho in 1896. But the nineteenth century would close, when Anthony was 80, with suffrage in only four sparsely populated western states. The reasons varied. Many men were loath to give up power. Many believed that woman suffrage would destroy family harmony and bring women from the safety of the home where they could be protected into the boisterous political arena. In some states, woman suffrage was linked with temperance, ensuring its defeat by men who feared that giving women the vote would lead to restrictions on alcohol. After the Civil War, as we have seen, woman suffrage was sacrificed to get black (male) suffrage through. In other states, even after passage of the Fifteenth Amendment, black men who now had the vote would not support it for women. Women were thought by many to lean Republican, so Democrats opposed giving them the vote.

But Anthony was winning converts if not legislation, among men as well as women. No longer routinely jeered, patronized, or ignored, she had, by the last quarter of the nineteenth century, lined up a number of members of Congress, senators, governors, and lesser state figures.

The power of women was gaining along with her own. By late century, many of the gains sought by the Declaration of Sentiments had been at least partially achieved. Women now had more access to a college education and jobs—and more money of their own as a result. With increasing education and economic independence came a lower birthrate and more domestic help that allowed them to be active outside the home. They formed associations for a wide range of social reforms, suffrage among them.

With increased acceptance of their right to speak on the public stage, women became more politically active. Their activity also became more acceptable. The spread of democracy, which in the first half of the nineteenth century empowered more men, was grudgingly but surely occurring for women. Anthony's focus on training women to use the tools of democracy—petitions, conventions, canvassing, letter writing, lobbying—and how to "read" politicians would in time empower a generation of women beyond her own to achieve what she had dreamed. With the spread of the press, railroads, and the telegraph, women would have the ability to communicate and engage in concerted national political action on a scale unimaginable even to men when the century began.

Yet in her lifetime, the "rub-a-dub of agitation" would have to suffice. Anthony spent the next quarter century in nonstop traveling, speaking, organizing, and preparing others to take the lead.

Seeing an historic opportunity, she sought press passes for the centennial July 4 celebration at Independence Hall. Civil War General Joseph Hawley, president of the Centennial Commission, refused her request and her proposal to present a women's Declaration. "We propose to celebrate what we have done...not what we have failed to do," he told her.[72] Nonetheless, when Richard Henry Lee, descendant of the signer of the Declaration of 1776 with the same name, finished reading the historic charter, she and several women (having obtained press passes elsewhere) rose and moved toward the stage. Once there, she handed Thomas Ferry, acting Vice President of the United States, a rolled up parchment copy of the "Declaration of Rights of the Women of the United States."[73] The women then marched back down the aisle, handing out copies as they went. Once outside, Anthony mounted the band platform and read the Declaration to the gathering crowd.

After the centennial, she and Stanton sat down in the latter's Tenafly, New Jersey home to begin what would eventually become a 46-year, six-volume work titled *The History of Woman Suffrage*. Characteristically, Anthony bristled at the sedentary task: "I am just sick to death of the whole of it—I had rather wash or whitewash or any possible hard work than sit here & go through digging into the dirty records of the past—that is rather *make* history than write it."[74]

Making history meant continuing to forge alliances. These ranged from the very small—the Women Taxpayers' Association of Monroe County founded during her trial to encourage women to refuse to pay taxes until given the franchise—to a working partnership with the Women's Christian Temperance Union, a national movement of 150,000 members. As Ward and Burns note:

> She set out to build bridges to as many organizations as she could. The Women's Division of the Knights of Labor, the Ladies of the Grand Army of the Republic, the Women's Conference of the Unitarian Association, the Universal Peace Union, the Daughters of the American Revolution, the National Association of Colored Women—Anthony would eventually reach them all.[75]

Perhaps the most significant was the merger in February 1890, after a two-decade split, of the two camps in the suffrage movement, to form the National American Woman Suffrage Association (NAWSA), with Stanton as president and Anthony as vice president.

"Failure is Impossible!"

It would be tempting to cast the remaining years of her life as filled with increasing assurance that the franchise would soon be granted. The truth was more mixed. In 1893, the World's Congress of Representative Women, brought 126 organizations from 27 countries together in Chicago, a signal achievement for women. Yet her sole focus on suffrage was dealt a blow when Stanton in 1895 published *The Woman's Bible*, an attack on the use of Bible to subjugate women. Pilloried by religious and lay leaders alike—and most women—Stanton brought just the negative attention that Anthony wished to avoid. Yet Anthony defended her friend's right to speak when the NAWSA censured Stanton with a resolution distancing itself from the book. They differed in tactics, but they shared core values. They had gone through too much to desert each other now. Stanton would die in 1902, a severe emotional as well as practical loss for Anthony. On her casket, surrounded by flowers, would be a photograph of Anthony.

In 1900, Anthony would preside over her last NAWSA convention, passing the leadership to Carrie Chapman Catt, a protégé. As Sherr notes, however: "In retirement she was not idle. Over the next six years she traveled to eighteen states...to Europe...finished the fourth volume of *History of Woman Suffrage*, privately interviewed President Roosevelt and publicly scolded ex-President Cleveland, attended six more suffrage meetings and four congressional hearings. And as honorary president of the NAWSA, she kept a close eye on its new leadership."[76]

Early in the new century, she bristled at the refusal of Congress to allow the legislatures of Hawaii and the Philippines to give women the vote and fumed when Roosevelt bellowed: "What, you would have the vote granted to those oriental women?"[77] In September 1900, she learned that her long campaign to make the University of Rochester coeducational would fail in 24 hours for lack of the remaining $8,000 the university trustees demanded to fund the change. At 80, she called upon friends and, with $2,000 still lacking, pledged her own life insurance policy to make up the difference.

But even the perpetual motion machine that was Susan B. Anthony wore down. The effort on behalf of her Rochester "girls" led to a stroke that left her bedridden for a week and speechless for a month more, leading her to worry about her ability to speak for the rest of her life.[78]

The 1906 NAWSA convention would be her last. She insisted on going to her eighty-sixth birthday celebration in Washington immediately following it. When told it would be too much, she responded characteristically: "The hammer may as well fall one time as another now. I am going."[79]

President Roosevelt sent a letter congratulating her. Anthony still had enough spunk to let him have it:

> I wish the men would do something besides extend congratulations. I have asked President Roosevelt to push the matter on a constitutional amendment allowing suffrage to women by a recommendation to Congress. I would rather have him say a word to Congress for the cause than to praise me endlessly.

As the meeting reached its end, she rose for a final time. With the aid of Anna Shaw, who had been by her side to assist with speeches since her stroke, Anthony thanked her followers and uttered her last public words: "There have been others also just as true and devoted to the cause...with such women consecrating their lives, failure is impossible!"[80]

Upon returning home, as double pneumonia set it, it took a full day before she could make it upstairs to her room. She never left it. At her side, Shaw heard, among her last words, an uncharacteristic if understandable lament: "Just think. I have been striving for over sixty years for a little bit of justice no bigger than that, and yet I must die without obtaining it." Anthony died at 12:30 a.m. on Tuesday, March 13. Contemplating this moment, her request, made years before to her family, had been simple: "When it is a funeral, remember that I want there should be no tears. Pass on, and go on with the work."[81] The work would go on, but there would be tears as well.

Susan B. Anthony's life was not a noble failure. Just as there may not have been a woman's movement without Elizabeth Cady Stanton, there might not have been a Nineteenth Amendment without Susan B. Anthony. If Stanton radicalized Anthony, Anthony radicalized generations to follow. Her tireless campaigning and teaching produced leaders that magnified her efforts across America. She invited, cajoled, and by example demonstrated to women what they had a right to demand, and this led them to demand it.

Within five years of her death, full suffrage for women had passed in a number of western states: Washington (1910), California (1911), Oregon, Kansas, and Arizona (1912), Nevada and Montana (1914). Then success spread east. Women not only began to vote, they began to use the power of the suffrage to threaten defeat to members of Congress who failed to support the amendment. When they made good on their threats, pressure built on Congress and the president. On June 14, 1919, the Senate approved the amendment it had scorned for 41 years on a vote of 56–25, it having previously passed the House.

When young Harry Burn, a 24-year-old legislator in Tennessee cast the vote that would ratify the Nineteenth Amendment on August 18, 1920, for a razor-thin margin of 50–49, in the hundredth-year anniversary of Anthony's birth, the work was finally done. That fall, 26 million women voted. Not one of them was arrested.

Saving Postwar Europe (and America): The Marshall Plan Speech

On the morning of June 5, 1947, Secretary of State George Catlett Marshall stood before an audience of graduates, parents, and guests to receive an honorary Doctor of Laws degree. After awarding 11 other honorary degrees to such luminaries as General Omar Bradley and poet T. S. Elliott, as part of Harvard University's 286th commencement, President James Bryant Conant, called Marshall forward. Conant cited him as "an American to whom freedom owes an enduring debt of gratitude, a soldier and statesman whose ability and character brook only one comparison in the history of this nation."[1] The audience knew the allusion to George Washington was well earned.

Like Washington, Marshall had an inauspicious childhood. The third of four children, born on December 31, 1880, he lacked signs of future greatness. He was a poor student (except in history). As biographer Ed Cray noted, "mathematics, grammar, and spelling gave him particular problems...The fear of failure and thus rejection lay heavy on the gangling boy."[2]

Yet, like Washington, what Marshall lacked in formal education, he made up for in determination. Despite the opposition of his older brother, who thought he would dishonor the family, Marshall entered Virginia Military Institute (VMI) at 16. Hazed as an entering "rat," he was forced to squat, naked, over a bayonet. When he collapsed and cut himself—he was still weak from a recent bout of typhoid fever—he refused to report the violation of hazing rules. This earned him the respect of his peers, a step on his way to election as First Corporal for his second year, First Sergeant for his third, and First Captain as a senior, the highest cadet military rank.[3]

Commissioned as a Second Lieutenant, Marshall rose slowly through the small, peacetime army until he came to the attention of General John "Black Jack" Pershing during World War I. Yet he did not earn his first star until nearly 56, with help through Pershing's intervention. By then recognized as a master at training and logistics, Marshall was summoned to head the War Plans Division in Washington, DC, reporting on July 1, 1938.

Like Washington, Marshall also developed a reputation for confronting authority. On November 14, 1938, he attended a White House meeting where Franklin D. Roosevelt (FDR) announced a plan for 10,000 planes, noting he would ask Congress for 20,000 but expected the request to be halved. After others agreed, he turned to Marshall, who was alarmed. "Mr. President, I am sorry, but I don't agree with that at all," Marshall said, knowing the army lacked enough trained pilots and munitions for the large fleet. As Marshall recalled, the president looked "startled" and the meeting ended. As everyone left, "they all bade me good-bye and said my tour in Washington was over."[4]

Yet Marshall earned Roosevelt's admiration not enmity. In selecting a new army chief of staff a few months later, FDR jumped over 33 more senior generals to select Marshall. On April 23, 1939, he offered Marshall the job. Marshall, characteristically, told the president he could take it only if he could speak his mind: "Is that all right?" "Yes," Roosevelt replied, to which Marshall retorted: "You said 'yes' pleasantly, but it may be unpleasant."[5]

Again like Washington, he took over a weak army. Sworn in on September 1, 1939, he had been awakened earlier and told that Germany had invaded Poland. He took the oath of office commanding a force of 174,000 men, in size just below the army of Bulgaria. By war's end, more than 8 million would be under arms, supported by 129,000 bombers, 4,000 ships, 12 million rifles, and 2 atomic bombs.[6] For this logistical achievement, as well as for his strategic sense, Winston Churchill hailed Marshall as the "organizer of victory."[7]

From Retired General to Civilian Peacemaker

On November 26, 1945, Marshall, recently retired, drove home to Dodona Manor in rural Virginia, the respite he and his second wife,

Katherine, had purchased in 1941 (his first wife, Lily, had died in 1927). While Katherine was upstairs resting, the phone rang. She came down to find that President Truman had called to ask Marshall to be Special Ambassadorial Envoy to China. The Chinese communists under Mao Tse-tung were in an intractable struggle with the Nationalists under Chiang Kai-shek. Marshall was handed the impossible task of negotiating a compromise to avert civil war. It proved beyond even his formidable talents. He was called back to Washington in January 1947 as Truman's nominee for Secretary of State.

He was entering a perfect storm. The Republicans had taken control of Congress in 1946. Isolationism, with its attendant reduction in military expenditures, was again in the air, even while the Soviets were exploiting war-devastated Europe. Speaking in Fulton, Missouri, the previous March, Churchill had proclaimed that "an iron curtain has descended across the Continent."[8]

The wrecked European economy was depressing U.S. exports, threatening a recession at home. What few postwar gains Europe had made were devastated by an extremely cold winter that could cause widespread starvation. There was still no peace treaty with Germany or Austria, retarding the German reconstruction essential to European recovery. Nations had to use monetary reserves to buy food, threatening not only recovery but, in England's case, her ability to honor international commitments. In the spring of 1947, wrote journalist Theodore White, "Like a whale gasping on the sand, Europe lay rotting in the sun."[9]

Arriving in Washington on January 21, Marshall immediately quelled speculation that he had presidential ambitions. He wanted to ensure his actions as secretary would be seen as above politics. Typically direct, he told reporters: "The popular concept that no matter what a man says he can be drafted as a candidate for some political office would be without any force with regard to me."[10]

Marshall next secured the continued services of Dean Acheson, Under Secretary of State, telling him that "I shall expect of you the most complete frankness, particularly about myself. I have no feelings except those I reserve for Mrs. Marshall."[11]

He reorganized State, adding hierarchy to counter poor coordination among area offices, and brought staff from 46 different locations into one Foggy Bottom building. He told Acheson to run daily operations and set up a Policy Planning Staff (PPS) to do long-range thinking. "I had no planning section," he later told biographer Forrest Pogue, "and you can't operate and plan at the same time. One or the

other is going to suffer from it. Well, as the operation is a forcing procedure...the result is that the other suffers."[12]

Marshall also brought his signature decision-making style to State.
"Don't fight the problem. Decide it!" he told subordinates. "I don't
want you fellows sitting around asking me what to do. I want you
to tell me what to do." And he expected to be told in short decision
documents.[13]

His approach was soon tested. On February 21, while Marshall
was preparing for an upcoming foreign ministers conference in
Moscow, the British informed Acheson that they could not continue
financial assistance to Greece and Turkey. The United States would
need to assume the world leadership that war had thrust upon it or
watch the Eastern Mediterranean and beyond open to communist
control. The response, which Acheson orchestrated, became known
as the Truman Doctrine. "I believe that it must be the policy of the
United States to support free peoples who are resisting attempted
subjugation by armed minorities or by outside pressures," Truman
told a joint session of Congress on March 12, asking for $400 million
in aid and the dispatch of civilian and military personnel to the two
countries.

Marshall knew that the situation was just as dire in Western
Europe. Stopping in France and Germany en route to Moscow, he
saw that 50 percent of the housing or more in major cities was gone.
In London, 3.5 million homes were destroyed. Infrastructure everywhere—rail lines, factories, machinery, roads, bridges, shipping—
was decimated, unable to sustain recovery. One hundred million
Europeans were being fed at 1,500 calories a day or less. As Lucius
Clay, the America military commander in Germany observed: "There
is no choice between becoming a Communist on 1,500 calories a day
and a believer in democracy on 1,000."[14]

In Moscow, Marshall made no progress. The Soviets were intent
on dominating Eastern Europe, to ensure it as a buffer against future
invasion and exploit its resources. Further, Soviet demands for repa-
rations and control over Germany would make recovery impossible.
After six weeks, he demanded to see Stalin. By now convinced that
Stalin wanted recovery to fail, Marshall told him on April 15, "We
are frankly determined to do what we can to assist those countries
which are suffering from economic deterioration which, if unchecked,
might lead to economic collapse and the consequent elimination of
any chance of democratic survival."[15]

Marshall returned home, ready to act. In a national radio address on April 28, he said: "We cannot ignore the factor of time involved here. The recovery of Europe has been far slower than had been expected... The patient is sinking while the doctors deliberate." The next day, he instructed George Kennan, whom had had brought in to head the PPS, to come back in two weeks with a proposal for European recovery. With no staff, Kennan was thunderstruck. Asking Marshall if he had any other instructions, he was told, simply, "Avoid trivia."[16]

Kennan delivered with a May 23 memo. He had help from a review Acheson had initiated on March 5 to identify what countries other than Greece and Turkey might make requests for help. Acheson himself had spoken at the Delta Council in Cleveland, Mississippi on May 8. "Without outside aid, the process of recovery in many countries would take so long as to give rise to hopelessness and despair," Acheson had said, in the address that Truman later called the "prologue to the Marshall Plan."[17] Will Clayton, Under Secretary for Economic Affairs, had been traveling in Europe and on May 27 sent a memo to Acheson with his own conclusions. A consensus emerged: Europe needed help. It needed it now. Help should focus on economic recovery (the Truman Doctrine was being criticized as too militaristic). It had to be more effective than the $10 billion already spent aiding Europe since the end of the war, and the public had to be sold on the idea.[18]

Marshall needed to proceed carefully. Sen. Arthur Vandenberg, Republican chair of the Senate Foreign Relations Committee, had expressed concern after the Delta Council speech about costly requests. Marshall wanted a venue to speak, but without unduly inviting opposition at home. As he later recalled, "[O]ur intention at all times was to spring the plan with explosive force in order not to dissipate the chances of acceptance at home by premature political debate."[19] He had been asked several times to accept an honorary degree at Harvard. During the war he had always declined. Convinced now that a speech to an academic audience would draw little press attention, he wired Harvard's president Conant that he would be pleased to accept, make a few remarks, and "perhaps a little more."[20]

Marshall's aide, Chip Bohlen, drafted the speech, drawing on the Kennan and Clayton memoranda. Marshall took the draft with him on the plane to Boston on June 4. Not fully satisfied, he reworked it for the next day's ceremony.

The Marshall Plan Speech: A Plan for a Plan

Following lunch after the morning commencement, the annual Alumni Association meeting began with the National Anthem, several addresses and the 78th Psalm. Republican Governor Robert Bradford of Massachusetts then rose and announced "the Secretary of State."[21] Six feet tall, dressed in gray suit, white shirt, and blue tie, Marshall stepped forward. While he preferred to talk extemporaneously, Acheson, had convinced him that reading a prepared text was essential as Secretary of State. In international affairs, words mattered.

At 2:50 p.m., he took eight pieces of paper, folded neatly in the middle, from his jacket pocket, adjusted his reading glasses and began. Truman's confidence in him was so high that Marshall was never asked to clear the speech, though the president was certainly aware of the direction he would take. Yet outside the president, "only three or four people...were aware of what I was going to do," Marshall later said.

He was not a charismatic speaker. His tone verged on the monosyllabic, and his words were delivered in almost matter-of-fact, emotionless fashion. The nearly 11 minutes it took to deliver the "little more" he had promised Conant did not immediately ignite the audience. Indeed, a student orator that day recalled that the speech was not "stirring" nor "did most of those present recognize Marshall's brief statement as a specific plan."[22] The power of poor delivery well suited the secretary's intention to be low key.

Marshall did not actually offer the "Marshall Plan" to his audience. That label was added only later. Instead, he offered a plan for a plan. The wisdom of that approach was carefully thought out. He would consciously plant a seed that would take nearly a year to bear fruit.

The Audience Beyond the Audience

As a leader, Marshall had to be conscious of his different audiences. Internationally, he was speaking to the Europeans and the Soviets.[23] The obstructionist intentions of the latter were clear. The former was both a collective and a set of individual nations, each with its own history, pride, needs, and preferences. Though the Eastern Europeans were under heavy pressure from the Soviet Union, the "Iron Curtain" was not yet, in Marshall's mind, an impenetrable wall. He would assume the best but anticipate the worst.

The domestic audience included segments within the American public. While public sentiment had supported European aid thus far, there was no guarantee about the future. Pent-up demand from the Depression and war years (and the rationing essential to the war effort) were counter pressures to the direction Marshall would set. He worried especially about the "Middle West," where farm machinery needed in Europe was in short supply, as was fertilizer. He worried also that "all America was opposed to appropriating anything else because of the way the first appropriation, right after the war, had been wasted."[24]

American business was another key audience. It needed overseas markets to stoke postwar growth, and right now those markets were empty of buyers, except for basic foodstuffs essential to survival.

In Congress, Vandenberg was leery, but Marshall hoped he could count on his help. Vandenberg had been an isolationist before Pearl Harbor, but the attack had dramatically changed him. He respected Marshall—in fact had pushed through his confirmation hearings and a unanimous confirmation vote—but that was not a blank check. The House would be even harder to convince. It had tried to cut foreign aid earlier in the year and gave Truman a hard fight on aid to Greece and Turkey.

Some in the press had already pushed to do more for Europe. *The Washington Post*, the day after Truman's speech to Congress on Greece and Turkey, had called it a "starter." Walter Lippmann had written columns pushing extensive aid, even outlining how the approach to Europe should be structured. Others had approved of Acheson's Delta Council speech.[25] While Marshall was not seeking wide press attention at the outset, their coverage would matter in shaping public opinion.

But the immediate audience, of course, was a highly intelligent one at Harvard on this bright June afternoon. Marshall would begin with them.

The Leader as Teacher

Marshall's opening paragraph was not in the prepared text. He added it extemporaneously despite Acheson's admonition. Marshall pronounced himself "profoundly grateful, touched" by Conant's comparison of him to Washington. He was "overwhelmed," "fearful of my inability," and noted that being there was "a tremendously impressive thing to an individual in my position." Clearly Washingtonian in tone, Marshall's humility placed him in debt to his Harvard audience and marked him as no better or wiser. This was not false deference; it was Marshall's character.

His reputation had been built not only on brilliant work but on steadfast subordination of self to national needs. Nothing exemplified this more than the process for selecting the commander of the D-day invasion. FDR initially wanted Marshall: "I want George to be the Pershing of the second World War—and he cannot be that if we keep him here [in Washington]."[26] FDR knew that success with OVERLORD would bring the kind of fame that could propel one into the presidency (as it would for Eisenhower).

Yet Marshall would not ask for the command that was his for the asking. Seeing Roosevelt at the president's request, Marshall later described the moment: "[A]s I recall, he asked me, after a great deal of beating around the bush, just what I wanted to do. Evidently it was left up to me...I just repeated again...that I wanted him to feel free to act in whatever way he felt was to the best interests of the country...and not in any way to consider my feelings. I would cheerfully go whatever way he wanted me to go and I didn't express any desire one way or the other. Then, he accepted that...because he said, 'Well, I didn't feel that I could sleep at ease if you were out of Washington.'"[27]

As Secretary of War Henry Stimson would say of Marshall on Victory in Europe (V-E) day:

> Seldom can a man put aside such a thing as being the Commanding General of the greatest field army in history. This decision was made by you for wholly unselfish reasons...I have seen a great many soldiers in my lifetime and you, Sir, are the finest soldier I have ever known.[28]

His deference at Harvard not only rekindled the admiration the audience felt for him, it also leveled the playing field. He was like them. This disarming beginning opened the audience to an honest effort to understand his words. Marshall would play the role of teacher to this academic crowd and the audience beyond, sharing what he had learned in the spirit of joint discovery.

Marshall would begin—and end—embodying this role. In his May 23 memo, Kennan had urged that the United States plan for

European recovery "be frankly stated to the American public."[29] In his May 27 memo, Clayton had argued: "[T]his problem can be met only if the American people are taken into the complete confidence of the Administration and told all the facts."[30] Adopting the advice, Marshall would say in his closing, also added extemporaneously, that "it is of vast importance that our people reach some general understanding of what the complications really are, rather than react from a passion or a prejudice or an emotion of the moment." That closing would stop with six pregnant, Socratic questions: "What are the reactions of the people? What are the justifications of those reactions? What are the sufferings? What is needed? What can best be done? What must be done?"

The teacher began in earnest in the second paragraph. After craftily inviting his audience into the collection of "all intelligent people," the secretary admitted that understanding Europe's situation was not easy: "I think one difficulty is that the problem is one of such enormous complexity that the very mass of facts presented to the public by press and radio make it exceedingly difficult for the man in the street to reach a clear appraisement of the situation." Further, "the people of this country are distant from the troubled areas of the earth, and it is hard for them to comprehend the plight and consequent reactions of the long-suffering peoples of Europe."

Setting Audacious Goals

The man who had conquered three Axis powers in a global war was aiming at a peace to end war. Almost buried amid the details of the speech were its lofty goals. Marshall did not shy away from bold endeavors. He gently inserted his goal at the very end of the second paragraph when he referred to "our efforts to promote peace in the world." This would be achieved through the supporting goal—"the rehabilitation of Europe."

While he built toward this vision slowly, by the end he left no doubt of its importance. Effective leaders not only issue challenges, they often raise the stakes, as Marshall did when he told his audience that "the whole world of the future hangs on a proper judgment."

His goals were not for Europe alone. He made clear that "the United States should do whatever it is able to do to assist in the return of normal economic health in the world, without which there can be no political stability and no assured peace." Peace for America depended on peace in Europe, political stability, and economic health. There was a strategy and a system at the heart of Marshall's world view.

A Systemic Problem Requires a Systems View

Marshall was a master of logistics. In World War I, Pershing had tasked him with planning an attack during the Meuse-Argonne offensive, for which Marshall earned the nickname "the wizard." Yet, his greatest contribution in World War II had been strategic. Dedicating the Marshall Arch at VMI in 1951, financier and wartime supporter Bernard Baruch would say of Marshall that he was "history's first global strategist."[31] Indeed, Marshall often cautioned subordinate generals on the dangers of "localitis"—thinking only of the needs of their theater of war.[32]

In the war, Marshall prevailed on three critical, strategic points. Correctly reasoning that Germany could fight on without Japan but not the reverse, he insisted on "Germany first" as the order of battle—despite the fact that the war began in the Pacific. Second, he fought for unity of command—across the services at home and among Allies abroad. Neither was easy, given a Navy that jealously regarded its own prerogatives and the stubbornness of Churchill and the British General Staff. Third, he insisted that the only way to conquer Germany was through a massive cross-Channel invasion that Churchill, remembering 60,000 casualties in one day at the battle of the Somme in World War I, put off as long as he could.

His strategic sense was no less evident now. He had seen the devastation in Europe and that aid thus far had little long-term impact. As he said in the speech, he wanted to "provide a cure rather than a mere palliative." Throwing money at the problem, on a "piecemeal basis" had not worked. A reconstructed Europe required a solution that spoke to the "enormous complexity" he had already referenced. The next three paragraphs would help the audience understand that complexity.

First, Marshall provided a *macroeconomic* view. The "visible destruction of cities, factories, mines and railroads" was a symptom of a deeper problem. The "dislocation of the entire fabric of European economy" was the result of a number of connected factors that represented a collective "breakdown." Among these were damaged or obsolete machinery, "disrupted commercial ties, private institutions, insurance companies, and shipping companies," and a lack of confidence in local currencies.

Second, Marshall provided a *microeconomic* view, which he labeled as "both interesting and serious." If the macroeconomic view was pitched to the businessman or economist, microeconomics spoke to the "man in the street." In concrete terms, Marshall explained how city dwellers lacked fuel and raw materials to produce things of value to the farmer. As a result, the farmer was producing food just for his family; there was no incentive to produce it for the city when there was nothing to buy with the money he might get for it. This led to near starvation for city dwellers, forcing governments to use money and credit needed for reconstruction to buy foodstuffs abroad. This "vicious circle" threatened the division of labor at the "basis of modern civilization."

Third, and as important from a leadership perspective, Marshall told his audience a story, replete with images that may have recalled the Depression for many in his American audience. The vivid depiction of Europe's devastation painted a real and compelling portrait—a story of the war-torn past and postwar present. But it was a story not yet finished.

It is a rare public paper that offers a systems view of the problem (see Figure 5.1). This was the diagnosis of the European disease.

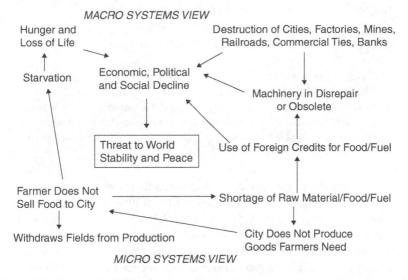

Figure 5.1   Europe in 1947.

Prescription, to produce a "happy ending" to the story, would come next.

Change Theory and the Marshall Plan

Marshall and other State Department planners had concluded that European recovery required European economic integration. The historical tendency of European nations to put their own economies first, erect trade barriers and—since the end of the war—press the United States to meet their aid requests irrespective of their neighbors' needs was not systemic change. Their economies were inextricably linked. At the same time, Marshall understood that if the United States dictated the manner of economic integration, it would be resisted by national pride. The result would be another piecemeal effort, inviting each nation to approach America on its own.

The solution had been suggested by both Kennan and Clayton. In his May 23 memo, Kennan had told Acheson:

> It would be neither fitting nor efficacious for this Government to undertake to draw up unilaterally and to promulgate formally on its own initiative a program designed to place western Europe on its feet economically. This is the business of the Europeans. The formal initiative must come from Europe; this program must be evolved in Europe; and the Europeans must bear the basic responsibility for it.[33]

Clayton, in his May 27 memo to Acheson had said:

> This three-year grant to Europe should be based on a European plan which the principal European nations, headed by the UK, France and Italy, should work out. Such a plan should be based on a European economic federation...Europe cannot recover from this war and again become independent if her economy continues to be divided into many small, watertight compartments.[34]

Marshall acted on the advice. His approach is consistent with the theory of social change that has emerged from universities in the postwar years. First, as noted, Marshall said that change "must not be on a piecemeal basis." It must be systemic. Second, "there must be some agreement among the countries of Europe as to the requirements of the situation and the part those countries themselves will take." Borrowing from Kennan, "[I]t would be neither fitting nor efficacious for our Government to undertake to draw up unilaterally a program." "The initiative...must come from Europe." Finally, echoing Clayton, "[T]he program should be a joint one, agreed to by a number, if not all, European nations."

Marshall knew that followers resist change when it is thrust upon them. In *Leadership Without Easy Answers*, Harvard professor Ron Heifetz notes that complex problems lack simple answers that an authority figure can decide and just announce. Marshall could not know how to integrate European economies nor the aid in each country that would help do so. Such complex, systemic problems require what Heifetz calls *adaptive thinking* that draws on the creativity of many people. But you cannot order creativity. You need emotional commitment to a goal to turn creativity loose. That comes from a compelling challenge.[35]

It is in this sense that there is no "plan" in the Marshall Plan speech. Marshall was issuing an invitation to create a plan—or, as he put it, "something between a hint and a suggestion."[36] This is vagueness as virtue. He suggests no specifics that can be argued with, no dollar amount that can be challenged, no timeline. Six weeks after the speech, Kennan would write: "Marshall 'plan.' We have no plan"— which was, of course, part of the plan all along.[37]

The vagueness went further. What role would the United States play while Europe prepared its program? What did "friendly aid in the drafting of a European program" mean? Who would convene the Europeans, when, and how? What level of integration of the economies of individual nations would be acceptable? How would aid be administered? By refusing to answer these questions, by challenging the Europeans to take the first steps, and thus by preserving maximum flexibility for the United States, Marshall was practicing the political astuteness essential to support at home and abroad.

The Political Savvy of a Nonpartisan Leader

Marshall was nonpartisan but not politically naive. Even before 1947, when he had firmly denied presidential ambitions on becoming Secretary of State, he had quashed, in 1944, an earlier bid to nominate him for the presidency as a Democrat. Marshall even refused to vote for fear that acknowledging a preference might compromise his objectivity and reputation.

Yet, on Pershing's staff, he had much earlier gained the ability to see war politically and the savvy to, as he later said, "make every minor concession without question, which usually resulted in settling the more important matters to our advantage."[38] When he went to Washington with Pershing, he frequently accompanied him to Harding's White House where he learned how to deal with a range of political actors and with Congress, skills he put to great use as army chief of staff. Indeed, his political astuteness, including the ability to deal with the micromanaging Churchill, the egos of Field Marshal Montgomery and General Patton, and the persistent Stalin no doubt played a part in FDR's decision to keep him home rather than give him the D-day command.

How, then, did Marshall address the political concerns of the segments of his audience? Just as he saw the need for a systemic approach to the problem of European recovery, he saw the need for a systemic approach to the political dynamics he faced.

He was least concerned with Europe: "Our principal concern was not with the European reception," he later told Forrest Pogue. "I was quite sure they would receive the idea only too willingly."[39] Yet he had to pay attention to European sensitivities, which is one of the reasons he insisted that they must take the initiative. Part of those sensitivities dealt with the "race for the leader" behavior he expected from British Foreign Secretary Ernest Bevin and French Foreign Minister Georges Bidault.[40] Both would want to launch—and take credit for—the program. Accordingly, he did not tell anyone in Europe in advance to listen to the speech for fear that the message would reach some and not others.

In regard to the Soviets, Marshall had two messages—one of inclusion and the other of warning. Kennan had advised Marshall to "play it straight" with them, and Acheson said it would be a serious mistake to exclude them and have the resulting division of Europe blamed on the United States.[41] Further, as Marshall later recalled, "[I]n 1947, many people in Europe were very timid about opposing the Soviet Union and I feared if we started our plan by throwing the Soviets out it would scare these people and perhaps keep some of the European countries out of the program."[42] Thus, the speech contains only references to "Europe," neither singling out nations by name nor excluding any. Even further, he added, "Our policy is directed not against any country or doctrine but against hunger, poverty, desperation and chaos." Marshall reasoned, it turned out correctly, that if the Soviets wanted to take themselves out of the Marshall Plan, this was better than the excluding them at the outset.

Of course, few within the State Department expected the Soviets to participate. Most expected them to obstruct. Thus Marshall also added a warning:

> Any government which maneuvers to block the recovery of other countries cannot expect help from us. Furthermore, governments, political parties, or groups which seek to perpetuate human misery in order to profit there from politically or otherwise will encounter the opposition of the United States.

For the American public, Marshall's approach was to invite them to the high plane of empathy with "the long-suffering peoples of Europe." He also held out a promise of" "peace in the world" and warned of "the consequences to the economy of the United States" if European recovery failed. He also appealed to Americans to "face up to the vast responsibility which history has clearly placed upon our country."

For American business, Marshall appealed to self-interest. Without European recovery, the markets that America needed would never develop. Clayton had made just this point to Marshall in his May 27 memo: "The immediate effects [of the failure of the European economy] on our domestic economy would be disastrous: markets for our surplus production gone, unemployment, depression, a heavily unbalanced budget on the background of a mountainous war debt."[43]

The decision to put the initiative on Europe helped Marshall deal with Congress. Any specific financial request would take time, and the failure to mention a budget figure dampened immediate opposition. Marshall also signaled that there were limits on what America could be expected to do (an important message to the Europeans as well) when he referred to, "Any assistance that this Government may render" and "later support of such a program so far as it may be practical for us."

Some in Congress were still upset over the cost and militaristic tone of the Truman Doctrine. Others were concerned that we were going it alone, weakening the new United Nations. No one in Congress, including the immensely influential Vandenberg, was informed ahead of time about the speech. Indeed, Marshall had been upset with Acheson's speech at the Delta Council and another speech on European recovery by Counselor to the State Department, Benjamin Cohen. "I gave Cohen hell for his West Coast speech," Marshall recalled, "for fear it would reveal my plans and start the much feared 'premature debate.' "[44] Knowing his audience on the Hill, Marshall said "I wanted to get at the money question very, very carefully."[45] "It is easy to propose a great plan," Marshall said later, "but exceedingly difficult to manage the form and procedure so that it has a fair chance of political survival."[46] Clearly, Marshall took some risk in springing the speech on Congress. But he counted on his strong reputation on the Hill and followed up, especially with Vandenberg, to smooth the way.

Was the Marshall Plan Really Marshall's?

It is fair to ask how much credit Marshall actually deserves for the speech. Some of its key ideas had been floating around the State Department before he took over. In early March, Acheson had put in motion a country-by-country assessment of Europe's needs and supervised much of that work while Marshall was in Moscow. Acheson had also worked with the White House on the Truman Doctrine speech, and, as Joseph Jones, a State Department specialist at that time, said later: "The fact is that had there been no Truman Doctrine, there probably would have been no Marshall Plan." Indeed, Truman called them "two halves of the same walnut."[47] Kennan had prepared a memo with many of the key points Marshall would draw upon, and Clayton's travels provided much of the vivid detail that ended up in the speech and the invaluable knowledge on how to approach the Europeans. Bohlen had pulled all this together in a draft of the speech.

Yet, it would be wrong to dismiss Marshall's contribution, though he did in his characteristically humble way years later. The speech was preceded by leadership acts that bear Marshall's indelible stamp. First, he had earned Truman's trust, initially through the respect he had shown when the latter was a Senator investigating war expenditures, then through his aid to the fledgling new president, and finally in his willingness to put his personal interests aside to serve in China.

Second, Marshall reorganized the State Department. He ended years of poor coordination by giving Acheson the authority he needed to bring integration to its work. As Jones noted, "George Catlett Marshall brought order to the conduct of foreign relations...he immediately straightened out the lines of authority in the State Department, placed them in the hands of the man best qualified to be his chief of staff, Undersecretary Acheson, and insisted upon orderly staff procedure."[48] Without such organization, it is doubtful that the department could have produced so effectively in a short time.

Third, Marshall delegated. Once capable people were in place, he let them act, and Marshall was a master at identifying and developing capable people. From 1927 to 1932, as Assistant Commandant of the Infantry School at Fort Benning, Georgia, he had led the "Benning Revolution," a total restructuring of the curriculum to prepare an officer corps for the next war. He taught a new way to think in battle and he remembered who learned and how well. As recalled by Katherine, "He always said that he possesses a wicked memory; and this is true—he never forgets a brilliant performance and he never forgets a dullard."[49] Among those who caught his attention, 150 would become generals before the end of World War II.[50]

How else, without such delegation and trust, could much of the work that went into the Marshall Plan speech have been done while Marshall was out of the country? An effective leader releases the capacity of his team. Again, Jones put it well: "Under the conditions created by Truman, Marshall, and Acheson, the staff of the State Department was able to make its fullest possible contribution...That this is so does not detract from, but enhances, the stature of their chiefs, who...were able to draw out and use the talents of those they commanded."[51]

Fourth, as Acheson described it, "General Marshall had the capacity for decision." In regard to the Marshall Plan, he made three key decisions to move things forward. "The first was to act, and to act immediately." Returning from Moscow in late April, Marshall knew that if the State Department did not act, others might take the initiative with uncertain consequences. "The second decision was that the plan for European recovery must come from and be devised by the Europeans themselves," a politically astute and masterful change strategy. "The third decision was perhaps the most difficult of all: that the offer should be made to all of Europe and not merely to Western Europe."[52] There were divisions on this question because, if the Russians accepted, they could sabotage the effort from inside. Marshall took the risk. It was his call to make.

Fifth, Marshall positioned the speech beautifully. He let the clamor for helping Europe build in the press, but he kept the government's intentions closely guarded to avoid premature opposition. He chose a venue to speak that offered intellectual respect and subdued publicity.

Finally, the speech was consistent with Marshall's understanding of history. He did not just bless the ideas of others. Marshall knew that the disruption of the European economy that followed World

War I was in no small measure due to the Treaty of Versailles and the United States' withdrawal from the world scene. Europe's failure contributed to Hitler's rise, and Marshall would not let history repeat itself. Indeed, in his first speech as Secretary of State, at Princeton, he had told his audience: "We have had a cessation of hostilities, but we have no genuine peace... Most of the other countries of the world find themselves exhausted economically, financially, and physically. If the world is to get on its feet... assistance from the United States will be necessary." Ever the teacher, he lectured that "I doubt seriously whether a man can think with full wisdom and with deep convictions regarding certain of the basic international issues today who has not at least reviewed in his mind the period of the Peloponnesian War and the Fall of Athens."[53] Democracies had ended in ancient Greece. They could end again.

The Marshall Plan Speech Becomes the Marshall Plan

Intent on creating history as well as remembering it, Marshall moved from words to action. "That's the thing I take pride in," he said years later, "putting the damned thing over. Anybody, well, you take a campaign or anything like that, there's nothing so profound in the logic of the thing. But the execution of it, that's another matter."[54]

The initial press reaction was minimal, just as Marshall sought. As historian Greg Behrman records in his comprehensive book on the Marshall Plan: "In the *New York Times,* Marshall's speech got second billing to comments Truman had made that same day about a recent Communist coup in Hungary."[55] American radio networks had not even broadcast the speech.

In Europe, the reaction was more striking, though even there Marshall's decision not to alert officials muted the immediate response. Ernest Bevin listened to who he thought was Marshall on the BBC, but it was Leonard Miall, a BBC commentator, reading the speech, which had only been released to the press late on June 4. The British Embassy in Washington, under orders to save money, had thought the speech was "just another university oration" and so didn't bother to cable it to London.[56]

Nevertheless, Bevin did not miss the point. As he later told the *New York Times,* the speech was "a lifeline to sinking men. It seemed to bring hope where there was none. The generosity of it was beyond belief."[57] The very next morning, he strode into the Foreign Office and said: "Get me Marshall's speech," and "I want to get Bidault on the telephone."[58]

Bevin went to Paris on June 17, and the two foreign ministers agreed to invite the Soviets to a three-way conference. Molotov joined them in Paris on June 27, but the conference ended on July 2 after it became clear the Soviets would not participate. They had no intention of opening their finances to Western, especially U.S., view, and they saw the plan as an effort to weaken their hold on Europe. On June 11, *Pravda Ukraine* had called the "Marshall Doctrine" a grab at "quick formation of notorious western bloc under unconditional and absolute leadership of American imperialism."[59]

Bevin and Bidault pressed on. They invited 22 European nations to a conference whose aim would be the preparation of a unified plan. Any hope that Eastern European nations might participate was quashed when the Soviets instructed them not to attend, and thus 16 Western European nations gathered in Paris on July 12. While they were at work, Marshall could attend to the sensitive subject of building support at home for the plan that was being hatched.

His most immediate task was to line up Vandenberg. While he thought the national interest should be enough to woo the Senator, he took advice from his staff to be more proactive.[60] "He soon became a full partner in the adventure...and we consulted together twice weekly at the Blair House...Vandenberg was my right hand man and at times I was his right hand man," Marshall would later say.[61] Vandenberg would eventually make the most powerful speech of his career in promoting the European Recovery Program in the Senate.

Truman helped by insisting (despite Marshall's objection) that the effort be called the "Marshall Plan," a name that had first been applied to it on June 6 by a *New York Times* reporter.[62] "Anything that is sent up to the Senate and House with my name on it will quiver a couple of times and die," Truman said, fully aware that the 1948 presidential election campaign would soon be underway.[63]

Convincing the public would take more work and was important to convincing Congress. A poll in late July found that only 49 percent of Americans had heard of the Marshall Plan, and 50 percent of those were not willing to pay more taxes for it.[64] By November 2, 61 percent had heard of the Plan, but only 47 percent approved of it.[65] Marshall understood what lay ahead:

> I worked on that as hard as though I was running for the Senate or the presidency. That's what I'm proud of, that part of it, because I had foreigners, I had tobacco people, cotton people, New York, eastern industrialists, Pittsburgh people, the whole West Coast going in the other direction...It was just a struggle from start to finish.[66]

Moving public opinion would require what a Dutch diplomat called "a Marshall Plan to sell the Marshall Plan."[67] It would consist of an orchestrated series of studies, commissions, committees, and speeches—all aimed at demonstrating the wisdom and feasibility of large-scale aid for Europe.

The best-known formal group was the President's Committee on Foreign Aid, suggested by Vandenberg and chaired by Secretary of Commerce Averell Harriman. The Harriman Committee looked at the policies that should guide U.S. aid. The administration also asked the Council of Economic Advisers to look at the impact of foreign aid on the economy, and the Secretary of the Interior, Julius Krug, examined the program's likely impact on natural resources.[68]

Other groups included a fact-finding mission, named the Herter Committee after Massachusetts Republican Representative Christian Herter, which took 18 members of the House for 45 days to England and Europe. Altogether, more than 200 members of Congress would make trips to form their own assessments.[69] A Committee for the Marshall Plan was also launched on November 17, with former Secretary of State and War, Henry Stimson, as national chair. The committee organized a vast network of supporters who were subsequently called upon to speak across the nation.[70]

Marshall himself spoke to groups as diverse as the Women's National Press Club, Governor's Conference, CIO Convention, Chicago Council on Foreign Relations, Pittsburg Chamber of Commerce, and the National Cotton Council.

Truman called a special session of Congress for November 17, aimed at passage of interim aid, which was critical since the overall package would take longer. On December 19, the president submitted "A Program for the United States Support of European Recovery" to the Hill. The 50,000 word bill asked for $18.8 billion from April 1948 through June 1952.

On January 8, Marshall was the first witness in front of Vandenberg's Foreign Relations Committee. His opening statement was blunt:

> This program will cost our country billions of dollars. It will impose a burden on the American taxpayer. It will require sacrifices...The vacuum which the war created in western Europe will be filled by the forces of which wars are made...Though the war has ended the peace has not commenced...Dollars will not save the world, but the world today cannot be saved without dollars.

It was also demanding:

> Either undertake to meet the requirements of the problem or don't undertake it at all.

And, in its last line, confident:

> But there is no doubt whatever in my mind that if we decide to do this thing we can do it successfully, and there is no doubt in my mind that the whole world hangs in the balance.[71]

Not without opposition, including calls that the program was "state socialism" or worse, the European Recovery Program passed the Senate 69–17 on March 30 and the House by 329–74 on April 3. It did not hurt that the Soviets assisted the communist coup in Czechoslovakia in February.

The Judgment of History

Shortly after 1 p.m. on Thursday, December 10, 1953, Marshall stepped forward in the University of Oslo's Festival Hall to become the first professional soldier to receive the Nobel Peace Prize. "George Marshall...arrived at the clear and passionate understanding," said Nobel Committee member Carl Hambro, "that the final object to be obtained by war, the only justifiable goal, is to make another war impossible."[72]

While Marshall harbored no illusion that such a vision was anywhere near reality, the Marshall Plan, for which he was being honored, had in the years 1947 to 1951 contributed to a dramatic increase in Western European industrial production, lifting it 35 percent higher than the prewar level.[73] With that achievement came a parallel rise in the living standards and hopes of the war-torn people in the

16 Marshall Plan countries. Their democracies were less threatened by communist postwar expansionism.

The $13 billion in Marshall aid eventually appropriated by Congress (roughly equivalent to $121 billion in 2011 dollars) played a key role in European recovery. Books such as Behrman's *The Most Noble Adventure* suggest that the impact went well beyond the dollar contribution. A key feature of implementation was the use of "counterpart funds." For example, an Italian farmer who needed a tractor would pay for it with Italian currency, deposited in an Italian bank. The United States would send the tractor using Marshall funds, but the bank was then required to take the farmer's money and invest it in other recovery projects, thus doubling each dollar of Marshall aid.

The State Department's figures show that by 1951, per capita GNP in Europe, on average, had risen 33 percent from 1947 levels and had exceeded prewar (1938) levels. Technical assistance provided by U.S. specialists also contributed, hastening the introduction of new methods and productivity growth.[74]

By the time of the 1948 election, 82 percent of Americans had heard of the Marshall Plan, and 62 percent were satisfied with it, a result that cannot but have helped Truman.[75]

In 2000, the Brookings Institution published the results of research on the "Government's Greatest Achievements of the Past Half-Century." "Rebuild Europe after World War II" was selected as the top achievement by its panel of 450 history and political science professors, being rated the most successful and the second most important undertaking of the federal government during that period.[76]

Some historians suggest that the Marshall Plan stoked the collaboration that in time would lead to the European Union. On the fiftieth anniversary of the plan, Germany's chancellor Helmut Schmidt said, "The United States ought not to forget that the emerging European Union...would never have happened without the Marshall Plan."[77]

There are, of course, dissenting views, suggesting that Marshall Plan aid played a small role in a recovery that would have happened anyway. Some argue that the Marshall Plan hastened the Cold War, creating a Western European bloc that the Soviets felt compelled to oppose—though Soviet designs on Western Europe may well have led to the Cold War, or worse, even without the Marshall Plan.

Convinced that his work was done, and having delayed a kidney removal surgery long enough, Marshall resigned in January 1949. Though he was not through with serving his nation (Truman would bring him back as Secretary of Defense at the height of the Korean

War in September 1950), he had achieved what the ceremony in Oslo so rightly honored.

Georges Bidault said, "[T]here has never been a finer, more far-sighted gesture in history than the Marshall Plan."[78] *Time* magazine, naming Marshall its "Man of the Year" for the second time in 1947 (the first time was in 1943), said that "[n]o one man was responsible for 1947's great step... But one man symbolized the U.S. action."[79] Churchill speaking in New York in March 1949 said, "[T]he Marshall Plan was a turning point in the history of the world."[80] Truman would say of Marshall, after he passed away on October 16, 1959, "[H]e was the greatest of the great in our time."[81]

George Marshall never sought such accolades. He would be uncomfortable hearing them. What he did seek was a world without war. Organizer of military victory, architect of the most successful postwar recovery program in history, Marshall hoped for a world where neither would be needed.

He had confronted nearly impossible challenges before. He knew that money and technology mattered in war and peace, but he knew something else mattered too. In June 1941, speaking at Trinity College while facing the near-certain prospect of American involvement in world war, he talked about the need to build a fighting force not just on "things of steel and the super-excellence of guns and planes":

> We are building it on things infinitely more potent. We are building it on *belief* for it is what men *believe* that makes them invincible. We have sought for something more than enthusiasm, something finer and higher than optimism or self-confidence, something not merely of the intellect or the emotions but rather something in the spirit of man, something encompassed only by the soul.[82] (emphasis in the original)

Standing in Oslo, in a speech he titled "Essentials to Peace," Marshall returned to that ephemeral element. He urged his audience to search as well for the soul essential to peace:

> For the moment the maintenance of peace in the present hazardous world situation does depend in very large measure on military power, together with Allied cohesion... but we must, I repeat, we must find another solution... Perhaps the most important single factor will be a spiritual regeneration to develop goodwill, faith, and understanding among nations... material assistance alone is not sufficient.[83]

The Movement in Crisis: King's Letter from Birmingham Jail

Surrounded by two dozen men in Room 30 of the Gaston Motel, the only place for blacks to stay in the steel city, the Rev. Martin Luther King, Jr. had a decision to make. The effort to desegregate Birmingham that began methodically ten days before was in trouble. Going to jail could jump start it. King had already been in jail many times, and he had picked this symbolic day, April 12, Good Friday, to go to jail again. He had announced it at a mass meeting and had fasted as usual. But now he was wavering.

The economic boycott of downtown merchants designed to hurt Easter season sales had not worked. Neither had the plan to fill the jails. Only three hundred people had been locked up for sit-ins and marches. There was no money left to bail people out, a problem magnified by the city's calculated notice that now only cash would be accepted for bonds and that the Movement's bondsman lacked sufficient assets. "Martin," someone said, "this means you can't go to jail. We need money. We need a lot of money. We need it now. You are the only one who has the contacts to get it."[1] His decision was also complicated because marching would defy a court injunction, served two days before, aimed at stopping Project C (for "Confrontation") in its tracks.

"Our most dedicated and devoted leaders were overwhelmed by a feeling of hopelessness," King recalled, and he could understand why.[2] "I want to meditate about this decision," he announced, and went alone to an adjoining room.[3]

The Unlikely Revolutionary

This moment would have been unimaginable when King took the pulpit at Montgomery's Dexter Avenue Baptist Church in 1954. "The first twenty-five years of my life were very comfortable," he later said. "Life had been wrapped up for me in a Christmas package."[4] Michael (his birth name) grew up in a middle class home and got the best education possible for his race at the time.[5] He entered Atlanta's Morehouse College at 15 and considered medicine and the law.

Yet the seeds of a different life were planted, if still dormant, in family history. The son, grandson, and great grandson of preachers, he grew up in the church. Its call would prove irresistible: "During my senior year in college," he said, "I finally decided to accept the challenge to enter the ministry. I came to see that God had placed a responsibility upon my shoulders and the more I tried to escape it the more frustrated I would become."[6] In 1947, at 18, he was ordained by and joined his father at Ebenezer Baptist Church in Atlanta.

After graduating as valedictorian from Crozer Theological Seminary in Chester, Pennsylvania, in 1951, he began his doctorate in systematic theology at Boston University. Near the end of his studies he selected Dexter because of its reputation for educated pastors and for congregations that responded to more intellectual preaching. The emotionalism of Southern Baptist "whooping" troubled him.

The decision to return to the South, made with his new bride, Coretta Scott, came with a clear understanding of what they would face. His father had suffered and fought against racism. Her father's home and sawmill had been burned down because he dared to succeed. At six, Martin's white friend was no longer allowed to play with him. "I was greatly shocked, and from that moment on I was determined to hate every white person." Yet his parents told him that it was "my duty as a Christian to love him."[7] At 14, he traveled to an oratorical contest, winning for his freedom speech on "The Negro and the Constitution," then had to stand for 90 miles on the bus back to Atlanta when ordered to give up his seat for a white person. "I was the angriest I have ever been in my life," he recalled.[8] After high school, he spent the summer picking tobacco in Connecticut. Returning home, he was told to move to the Jim Crow car of the train as it left Washington, DC. "The first time I was seated behind a curtain in a dining car, I felt as if the curtain had been dropped on my selfhood," he later said.[9]

Yet these experiences registered as a desire to help his race not lead a revolution. On his Crozer application, he had said that "I felt an inescapable urge to serve society."[10] Though Coretta's career (as a vocalist) would be advanced by staying in the North and he had been offered a pulpit in Detroit, "we agreed that, in spite of the disadvantages and inevitable sacrifices, our greatest service could be rendered in our native South. We came to the conclusion that we had something of a moral obligation, to return."[11] "[We] had a feeling that something remarkable was unfolding in the South, and we wanted to be on hand to witness it," King would later say.[12]

The postwar period had prepared the way. As King would later note, more than four dozen nations would declare their independence from colonial rule, freeing many people of color in Africa and Asia to chart their destiny. Having fought for freedom overseas, returning black soldiers expected it at home. In 1948, Truman sent a civil rights message to Congress, calling for a permanent Civil Rights Commission and federal action to stop lynching and protect the right to vote. In 1949 he integrated the Armed Forces by executive order. In 1954, the Supreme Court's 9–0 decision in *Brown vs. Board of Education* ended 58 years in which "separate but equal" had been the law of the land.[13]

In this fertile ground, a 42-year-old seamstress, Rosa Parks, boarded the Cleveland Avenue bus in downtown Montgomery on her way home from work on Thursday, December 1, 1955. When she refused to give up her seat to a white passenger, she was arrested for violating the segregation ordinance. Respectful and respected, secretary of the local National Association for the Advancement of Colored People (NAACP), she offered the perfect case on which to take a stand. Within hours, E. D. Nixon, Pullman Porter Union leader and local NAACP president, and Jo Ann Robinson, an Alabama State College professor and a member of Dexter's Social and Political Action Committee, began organizing a boycott of the buses, to begin Monday morning.

Having only recently turned down the presidency of the local NAACP to focus on his church and his new daughter, Yolanda, born just two weeks before, King was reluctant to assume leadership. Yet at the group's second meeting, on Monday, he was elected president of the newly formed Montgomery Improvement Association. He was young, articulate, and a compromise choice.

The first mass meeting was that evening, December 5. "I had only twenty minutes to prepare the most decisive speech of my life," King recalled. "I became possessed by fear...In this state of anxiety...I turned to God in prayer."[14] His speech electrified the crowed: "If we are wrong, then the Supreme Court of this Nation is wrong. If we are wrong, then the Constitution of the United States is wrong. If we are wrong, God Almighty is wrong. If we are wrong, Jesus of Nazareth was merely a Utopian dreamer and never came down to earth. If we are wrong, justice is a lie."[15]

While King expected the protest to be brief (blacks comprised the great majority of the private bus company's riders and the boycott was nearly 100 percent effective), success took almost a year. It came not when the local government backed down but when the Supreme Court upheld a district court decision that the city's bus segregation law was unconstitutional. During that year, King was arrested and his home was bombed. Yet he earned national recognition. *Jet* magazine called him "Alabama's Modern Moses." Ten thousand attended his first northern fund-raiser. New Yorker and popular singer Harry Belafonte grew to respect King for his humility. "I need your help," King told him. "I have no idea where this movement is going."[16]

A Movement Going Nowhere

Success in Montgomery must have seemed like an oasis in the desert over the next seven years. Despite *Brown*, despite Montgomery, one hundred years after the Emancipation Proclamation, in 1963, the Negro was far from free.[17]

In 1955, the Court had issued *"Brown II,"* which called for school desegregation with "all deliberate speed." This step back from immediate compliance became a march to the rear with the Court's approval, in the same term, of "pupil placement laws." These gave schools wide latitude on whom they could accept, provided only that race was not an overt criterion. By 1963, King noted, only 9 percent of southern Negro students were attending integrated schools.[18]

Civil rights legislation enacted by Congress in 1957 and 1960, aimed at securing voting rights, was weak in content and enforcement. Blacks were routinely prevented from registering. Segregation laws kept them separate in almost all public places in the South—lunch counters, fitting rooms, rail and bus stations, parks, rest rooms, even libraries. Montgomery itself illustrated the one-step-forward, two-steps-back pace. Bus integration proceeded after the Court's order, but five of seven white men arrested for Montgomery bombings signed confessions, were indicted, and acquitted anyway. New city ordinances prevented Negroes and whites from even playing checkers together.

In Birmingham, Rev. Fred Shuttlesworth created the Alabama Christian Movement for Human Rights (ACMHR) when an injunction barred the NAACP from operating in the state, petitioned the city for bus desegregation and sought to integrate schools and store lunch counters, for which he was in due course arrested, beaten, and had his house and church bombed.[19]

King was active, but results were meager. Still, he had detected a split in the white community: "it was clear," he said in *Stride Toward Freedom*, his 1958 book on the bus boycott, "that the vast majority of Montgomery's whites preferred peace and law to the excesses performed in the name of segregation."[20] That split, infused with determination and hope, led to the creation of the Southern Christian Leadership Conference (SCLC) in 1957, with King as president. Its focus would be Negro registration and voting, the theme of his first national speech. On May 17, 1957, the third anniversary of *Brown*, King told the crowd at the Prayer Pilgrimage for Freedom in Washington, DC: "Give us the ballot, and we will no longer have to worry the federal government about our basic rights." King of course knew that the federal government was not worried enough on its own.[21]

Despite gaining international prominence with a trip to Ghana for its transition from colonial rule in 1957 and a tour of Gandhi's India in 1959, King and the SCLC struggled. At home, he was what *Jet* magazine labeled a "Man on the Go," traveling some 780,000 miles and making 208 speeches in one year.[22] Yet the Eisenhower Administration largely ignored him, as did most of the white press, and the SCLC suffered financially and organizationally.

The SCLC was not just too weak. It was often too late, especially to students who bristled at the more cautious King. Student lunch-counter sit-ins began in Greensboro, North Carolina, on February 1, 1960, without his involvement, though he flew to Durham on February 16, encouraged the students to form what became the Student Nonviolent Coordinating Committee, and lent it SCLC support. He played catch up again when the Freedom Rides began on May 4, 1961 to integrate interstate transportation facilities. Attacked and their bus burned outside Anniston, Alabama, and then set upon by the Birmingham Klan under the calculated absence of Chief Bull Connor's police, the student riders were not joined by King until he arrived in Montgomery on May 20. Even in voting rights, the SCLC had little to show for its work.

King had been thrust into a leadership position for which he was not prepared. Just 26 when the Montgomery boycott began, he had to learn to be not just a minister but a civil rights leader, politician, strategist, organizer, fund-raiser, office and staff manager, and national and international spokesman. He felt he had little other choice:

> If anybody had asked me a year ago to head this movement, I tell you very honestly that I would have run a mile to get away from it...As I became involved, and as people began to derive inspiration from their involvement...The people expect you to give them leadership...you can't decide whether to stay in or get out of it, you must stay in it.[23]

Stay he did, seeking a way forward. Since Montgomery, he had championed Christian love and nonviolence, and while that message characterized protests, it was a philosophy not a plan. The SCLC was hope looking for a method. As King biographer Taylor Branch would note: "Nonviolence, like the boycott itself, had begun more or less by accident...Not until Birmingham, more than six years later, would King's ideal of leadership encompass the deliberate creation of new struggles or the conscious, advance selection of strategies and tactics."[24] But first he had to endure yet another baptism in the streets and jails of Albany, Georgia.

On the heels of the Interstate Commerce Commission's November 1 start date for integrating interstate transportation facilities, a victory of the Freedom Riders, five black members of the Albany Movement tested the ruling on November 22, 1961. They were promptly arrested for trying to eat in the bus station dining room. On December 10, a group of eight Freedom Riders arriving from Atlanta were jailed for trying to integrate the railroad station. By December 15, 471 marchers were in jail and Dr. William Anderson, a local osteopath and the Movement's leader, invited King to Albany. On December 16, in town for less than a day, King and Abernathy led a protest march of 265 people, all of whom were jailed. King had planned only to offer advice, yet once there he felt compelled to march. For good and ill, his and the SCLC's reputation were at stake, with no plan to guide them.

The protests collapsed almost as quickly as they began when a tentative settlement was announced, an unwritten agreement that the city government would soon ignore and in which the jailed King played no part. Released on bond, he left town dogged by press accounts that gave credit to Albany police chief Laurie Pritchett, who had managed to arrest people politely. The only black leader with national recognition, King took the heat for failure. And the worst was not over.

Convicted for the protest in February 1962, King was sentenced on July 10. He accepted jail rather than pay a fine, yet his self-sacrifice was thwarted when Albany's mayor secretly arranged to have his fine paid so he could not be a martyr. "This is one time that I'm out of jail and I'm not happy to be out," King announced, insisting he would remain in Albany until the Albany Manifesto's demands were met.[25] He next confronted an injunction against further marches. After agonizing, he honored it (a decision he later regretted), stopping the Albany effort cold. When lawyers got the injunction lifted, King marched again, was arrested again, and then freed with a suspended sentence. Concluding that his presence was doing little good, he returned to Atlanta under cover of a statement that he trusted his departure would make negotiations easier.

Trying to put the best light on failure, King convinced no one. The New York *Herald Tribune* summed up the general consensus in saying that Albany had been "a devastating loss of face" and "one of the most stunning defeats" of his leadership.[26] Even the NAACP piled on, observing that "Albany was successful only if the objective was to go to jail."[27]

Seeing is Deceiving

Chief Pritchett's boast that integration had been set back "at least ten years" by King's failure mistook observable events for unobservable change.[28] Beneath the surface, King was growing in intellectual depth and political savvy. He learned a lot in Albany and would marry it with much he had learned before.

Missed by the press and opponents was King's sophisticated theory of nonviolent social change. While struggling with how to act on that theory, his guiding philosophy—only partly formed in Montgomery—had taken shape. As he later said: "From the beginning a basic philosophy guided the movement. This guiding principle has since been referred to as nonviolent resistance, noncooperation, and passive resistance. But in the first days of the protest none of these expressions was mentioned: the phrase most often heard was 'Christian love.' "[29]

King had struggled with the command to "love thy neighbor" even if that neighbor was a racist. He resolved the dilemma by relying on the Greek differentiation among three kinds of love. *Eros* (aesthetic or affectionate love) and *philia* (mutual respect, friendship) were neither appropriate nor possible. What he did ask was that Negroes practice *agape*, the love of others as human beings. You do not need to like your opponents, but you must love them because God loves them.[30] Yet love is a feeling not a method. In Montgomery and for some time after, King struggled to find a technology to go with the feeling.

King had been interested in social issues from his youth. Exposure to Walter Rauschenbusch's *Christianity and the Social Crisis* in his first year at Crozer convinced him that the social gospel movement, which asked Christians to improve society not just show up in church, could be a driving force in his life. He admired Thoreau's *Civil Disobedience* as a student and found the incarnation of Thoreau in Gandhi in a lecture by Dr. Mordecai Johnson, president of Howard University, that he attended in Philadelphia while at Crozer. It was not until he traveled to India in 1959, however, that he absorbed the potential of merging Gandhi with Christ in the civil rights movement. The attraction to Gandhi was his adherence to Satyagraha (translated from Sanskrit as "love" plus "force"). "My study of Gandhi," King said, "convinced me that true pacifism is not nonresistance to evil, but nonviolent resistance to evil." Further, he noted, "a courageous confrontation of evil by the power or love...may develop a sense of shame in the opponent, and thereby bring about a transformation and change of heart."[31]

"The balanced Christian," King concluded, "must be loving and realistic."[32] The realism was underscored by King's encounter with Reinhold Niebuhr's *Moral Man and Immoral Society*, which helped balance the optimism of the social gospel movement with the understanding that education and faith were not sufficient to eradicate evil. As Niebuhr put it, "The white race in America will not admit the Negro to equal rights if it is not forced to do so."[33]

The final piece in the eclectic intellectual puzzle was provided by King's doctoral work. At Boston, he took ten courses from Edgar Brightman, the chief proponent of the school of theology called personalism. King's conclusion that religion must nurture the individual personality, and his awareness that loss of dignity and self-respect was the insidious result of racism, would underlie the Movement's emotional force and tactical approach.

To philosophy, King added political insight. Even though Kennedy had been elected in 1960 with a 40 percent margin among blacks, King learned he could not count on the White House to take the initiative. But he could force it. Kennedy was too dependent on segregationists in Congress and insisted he had no authority to intervene in state and local affairs unless public order was threatened. King learned that some Negroes would willingly risk their lives in protests but that disunity in the Negro community, especially at the local level, allowed the white city government to exploit divisions. He learned that: "You don't win against a political power structure where you don't have the votes. But you can win against an economic power structure when you have the economic power to make the difference between a merchant's profit and loss."[34] He learned that *he* had to control when he came out of jail and that obeying an injunction may make legal but not political or symbolic sense. In Albany, he learned that a protest movement had to be focused: "The mistake I made there was to protest against segregation generally rather than against a single distinct factor of it. Our protest was so vague that we got nothing."[35]

King also learned how to use his strengths. His intellectual and rhetorical skills had earned him the admiration of black masses and at least some in the Northern white community. Working with whites, he had acquired a political sensitivity to the latitude they had to act. Attacked from both sides—as too timid by black student activists and too radical by whites and moderate blacks—he understood both sides and could be a bridge between them. As he said, finding strength in a fault: "It is one of my weaknesses as a leader. I'm too courteous and I'm not candid enough. However, I feel that my softness has helped in one respect. People have found it easy to become reconciled around me."[36]

All these strands were woven through Hegelian synthesis, a capacity that King admired in the philosopher and mastered in practice. The test of his learning, of course, would be in the application. Birmingham would soon be that test.

Why Birmingham?

"I don't want to be a fireman anymore," King resolved after Albany.[37] Since Montgomery, he had always been pulled into protest movements, not in a place, time, or manner of his choosing. With his leadership in question and the SCLC floundering, it was time to take command of his destiny.

The SCLC had already failed in Birmingham. Its aborted voter registration drive in 1959 had relied on the moderate Negro middle class—not the charismatic Shuttlesworth. King would not repeat that mistake. Shuttlesworth, who was on the SCLC board, asked King in

May 1962 to come to Birmingham—and kept asking. Earlier that spring, Shuttlesworth had supported a student-led Easter season boycott of downtown stores. Despite initial success, the boycott failed in the face of intransigent city commissioners. Yet, he told King and the SCLC: "Birmingham is where it's at, gentlemen...If you win in Birmingham, as Birmingham goes, so goes the nation."[38] Bogged down in Albany, King had deferred the request until the September SCLC Board meeting, coincidentally scheduled for Birmingham.

Extricated from Albany and desperate for success, King warmed to the idea. Birmingham, he would later say, was "the most segregated city in America,"[39] its racism entrenched since only 10 percent of the black population had even been allowed to register to vote.[40] In addition to the Freedom Rider violence in 1961, Birmingham had been the site of more than 50 unsolved bombings in the last two decades.[41] It was the only 1 of 82 southern cities that a 1952 report found had no blacks on its police force. Since Eugene "Bull" Connor was in charge, that would not change. Local courts had separate Bibles for blacks and whites for taking the oath, and when the city was ordered to integrate its recreational facilities, the three city commissioners (Connor being one) closed them instead. Laundry trucks that traversed the city were inscribed with "We Wash for White People Only."[42] Such realities led *New York Times* reporter Harrison Salisbury to write in April 1960 that "Some Negroes have nicknamed Birmingham the Johannesburg of America."[43] Others had more colloquially labeled it "Bombingham."

While progress in Birmingham would be difficult, the level of racism would magnify anything King could accomplish. The partial success of the student-led boycott in 1962 suggested a strategy. So did other fissures in white opposition. Businessman Sidney Smyer, a former staunch supporter of segregation, had been appalled at the international notoriety Birmingham suffered after beating the Freedom Riders. Since then, he had led a campaign to replace the city commission with a mayor-council form of government, a way of ousting Bull Connor from power. A vote on this change was on the November 1962 ballot.

How Birmingham?

Events connected with the SCLC board meeting were promising and predictive. Hoping to head off demonstrations in connection with that meeting, Smyer formed a Senior Citizens Committee and sought negotiations. When Shuttlesworth threatened to put people in the streets, the merchants agreed to remove "whites only" signs from drinking fountains and restrooms. Shuttlesworth called a truce and the SCLC board arrived, though he was under no illusions: "They took those signs down because you were coming to town, and they'll put 'em up again just as soon as you leave," he told King.[44] Even if the business community had an interest in negotiations, they could not control Connor. When the SCLC left, he sent inspectors into the stores. They started finding multiple violations, the stores got the message, and the segregation signs returned. Anticipating this, the SCLC board had already approved a move into a southern city but kept the choice of Birmingham a secret.

On November 8, the mayoral form of government was approved. The election for mayor was set for March 5. Since Connor could no longer be a commissioner, he announced his intention to run. His chief opponent would be Albert Boutwell, considered the more moderate choice though as a state senator he had helped write the School Placement Act that the U.S. Supreme Court upheld in 1955.

The last chance to avoid a confrontation slipped away when King, Ralph Abernathy (SCLC vice-president), and Shuttlesworth met with President Kennedy in January and left convinced he had no intention of supporting civil rights legislation in 1963. He had to be forced.[45] They set March 12 for the start of demonstrations, to impact the Easter shopping season. Local black leaders had asked them to delay until after the mayoral election to avoid a confrontation that might sway votes to Connor.

The Movement now had a mechanism. Limited goals, meticulous planning, engaging the local community through church-based mass meetings, demonstrations conducted by trained volunteers who signed Commitment Cards promising nonviolence, and getting arrested to generate the press coverage needed to pressure change were its elements. King directed SCLC executive director Wyatt Tee Walker to travel to Birmingham to prepare. The initial focus would be sit-ins to concentrate the effort and hit businesses directly. As King recounted in *Why We Can't Wait*, his post-Birmingham book, as a result of Walker's efforts: "By March 1...250 people had volunteered to participate in the initial demonstrations and had pledged to remain in jail at least five days."[46]

The mass meetings, held every night once the campaign began, are often overlooked as an element of the Movement. Conducted in churches, the central gathering place for blacks in the South, their

content paralleled a church service. Freedom songs replaced spiritu-
als, rousing talks by King and others replaced sermons, and a call for
nonviolent volunteers at the end took the place of the invitation to
respond or altar call. More importantly, they gave everyone a chance
to participate even if they could not march, kept information flowing
to the community, maintained the emotion needed in a long campaign,
and strengthened the sense of selfhood central in King's philosophy.
Daily, they pumped energy into the Movement. As King would tell the
New Pilgrim Baptist Church mass meeting in early May: "Keep climbing. If you can't run, walk. If you can't walk, crawl, but by all means
keep moving."[47] A Movement without movement was a failure—and
a possible failure is what King soon faced.

Toward a Crucial Decision

The first roadblock came on March 5 when Boutwell beat Connor but
failed to gain the required majority in the three-person race, forcing
a runoff on April 2. King again felt compelled to delay, pushing the
start of the campaign to April 3, just 11 days before Easter. Boutwell
beat Connor by 8,000 votes in the second election. The *Birmingham
News* on April 3 featured a golden sun rising over the city and the
caption "New Day Dawns for Birmingham." Yet Connor and the two
other commissioners refused to step down, challenging the new form
of government in court and claiming that, in any case, their terms
of office did not end until 1965. Project C would confront two city
governments.

On April 3, only 65 of the 250 who signed pledge cards showed up
to protest, a result of the month-long delay. Shuttlesworth delivered
copies of the "Birmingham Manifesto" to reporters. On behalf of the
ACMHR, it demanded (1) immediate desegregation of store facilities, (2) fair hiring practices, (3) dismissal of charges against previous
nonviolent ACMHR protesters, (4) a merit system to open city jobs to
Negroes, (5) reopening of parks and pools on an integrated basis, and
(6) a biracial committee to focus on other areas.

Protesters went to lunch counters in downtown stores. In four
stores, waitresses simply closed up rather than serve them. Only at
one did a manager call police. The arrest count was a meager 21, and
at the end of the third day only 30 had been jailed. With scant success,
King changed the plan with a Shuttlesworth-led march on city hall.
Even that led to only 25 arrests as Connor reacted in Pritchett style,

not with the violence the SCLC had counted on. Then, on April 10, the state court's injunction banned further marches.

Unable to provoke Connor, King also met opposition in the black community. Moderates, including black businessmen, had more to lose and resented King's disruption of their accommodations with the city. Some felt he should give Boutwell a chance before protesting. Even black pastors withheld support, leading King to castigate them at an April 8 meeting for paying too much attention to man's condition in Heaven and not enough to his plight on earth.[48] The Negro *Birmingham World* criticized the campaign on April 10 as "wasteful and worthless."[49] King was asking people to take a big risk with little guarantee of success. He had also misjudged the level of support for Shuttlesworth, a grating personality who had moved to a pastorate in Cincinnati and come back to lead the effort, causing some ministers to label him an "absentee aristocrat."[50]

King's problems went beyond Birmingham. Rather than support from the white press and the White House, he met skepticism and opposition, when not totally ignored. The *New York Times* titled its first story "Integration Drive Slows...Sit-Ins and a Demonstration Plan Fail to Materialize," and Project C got no further than page A6 of the *Washington Post* by April 12.[51] President Kennedy was silent, and Attorney General Robert Kennedy let King know, through Burke Marshall, Assistant Attorney General for Civil Rights, that he thought the demonstrations "ill-timed" since Boutwell had just taken office.[52]

Amid all this, King soldiered on, making some progress among the black community by forming a cross-cutting Central Committee. But it was not enough. Tentative efforts at negotiation between the ACMHR, SCLC, and Smyer's Senior Citizens Committee faltered almost as soon as they began. Birmingham was threatening to become another Albany.

Alone in the Gaston Motel, King weighed all this. He was just 34. His background and instincts urged caution. As Coretta would say of him, "Martin never abruptly forced an issue."[53] He had been reluctant in Montgomery, in the sit-in movement, at the start of the Freedom Rides, in Albany, and even in deciding to come to Birmingham. Nevertheless, he had been vilified, physically attacked, and seen others get beaten, go to jail, and die on his behalf. The burden seemed overwhelming. Some likened him to Moses and Christ, and he felt a messenger for both.

If he obeyed the injunction and cancelled the march, Project C would collapse. If he allowed the march, he would violate the law. If others marched without him, he could not bail them out and would be seen as a coward: "What would be the verdict of the country about a man who had encouraged hundreds of people to make a stunning sacrifice and then excused himself," he later observed. Confronting a decision, he recalled, "I think I was standing also in the center of all that my life had brought me to be."[54]

Going to Birmingham Jail

"I must go," King said to himself. In the end, he trusted the morality of his choice and the belief that creating tension was the only chance for success, even if he could not control where the tension led. He changed into blue jeans, a work shirt and draped a coat over his arm (jail would be cold). He rejoined his advisers, telling them: "I don't know what will happen. I don't know where the money will come from. But I have to make a faith act. If we obey this injunction we are out of business. I have to go."[55] "That, I think," civil rights leader Andrew Young later recalled about King, "was the beginning of his true leadership."[56]

"Wait a minute," Ralph Abernathy said. "Let me see if I can get in touch with my deacons, because I'm gonna spend Easter in the Birmingham Jail."[57] King, Abernathy, and Shuttlesworth emerged in the soft, 73-degree spring air, and went one block to Zion Hill Baptist Church where King told the audience that only the "redemptive influence of suffering" could transform Birmingham.[58] Only 50 marchers joined him. Singing "We Shall Overcome," King and Abernathy, walking side by side, led the way onto the street. Three blocks later, facing Connor and more than 80 officers, they fell to their knees to pray and were promptly arrested.

King was put in solitary confinement, a 54-square-foot cell, with a 6-foot cot that had metal slats and no bedding. He had never been isolated before, and being alone frightened him perhaps more than being in jail. He was allowed neither phone calls nor the chance to meet privately with his lawyer. As he recalled, "Having no contact of any kind, I was besieged with worry. How was the movement faring?"[59]

His worry got no relief until Monday, when he learned from his lawyer, Clarence Jones, that "Harry [Belafonte] has been able to raise fifty thousand dollars for bail bonds."[60] On the same day, he was allowed a call. Wyatt Walker had been phoning people, urging them to call the White House. President Kennedy had subsequently called

Coretta and, though not willing to intervene, got word to Birmingham officials of his concern for King's safety. When King heard from Coretta of the President's call, his spirits soared. "Let Wyatt know," he instructed her.[61] A call from the president meant that pressuring the White House might work. Walker would need to ramp up the demonstrations and get more people arrested.

Despite these hopeful signs, the outside world took little notice. What attention it paid was negative. The *Washington Post's* Sunday editorial opined that the marches were "of doubtful utility" and that "Boutwell deserves a fair trial."[62] On the previous day, April 13, the *Birmingham News* carried a story on page 2 titled "White Clergymen Urge Local Negroes to Withdraw from Demonstrations." The story contained an open letter, composed by eight religious leaders on Good Friday, the day King was arrested. The same group of eight had written to Governor George Wallace after his January 1963 inaugural address had pledged "segregation now, segregation tomorrow, segregation forever." Their earlier letter called for "law and order and common sense," for which they were attacked by segregationists, and they now issued the same call to Birmingham's moderate Negroes, refusing to mention King by name. Sometime over the weekend, King appears, through his lawyers, to have read or heard about the clergy's missive. He got a copy of the newspaper and began writing a reply.

Writing the Letter from Birmingham Jail

The letter from the clergy was addressed to local public opinion, not King directly. His reply would be addressed to world opinion, not the clergy directly. He never signed the letter or sent it to them. They were the vehicle, not the destination. He never met with them and even misspelled two of their names. Why he wrote the letter is thus subject to some speculation.

During Albany, Harvey Shapiro of the *New York Times* had suggested to SCLC officials that King write a letter while in jail.[63] On Sunday, April 14, the *Times* wrote that individuals in Birmingham were "drawing up an answer" to the eight clergymen, possibly a leaked message from Walker.[64]

King had a keen sense for history. Perhaps the timing was right. He had been frustrated with the white clergy for some time. In *Stride Toward Freedom*, he had said that "Many white ministers can do much more than they are doing."[65] Perhaps his frustration just boiled over when he saw them urging moderation and praise for Bull Connor for his handling of the demonstrations. Perhaps, in solitary with nothing else to do, he chose this moment to do what he did best.

Whatever else a letter might achieve, it *would* respond to two challenges. First, Project C might collapse and the Movement with it. If it did, a justification of the failed effort would be essential and perhaps the only way to rescue the Movement and his reputation. Second, moderates, and in fact most of the nation, were viewing the civil rights movement as a legal battle, in which the courts not the streets were the proper battleground. Yet for King, the Movement was primarily a moral issue, in which hearts not heads were the place to make the appeal. A letter could make that argument, even if it was unlikely to have impact on events "on the ground" in Birmingham itself.

The letter, in its present form, was not composed solely while King was in jail. Since it was intended for publication, not for private, immediate delivery, much care was taken with it. A master at memorizing sermons and retaining whole passages of previous writings in his head, King no doubt drew on these skills as he wrote on the margins of the newspaper and even on toilet tissue supplied by a prison trusty.[66] Later on, when his lawyers supplied him with writing paper, he used them as messengers to send sections of the letter to Wyatt Walker for typing. Typed sections were snuck back in by lawyers for his review. While the letter would be dated Tuesday, April 16, evidence suggests that he continued to work on it after it was released on April 18 and after his release on bond on April 20. The original manuscript may even have been as much as 15,000 words longer than the eventual published version.[67]

The Audience, the Challenge, the Tools

If the eight clergymen were just a vehicle, to whom *was* King writing? The simplest answer would be white clergy in general, since the greatest criticism in the letter would be reserved for them. But this would underestimate King's political calculus and the power of his words. The broader audience included all white moderates—those who were sitting on the political and moral fence—and politicians (who were almost universally white). It also included moderate black leaders whose caution posed its own threat to the Movement, the black masses who needed a demonstration that King was their champion, and black extremists for whom violence was an acceptable tool that threatened his leadership and the cause. The Letter was thus part of the leadership task of forging relationships and a shared understanding between King and all these groups.

Each audience had its own interests, which were by no means compatible with other audiences. Yet King was the ultimate "crossover man." He could speak to them all because he had lived in all of their worlds. He was a member of the black middle class and had worked with black leaders in the church, NAACP, CORE (Congress of Racial Equality), and the student movement. He had suffered the emotional and physical attacks of racism and was respected by poor blacks. He was a preacher and intellect who had attended northern white universities, had a small but growing network of influential white supporters, and had met with white leaders in two presidential administrations.

Speaking to them without losing them was a task of political craftsmanship, and he needed not just to address their concerns but to gain their active support. That support, until now, had been aimed at a legal battle in the courts. The tools had been filings, appeals, and judicial orders, which often took years and, given the number of segregationist judges, carried no certainty of success. King was asking people to engage in a moral battle, fought nonviolently with their bodies in the streets. The stakes could hardly be higher. They called for his most effective tool: rhetoric.

King had loved words since childhood. As his father recalled, "M.L. liked to listen to good preachers before he was old enough to understand them. If he heard that some outstanding man was going to speak, he would ask me to take him."[68] "He learned to recite the Scriptures before he was five," Coretta recalled.[69] At six, he told his mother: "Just wait and see. I'm going to get me some big words."[70] His younger brother, A. D., recalled that even as a child King "had the gift of talking himself out of unpleasant situations."[71] King perhaps first realized this power when he was selected as a devotional leader for his work camp in Connecticut. At Crozer, he took ten classes on the structure and art of giving sermons. Yet, as Coretta noted, "[H]is preaching style grew out of the traditions of the southern Baptist ministers, with cadences and timing which he had heard from his father and other ministers as long as he could remember."[72] As the new minister at Dexter, he would spend 15 hours preparing each sermon, memorize the text, and then deftly (but noticeably) tuck away his notes as he mounted the pulpit. And, as Taylor Branch noted, "King came to accept the shorthand description of oratory as 'the three P's': proving, painting, and persuasion, aimed to win over successively the mind, imagination, and heart."[73]

Not technically a sermon, the Letter nevertheless reflected the rational and emotional approach King had learned to take. In his early years, he was more erudite and focused on reason, drawing heavily on white Protestant sermonic forms encountered at Crozer. As he and the Movement grew, his sermons began to draw on black traditions, blending reason with an increasing emotionalism. He departed from his early scorn of "whooping" and physical preaching. In short, his style became more eclectic and inclusive. As in the man, so in the Letter, which for all its printed silence was definitely a public oration.

Leadership and the Letter from Birmingham Jail

The Letter is an act of leadership courage. As sociologist Jonathan Rieder notes of King: "For a black man of that time to establish the relationship of moral teacher to whites was an act of great boldness."[74] Yet King began humbly. Writing to "My Dear Fellow Clergymen," he mixed warmth and community, focusing on their shared devotion to God. They are "men of genuine good will" who have "sincere criticisms" with which he hoped to be "patient and reasonable."

At the same time, he called attention to the gulf separating them. He is in jail; they are free.[75] Yet rather than this distinction making him a lesser man, he subtly recalled for them that he is so busy that "seldom do I pause to answer criticism" and that his "secretaries" are always at work.[76] In this deft and defusing opening, he invited himself into the same social (if not physical) space as his white colleagues. If the audience expected an angry black man, they must take a step back. In the space he thus created to be heard without judgment, King moved to tackle their charge that the demonstrations were "directed and led in part by outsiders." He rejected the "outsider" label in three arguments that build moral claims to his legitimacy. These arguments must come first; without legitimacy, he had no right to followers.

He first noted that "I am here because I have organizational ties here." As president of the SCLC, he was "asked...to be on call" by the local (Shuttlesworth-led) affiliate and so "consented." Not just an organizational duty, it was a moral duty: "We lived up to our promise." Second, he was in Birmingham on a religious duty—"because injustice is here." Boldly comparing himself to the apostle (Acts 16:9–10), he was here to "carry the gospel of freedom": "Like Paul, I must constantly respond to the Macedonian call for aid." If his audience wanted to label him an outsider, they must label Paul an outsider, a logical impossibility for men of the cloth. Third, King argued, no one who lives in the United States can ever "be considered an outsider anywhere within its bounds." He was in Birmingham as a duty of citizenship: "[I]njustice anywhere is a threat to justice everywhere."

King next turned to several other charges against him. The clergymen had called "for honest and open negotiation." He disarmed the criticism by agreeing with it. In the four-step process of nonviolent change, fact gathering (step one) is followed by negotiation (step two). The facts, King noted, showed that Birmingham was "probably the most thoroughly segregated city in the United States." Indeed, the clergy did not dispute the existence of segregation—they just favored gradual change. King recalled the negotiated promises made and broken to Shuttlesworth the previous September. In short, negotiation *had* been tried—and failed.

Broken promises led to self-purification (step three), the preparation for nonviolent protest. Direct action (step four) was the only recourse left. Even that had been twice delayed, in deference to the mayoral election and runoff. But the aim of direct action was nothing more than negotiation itself: "[I]ndeed, this is the very purpose of direct action." King admitted that direct action "seeks to create a crisis and foster such a tension that a community which has constantly refused to negotiate is forced to confront the issue." The failure to negotiate thus rested not with the black community but with the white power structure.

Next, King dealt with the charge that the demonstrations were "untimely." He rejected the clergy's contention that "recent public events [the election of Boutwell] have given indication that we all have opportunity for a new constructive and realistic approach to racial problems." Aware of Boutwell's segregationist history, King only admitted that he was "a much more gentle person" than Bull Connor. More importantly, King stated, "We have not made a single gain in civil rights without determined legal and nonviolent pressure."

A more devastating attack against the charge of "untimely" demonstrations was made on both a legal and moral basis—the twin pillars of the Movement. First, King quoted the dictum traced by some to British prime minister William Gladstone and by others to Chief Justice Earl Warren (of *Brown* fame), that "justice too long delayed is justice denied."[77] Second, he argued on moral grounds: "For years now I have heard the word 'Wait!'...This 'Wait' has almost always meant 'Never.'" What followed built quickly to the emotional crescendo of a single, 310-word sentence, excerpted here, that described in emotional language why it was so hard to "wait":

> ...when you have seen vicious mobs lynch your mothers and fathers at will and drown your sisters and brothers at whim; when you have seen hate-filled policemen curse, kick and even kill your black brothers and sisters; when you see the vast majority of your twenty million Negro brothers smothering in an airtight cage of poverty in the midst of an affluent society; when you suddenly find your tongue twisted and your speech stammering as you seek to explain to your six-year-old daughter why she can't go to the public amusement park that has just been advertised on television, and see tears welling up in her eyes when she is told that Funtown is closed to colored children, and see ominous clouds of inferiority beginning to form in her little mental sky, and see her beginning to distort her personality by developing an unconscious bitterness toward white people...then you will understand why we find it difficult to wait.

King aimed at the hearts of whites and blacks. The latter would see that he understands their suffering, and the former would feel the sting of segregation. The portrait painted images: "lynch," "drown your sisters and brothers," "kick and kill," "smothering in an airtight cage" and evoked sounds: "curse," "speech stammering," "Daddy, why...?" "your first name becomes "nigger." Use of the repeating phrasing "when..." and the semicolon rather than the period created a stream of consciousness that leaves the reader breathless and emotionally spent. King did not allow escape from the horror of racism until he was ready, in part to sear the conscience and in part to prepare for his argument against the most dangerous charge of the clergy—that the demonstrations broke the law.

"This is certainly a legitimate concern," he told them. Again he had a three-part answer. First, he made the distinction between just and unjust laws, arguing that "one has a moral responsibility to disobey unjust laws." Beginning a near-continuous effort through the remainder of the Letter to anchor his actions in history and association with famous men, he linked himself to St. Augustine, who said that "an unjust law is no law at all."

Second, he adopted the natural law reasoning of the Declaration of Independence, though he echoed St. Thomas Aquinas, not Jefferson: "An unjust law is a human law that is not rooted in eternal and natural law." Finally, he argued on Constitutional grounds: "An unjust law is a code that a numerical or power majority compels a minority to obey but does not make binding on itself." He even accused segregationists of misusing laws that seem just, such as the law he had broken, parading without a permit. In essence, this was a fourth argument—even just laws can be unjustly applied: "But such an ordinance becomes unjust when it is used to maintain segregation and to deny citizens the First Amendment privilege of peaceful assembly and protest."

He then linked the Movement to Thoreau, Shadrach, Meshach, Abednego, Socrates, and the Boston Tea Party—all cases of civil disobedience against unjust laws. If this were not enough, he reminded the audience that Hitler's laws were legal and rhetorically asked them to consider if they would have obeyed them. Rabbi Milton Grafman, one of the eight clergy writing to King, cannot have missed the point.

Having begun to respond to the clergy's call for "law and order," King moved to the related charge that lawbreaking was an "extreme measure." Since the Northern press and the Kennedy Administration agreed, refuting it was essential. King at first denied being an extremist. He placed the Movement in the political center, as a force for moderation between the extremes of white racism and violent black nationalism. The Movement could thus lay claim to public support as the best bet against a descent into chaos.

Next, he threw moderates off guard, attacking their moderation: "I have been gravely disappointed with the white moderate...Shallow understanding from people of good will is more frustrating than absolute misunderstanding from people of ill will." The shallow understanding of moderates occurred on two levels. They blamed the black protester for racism: "Isn't this like condemning a robbed man because his possession of money precipitated the evil act of robbery?" Also, they acted as if time alone would bring change: "Actually, time itself is neutral...Human progress never rolls in on the wheels of inevitability...the time is always ripe to do right."

Having logically removed the white moderates from their presumed position, he occupied it: "I stand in the middle of two opposing forces in the Negro community. One is a force of complacency...The other force is one of bitterness and hatred, and it comes perilously close to advocating violence." King offered "the more excellent way of love and nonviolent protest," reminding his white audience that if his approach was dismissed, a "frightening racial nightmare" could follow.

His final act of positioning redefined extremism itself, from a negative to a positive. In a single paragraph he reminded his audience that

Jesus, Amos, Paul, Martin Luther, John Bunyan, Abraham Lincoln, and Thomas Jefferson were all extremists—for love and justice. "Perhaps the South, the nation and the world are in dire need of creative extremists," he concluded.

Having dealt with the charges in the clergy's letter, he finally attacked the church itself. Had he started with this, as a frontal assault, it could have been seen as simply angry. Coming after his powerful, respectful, and logically disarming refutation of their charges, they were left defenseless as he told them of his great "disappointment with the white church and its leadership."

King had been angry with the white (and many in the black) church for some time. In a December 1962 speech in Chicago, titled "A Challenge to the Churches and Synagogues," he attacked them for remaining "silent behind the anesthetizing security of stained-glass windows," the very words he used again in the Letter.[78] His belief in the social gospel strengthened him in chiding the clergy for making "a strange, Biblical distinction between body and soul, between the sacred and secular." Urging parishioners to comply with desegregation laws was not enough; the clergy must extol their flocks to a higher, moral standard, "because the Negro is your brother."

He also turned their attack on his legitimacy against *them*: "If today's church does not recapture the sacrificial spirit of the early church, it will lose its authenticity" and become "an irrelevant social club." Lest he lose them, however, he noted that he "wept over the laxity of the church" but that "my tears have been tears of love. There can be no deep disappointment where there is not deep love." Faithful to the power of love, King was able to use it as a leadership device to defuse anger and criticism of his own anger and criticism.

The remainder of the Letter returned to the leadership of hope: "I have no despair about the future" because "the goal of America is freedom." Recalling that blacks helped build America, and that their sacrifices stood up for "what is best in the American dream," he looked forward to the day when "the radiant stars of love and brotherhood will shine over our great nation." His humble ending disarmed critics for the final time:

> If I have said anything in this letter that overstates the truth and indicates an unreasonable impatience, I beg you to forgive me. If I have said anything that understates the truth and indicates my having a patience that allows me to settle for anything less than brotherhood, I beg God to forgive me.

The Letter as a Vehicle for Social and Psychological Change

On one level, the Letter is a work of leadership artistry. Blending structured reasoning, an appeal to core values, political savvy, coalition building, and forcefulness of character and expression, King defuses critics and builds allies.

On a second level, the Letter is a demonstration of the assertion of power without position. Sitting in jail, condemned by whites and many blacks, leading a nearly bankrupt organization, politically weak, King gathers power. As social psychologists French and Raven noted, when the power of formal position is absent or inadequate, one may still exert social power through command of information and expertise, communication skills, interpersonal effectiveness, and association with others.[79]

The Letter also works as a macro- and micro-level attack on racism, as a black "Declaration of Independence" calling for fundamental social change, and as a plea to reverse the psychological damage of two centuries in which the Declaration's promise went unfulfilled.

Jefferson said near the end of his life that the Declaration was "an expression of the American mind," that his aim, as author, was "to place before mankind the common sense of the subject, in terms so plain and firm as to command their assent."[80] King's aim is similar, and the Letter contains many of the same elements as the Declaration—a natural rights argument, a list of abuses, scathing criticism of disenfranchisement by an overbearing power, a call to throw off oppression and the pledge of one's honor and self to the struggle.[81]

The parallel to the Declaration exists in another context as well. Writing in 1818, John Adams noted that: "The Revolution was effected before the war commenced. The Revolution was in the minds and hearts of the people; a change in their religious sentiments of their duties and obligations."[82] For blacks, the "real revolution" in a sense also preceded Birmingham, and the Letter reflects the change in mindset that evolved in at least the period since 1955.

It is at this psychological level that the power of the Letter is missed in a casual reading. King's doctoral work and faith convinced him that the health of the individual psyche is a birthright and an obligation of social justice. In his first published article, in 1956, King acknowledged that the force of history meant that "many Negroes lost faith in themselves and came to believe that perhaps they really were what they had been told they were—something less than men."[83] In *Stride Toward Freedom*, he noted "their corroding sense of inferiority, which often expressed itself as a lack of self-respect" that "scars the soul and degrades the personality."[84] The Movement aimed to free them socially, but it also sought to build them psychologically. Indeed, success in the former depended on success at the latter. As he noted during the Albany protests: "the salvation of the Negro in Albany, Georgia is not in Washington...The salvation of the Negro in Albany, Georgia, is not forthcoming from the governor's chair in the state of Georgia...The salvation of the Negro in Albany, Georgia, is within the hands and the soul of the Negro himself."[85]

The Letter thus forces whites to face the damage inflicted on Negro selfhood. When King explains to his daughter why she cannot go to Funtown in Atlanta, he cannot help but observe: "ominous clouds of inferiority beginning to form in her little mental sky, and see her beginning to distort her personality by developing an unconscious bitterness toward white people." The Letter is an argument to blacks and whites on the critical importance of seeing the value of nonviolent protest in helping the Negro regain his sense of "somebodyness."

As King would say in his last book, *Where Do We Go from Here?*: "The Negro will only be truly free when he reaches down to the inner depths of his own being and signs with the pen and ink of assertive selfhood his own emancipation proclamation."[86] It is hard to find a better statement of the art of a leadership that empowers followers.

Risking Everything: The Children's Crusade

However much we respect the Letter now, it did nothing for King in Birmingham, and when he emerged on bail on April 20, he surely needed help. The protests had sputtered (only 339 people were arrested between April 3 and April 27). As historian Glenn Eskew notes, "[T]he campaign appeared to be on the verge of collapse." Getting volunteers to march proved almost impossible. At an emergency meeting of the ACHMR-SCLC Central Committee on April 29, King despaired: "The press is leaving, we've got to get going."[87]

King's aide, James Bevel, understood that adults who could and would march already had. The black community was simply not strong enough to produce more. It was time to use children. Students knew each other, felt a common bond, and had no other obligations. Bevel proposed to train and send them forth to confront Bull Connor, beginning on "D-day," May 2, despite the city's denial of a march permit.

On that morning, King again confronted division in Room 30 of the Gaston Motel. Thousands of students had skipped school and were gathering at the Sixteenth Street Baptist Church, yet middle class black leaders castigated King for his plan to use them. Walker, Shuttlesworth, and Bevel not only argued for a youth march but pushed King to lower the age of protesters using a simple formula— old enough to belong to church, old enough to march.[88] King seemed paralyzed—caught between the necessity of using children and his abhorrence at exposing them to Connor's police. Once again, as on April 12, he felt forced to risk everything.

After no word from him arrived by the Movement's noon deadline, Bevel and Walker opened the doors of the church and students began pouring out, two by two. By the end of the day, nearly 1,000 had been arrested. As King later recounted, about what *Newsweek* labeled the "children's crusade" that continued for days: "At one school, the principal gave orders to lock the gates to keep the students in. The youngsters climbed over the gates and ran towards freedom." Finally, he said, "We were able to put into effect the Gandhian principle: 'Fill up the jails.'"[89] Children as young as six were arrested. The jails overflowed, and some were bused to open-air holding pens, subject to whatever the elements might do to them—a fact King sought to conceal fearing that parents would keep their children at home if they knew.

Finally, Connor lost control of himself. On May 3, with no place to put more children, he resolved to keep them from demonstrating and turned on the fire hoses as soon as they left the church. When one hundred pounds of pressure sent students careening down the street and ripped off flesh, orderly black observers turned into a mob, hurling bricks and bottles at the firemen. Connor responded with police dogs.[90] Even black moderates like A. G. Gaston were appalled and threw their support to the protests. As Walker would later comment, "Bull Connor had something in his mind about not letting these niggers get to City Hall...Birmingham would have been lost if Bull had let us go down to City Hall and pray."[91]

The violence, covered graphically and nationally, finally forced Kennedy's hand. He dispatched Burke Marshall to engage in shuttle diplomacy between the SCLC and Smyer's Senior Citizens Council. King was also bolstered by two observations. Despite the demonstrations, most whites were not engaged in them—they were leaving the police to handle things. Also, the downtown business district was nearly deserted; whites were staying away out of fear. Economic pressure was working.[92]

Convinced that the strategy he was reluctant to embrace was succeeding, King became an ardent supporter. At the same time, Walker increased the pressure. On Monday, May 6, 1,000 children were arrested, and on Tuesday so many students converged on downtown from so many directions that the police were powerless to intervene. The SCLC was shutting down the city. When the Senior Citizens Council negotiating committee, meeting downtown, broke for lunch that day, they were confronted by what King would call "square blocks of Negroes, a veritable sea of black faces."[93] This broke the back of their resistance.

It would be inaccurate, however, to say the Movement scored a resounding success. The settlement announced on May 10 fell far short of initial demands. Desegregation in downtown stores was to be phased in, not immediate, and the reopening of parks and pools on an integrated basis was not even in the agreement. Fair hiring was only a goal, to be reached after further discussion. Charges against protesters were not dropped. The "required" biracial committee would be established but with a vague mandate and little commitment to action.

Success in Birmingham?

King needed a victory and he took what he could get. Perhaps he understood that Connor and Wallace were on the verge of sending in state troopers; perhaps he sensed that Kennedy had done all he could (or would); perhaps he felt the wedge between white businessmen and politicians would not get wider. Or perhaps it was the realization that it was he and the SCLC who would get the credit or blame, survive or fade away, depending on the perceived results in Birmingham. As Burke Marshall put it a year later: "I think he wanted success...for himself and he wanted success for his people. It was partly cynical, and it was partly sincere...Partly cynical in the sense he wanted it for himself. He, King, as a Negro leader, wanted to be *the* Negro leader who had a success. In part, he was just trying to accomplish something."[94]

Both city governments denounced even the limited concessions in the settlement. Mayor Art Hanes called it "a capitulation by certain weak-kneed white people under threats of violence by the rabble-rousing Negro, King,"[95] and "moderate" Mayor Boutwell said he was "unwilling to make decisions virtually at gunpoint or as a result of agitation."[96] Sidney Smyer was the only white leader willing to publicly endorse the accord.

On the night of May 11, more than 2,500 Klansmen rallied. Shortly after, the home of Rev. A. D. King, Martin's brother, was bombed as was the Gaston Motel. Rioting followed, state troopers intervened, and the racist effort to sabotage the settlement seemed on the verge of working. King and his brother calmed local blacks, and Kennedy responded by authorizing the deployment of 3,000 army troops. Halting progress followed.

In mid-May, businesses integrated fitting rooms, and the next month they removed "colored only" signs from water fountains and rest rooms, though politicians refused to take the segregation ordinances off the books until July. On May 20, the Birmingham Board of Education expelled more than 1,000 black students who had left school to join the protests, forcing King back to Birmingham to help reverse the expulsions. On May 23, the Alabama Supreme Court ruled that Boutwell was the legal mayor and ordered the commissioners to step down. The federal courts ordered desegregation of city schools, yet Wallace used Guard troops to enforce segregation in September. Kennedy federalized the guard and integration went ahead. Then, on Sunday, September 15, a bomb placed by the Klan under the steps of the Sixteenth Street Baptist Church exploded, killing four young girls. Two weeks later, King threatened to resume demonstrations since the sham "Community Affairs Committee" Boutwell had created for biracial discussions had made no progress (he had refused to appoint any of its blacks to key subcommittees) and no blacks had been promoted to white jobs in local businesses and no black policemen had been hired.

Yet King backed down. He and the Movement had emerged in the national consciousness as oppressed, nonviolent, and moderate in demands for which they should no longer be asked to wait—and as victorious, exactly the positioning that King had written the Letter to create. If the result on the ground was less than the outside world imagined, that was the beauty of the press and the Administration telling the story the way they wanted. King's job was to use that story for all it could achieve.

Five days after the settlement, he spoke to the first mass meeting for civil rights in the North, in Cleveland, and major events followed in Los Angeles, Chicago, and Detroit, among other cities. SCLC fund-raising took off ($150,000 in a single week). In mid-June, President Kennedy gave a national address on civil rights, uttering words King had despaired of hearing: "We are confronted primarily with a moral issue." Kennedy introduced civil rights legislation a week later. Earlier plans for a March on Washington took concrete shape, now concentrated on pressuring Congress to pass Kennedy's bill. On August 28, a peaceful crowd of well over 200,000 and King's concluding "I Have a Dream" speech demonstrated for a national TV audience that blacks were neither outsiders nor extremists. King would later note that the number of SCLC affiliates jumped from 85 to 110 that summer, and "hundreds of national civic, religious, labor and professional organizations speaking for tens of millions...called upon their supporters to join the demonstrations." In the ten weeks following Birmingham, 758 demonstrations led to 14,733 arrests in 186 American cities as the demand for racial progress spread virally. By the end of the year, King had traveled more than a quarter million miles, made some 350 speeches, and would be featured in January as *Time's* Man of the Year. The Nobel Peace Prize would follow in 1964, when the Civil Rights Act was finally passed in homage to the slain Kennedy.[97]

The Letter in History

Birmingham was a turning point, and the Letter signaled that change and became its manifesto. The shift in national consciousness evoked in the Letter formed the psychological foundation for decades of (often halting) progress. A Gallup Poll released on April 3, 1963, at the start of the Birmingham campaign, showed that only 4 percent of Americans considered "racial problems" one of the nation's "most important problems." By October 2, that figure jumped to 52 percent and "racial problems" ranked first.[98]

Yet the Letter also offered a practical change strategy. This consisted of fact gathering, self-purification and training, direct action through marches, mass meetings, and public appeals, arrests, violence by racist resistance, and an escalation that forced negotiation and engagement of the federal government to use its power to tear down racial barriers. While the ingredients of this nonviolent protest recipe might be mixed in a different order in other situations, they were all present (and at least somewhat effective) in Birmingham.

Wyatt Walker initially saw the Letter's potential mostly for fund-raising, releasing it to the press in the first half of May. It did not get much attention, however, until the Birmingham settlement took pictures of police brutality and riots off the front pages. The first northern paper to pick it up was the *New York Post*, which published excerpts on May 19. The Quaker American Friends Service Committee distributed 50,000 copies beginning May 28, but it was not until June 12 that the *Christian Century*, a liberal Protestant weekly, became the first to publish the Letter in its entirety. Not until July 30 did the *Birmingham News* mention the Letter and it did not hit the mainstream media until *Atlantic Monthly* printed it in August. After the March on Washington, interest grew, with King including it as well in his 1964 book on Birmingham, *Why We Can't Wait*.[99]

The reception of the Letter by the eight clergymen was less positive. Most felt their letter had been misunderstood at best and ill-used at worst by King. They had, after all, chastised Wallace for his inaugural speech in January, for which they had taken considerable criticism, and the Letter had instead falsely chided them being silent ("Where were they when Governor Wallace gave a clarion call for defiance and hatred?"). Rabbi Milton Grafton said that "He did us an injustice and said things that hurt us."[100] Bishop Charles Carpenter said that "This is what you get when you try to do something."[101] Reverend Stallings, as the Letter acknowledged, had welcomed a black delegation to Easter services while King was in prison, as had Pastor Ed Ramage, whose act King did not acknowledge. All eight took criticism and threats from their white congregants.

The impact on their careers was profound, in both negative and positive ways. By the fall of 1964, only three of them were still in Birmingham, the rest driven out by congregations that no longer welcomed their moderate views. By 1971, only one remained.[102] Yet despite their sense that King had treated them poorly, they responded to his message. Four days after the bombing that killed four black girls, Rabbi Grafman told his congregation that "You're going to have to put up or you're going to have to shut up" in their supposed support for racial harmony.[103] Catholic bishop Joseph Durick would say, in 1971, that "I had seen segregation as wrong, but not as he had portrayed it," and would go on to fight for equal employment opportunities for blacks when he moved to Tennessee. He also marched with black sanitation workers in Memphis in a memorial protest after King's assassination.[104] Rev. Stallings would publicly castigate white churches after the violence following the May 10 settlement.[105] Bishop

Paul Hardin, who initially bristled at King for attacking those clergy trying to "make the situation better," would in the late 1960s be the first to order black and white Methodist groups to merge for their annual conference.[106]

If the reaction of these clergy seems a mixture of pain and progress, the same could also be said of the effort to advance civil rights after the Letter, itself a mixture of pain and hope, emerged from King's jail cell. In Birmingham, 5,000 black students were in integrated schools by the end of the decade, compared to 7 in 1963. The number of black voters continued to rise and with that the emergence of elected black officials, including the first black on the City Council in 1969 and the first black mayor in 1979.[107] Yet white flight accompanied these changes in a pattern that would repeat itself in much of the South. King's dream of integration not just desegregation still struggles to be realized, though it is hard to conceive of today's prosperous, modern South emerging had not King forced its conception and birth.

King would also see victory mixed with defeat in the five years remaining to him after Birmingham. St. Augustine, Chicago, Los Angeles, Selma, and Memphis would prove hard tests as would his effort to add a focus on international peace and economic justice to his earlier emphasis on equal rights, especially after winning the Nobel Peace Prize. He would be celebrated as a modern-day Moses by many blacks and liberal whites yet castigated as out-of-touch by ghetto blacks, as abandoning the Movement by those who resented his vocal opposition to the Vietnam War, and even as an Uncle Tom by black nationalists.

This may have hurt King, but it probably did not surprise him. The complexity of racism and racial progress in America—and his ability to thrive amid that complexity—were strengths of character and leadership that marked his life. He understood people and could place himself within their world view and their hearts. He could blend reason and emotion in a resounding moral argument that grasped the situation with realism yet unbounded hope. There were sinners, in King's worldview, yet each held the power of climbing the lofty path to redemption. Understanding human nature as he did, he also understood that only some would choose that road. But that some, in time he believed, would become a multitude. For the Letter not only marked the black transition to self-respect and empowerment, it helped whites understand that they held the keys not only to black liberation but to their own transcendence into a greater humanity.

As the arc of his life moved toward Memphis, where an assassin's bullet awaited him on April 4, 1968, it would be easy to see King as a tragic hero whose fatal flaw was that he believed in nonviolent change in a violent society. Though King himself became more fatalistic with time, his fatalism did not—nor would he have wanted it to—define him.

Nor would he have wanted the hagiography that now surrounds him. The Movement had countless leaders who supported and sometimes even led King on his leadership journey. His success would have been impossible without field workers who did the tactical and logistical work as "advance men," fund raisers who kept money coming for everything from bail to travel costs, political advisers who helped the initially ill-adept King sort out the players and develop strategy and who could speak and lobby for King when he was imprisoned, publishers (and ghost writers) who helped move his books to a wider audience, an inner circle of preachers and close friends who served as everything from sounding boards to downtime buddies to moral supporters in the darkest of moments and of course the millions who marched, risked beatings and jail, and spoke with their bodies the words King fashioned in the Letter from Birmingham Jail.

King returned to that jail in November 1967 to serve a five-day sentence after the U.S. Supreme Court upheld his conviction for the April 12, Good Friday, 1963, march. He would be buried in Atlanta just three days before April 12, Good Friday, 1968. Coretta received many letters of condolence, yet one from Harry Belafonte and Stanley Levison, among his closest black and white friends, captured for her the essence of his life. They spoke of his achievements, yet they heralded his humility:

> He drained his closest friends for advice; he searched within himself for answers; he prayed intensely for guidance. He suspected himself of corruption continually, to ward it off. None of his detractors, and there were many, could be as ruthless in questioning his motives as he was to himself...Today, when millions of his portraits hang in simple cabins, in ordinary homes, and in stately halls, it is hard to recall that he forbade his own organization to reproduce his picture. He did not want to be idolized; he wanted only to be heard.

A month before he died, King spoke to a gathering of rabbis in the Catskill Mountains of New York. They welcomed him to the podium by linking arms and singing "We Shall Overcome"in Hebrew. If any act could serve as testimony to the power of his life, the Letter from Birmingham Jail, and the fact that he was heard, that would seem to be a good choice.

Constitutional Crisis: Ford Assumes the Presidency and Pardons Nixon

After a series of phone calls to Congressional leaders and Vice President–designate Nelson Rockefeller, President Gerald Ford entered the Oval Office to face a single camera and about a dozen hastily assembled reporters.[1] He was at peace with what he was about to do. As was his custom, he had gone to church earlier, and he would play a full round of golf at Burning Tree in Bethesda later, as he had the day before.

On this same Sunday, September 8, 1974, Evil Knievel would launch an ill-fated attempt to propel his motorcycle over Idaho's Snake River Canyon, and Hurricane Carmen would lurk off the Louisiana coast. It would become the deadliest storm of the season. At 11:16 a.m., Gerald Ford would invite his own storm by signing a full pardon of disgraced former president Richard Nixon.

The *Washington Post* that morning reported the results of the first Gallup Poll pitting Ford against Ted Kennedy in the 1976 presidential race. Ford had a commanding 57–33 percent lead.[2] But if he had any sense of how that could change, it did not seem evident. The paper's front-page photo showed a beaming, plaid-jacketed president eating crab at Saturday's annual Alexandria Police Department picnic, with Soviet cosmonauts and American astronauts of the coming joint Soyuz-Apollo mission.[3]

A year ago, Ford had been the minority leader of the House and had already told his wife, Betty, that his thirteenth term in Congress would be his last. Yet, since then he had become the nation's fortieth vice president and just 31 days earlier the thirty-eighth president elected to neither office.

Why would he pardon—and link himself to—a man whose politically disastrous shadow he had spent most of the last year trying to avoid? Did he think the pardon would put Nixon behind him? Did this veteran politician miss the impact of his highly political act?

Ambition with Limits

Ford had never aspired to reach the Oval Office. Named the most popular high school senior in Grand Rapids, which won him his first trip to Washington, he had become enamored with the House of Representatives, where he stood in the gallery and resolved to become a lawyer.[4]

Completing law school in 1941, he entered practice with friend—and later presidential counselor—Philip Buchen. Pearl Harbor changed his plans. His war service brought respect for his abilities—his captain called him "steady, reliable, and resourceful" with "unfailing good humor...and natural ability as a leader."[5] Returning to Grand Rapids in early 1946, he resumed his law practice and threw himself into community service. "I was a competitive 'joiner,' but the truth is that I really enjoyed the challenges," he recalled.[6] He was also building a network that would soon prove useful.

Intent on unseating five-term Republican Congressman Bartel Jonkman in Michigan's Fifth District, he had to lure his opponent into thinking he was unopposed in the primary for the safe Republican seat. Shocking Jonkman, Ford won by more than 10,000 votes, and on November 2, 1948, he was elected with 60.5 percent of the vote. His margin of victory would grow to 66.7 percent two years later.

Election to Congress was not a stepping stone but a destination. Ford declined to run for the Senate in 1954, and he turned down a run for governor two years later. His lifelong goal was to be Speaker of the House.

An avid learner, Ford became a master of the inside game. In his first vote, he set himself apart by opposing both the House leader and Republican Whip, and then formed, in the first of a career-long series of collaborations with Richard Nixon, the Chowder and Marching Society, composed of young Republican members.

In only his second year, he secured a spot on the Appropriations Committee, despite bucking his own state delegation on a public works project, perhaps his first test of political conscience. By his third term, he was on the Defense Appropriations Subcommittee. His Democratic boss, George Mahon of Texas, would recall being "impressed with his calm judgment and steady hand" and would remember Ford as "a man you could deal with" no matter who was in the White House.[7]

By 1956, Ford was on the Intelligence Subcommittee of Appropriations, a sign of the trust he had built, and in late 1963, President Johnson selected him as the only House Republican to serve on the Warren Commission after the assassination of JFK.

Ford had a way of being a combative Republican yet a collaborative legislator. As his biographer, Lou Cannon, put it:

> In House debate, Ford could be vigorously partisan; but at the end he would make a point of shaking hands and enjoying a laugh with his Democratic adversary. In negotiations, his affable nature and hearty laugh could ease the tension in the clash of philosophy and ego. He was not an initiator of programs or a creator of ideas; but he sought out policy discussion and kept his mind open to a new approach. He was an unembarrassed eclectic, picking and choosing among proposals, finding the solid middle ground, and then giving full support and credit to a colleague... Safe in his District, secure in the hierarchy of the House, he had no need to preen on the House floor or to the press... Ford was a workhorse, not a showhorse.[8]

Ford's affability and diligence moved him into the House leadership. In 1962, after Republicans lost heavily in midterm elections, he was approached to challenge Charles Hoeven as chairman of the House Republican Conference. "If I defeated Charlie Hoeven, and I felt sure I could, that would be recognition. I would get a head start on the possibility of becoming the Republican Leader,"[9] Ford recalled.

That win in early 1963 was followed by a six-vote margin in his effort to unseat Minority Leader Charles Halleck in January 1965. Now he was just a national election away from the Speaker's chair.

The Bitter Fruit of Loyalty

Yet, on election night, November 7, 1972, Ford watched his lifelong goal fade away. Though Nixon won every state but Massachusetts and the District of Columbia, his coattails were woefully short. The Democrats held control of Congress. Despite Nixon's lack of interest in helping the party, Ford resolved to maintain his career-long loyalty through the president's (and his own) last term, as best as he could.

Ford's best could not be enough. On June 23, 1972, while Ford was on his way to China to meet with Premier Chou En-Lai, Richard

Nixon had met with Bob Haldeman in the Oval Office and approved a plan, dutifully recorded on the White House taping system, to have the CIA choke off FBI efforts to trace the money used to pay for a bumbled Watergate break-in days before. In that moment, the 25-month chain of events that would make Gerald Ford president began.

Nixon's unraveling would start slowly, but by May 1973, the Senate Watergate Committee began hearings. On June 3, John Dean told the committee that he discussed a cover-up with Nixon nearly three dozen times, and on July 13, a virtually unknown former presidential appointments secretary, Alexander Butterfield, told the committee about the tapes that would provide the "smoking gun" to bring down the president. On July 23, Nixon refused to turn them over to the Watergate Committee or to special prosecutor Archibald Cox.

Nixon received a reprieve, of sorts, when Vice President Spiro Agnew was forced to resign on October 10 for accepting bribes and income tax evasion while he was the governor of Maryland and even in his vice presidency. Under the Twenty-Fifth Amendment, Nixon had to nominate a vice president, to be confirmed by the House and Senate.

Nixon preferred John Connolly, former Democratic governor of Texas, who had switched parties in May and who Nixon saw as his successor. But a Democratic Congress was not about to reward Connolly's behavior or help him gain the presidency. Instead, they looked for someone without a national political future. Who they saw was Gerald Ford. "We gave Nixon no choice but Ford," House Speaker Carl Albert later said.[10] Nixon sent Ford's name forward on October 12.

On October 20, in what became known as the "Saturday Night Massacre," Nixon got Solicitor General Robert Bork to fire Archibald Cox in a vain attempt to stop his demand for the tapes, and announced the dismissal of Attorney General Elliott Richardson and the resignation of Deputy Attorney General William Ruckelshaus, both of whom had refused to fire Cox.

Ford's reputation for honesty became central to his confirmation, and his effort to retain that reputation amid Watergate would be central to his vice presidency. He insisted on a full investigation before his confirmation hearings. "Hold nothing back," he told his aides. " ...Anything they want, if we have it, give it to them."[11] After interviewing more than 1,000 people and producing a 1,700-page report, the FBI had one finding—and Ford dutifully reimbursed the government $435.77 for two suits he bought and improperly deducted for an appearance at the 1972 Republican National Convention. On November 27, the Senate confirmed Ford on a vote of 92–3, and the House voted 387–35 to do so on December 6. Ford chose the House chamber for his 6:10 p.m. swearing in that same day, after convincing the White House that the president would not be booed at the ceremony.

A man known for being trustworthy now owed his loyalty to a man considered a liar. Ford sought to balance his desire to support the president with the need to maintain his integrity. If he supported Nixon despite the accumulating evidence, he could be tarnished with Watergate. If he distanced himself from the president, he could be seen as advancing at the expense of his boss. Ford's dilemma was complicated by his character. He trusted people. As Robert Hartmann, his vice presidential chief of staff and later counselor to Ford as president would say, "Ford demonstrated a disconcerting blind spot in dealing with people. He had difficulty seeing the obvious when ingratiating scoundrels were trying to use him, and he rather resented suggestions that their motives might be less than pure."[12]

He had always trusted Nixon. Of his first conversation with Nixon about Watergate in the spring, he said "You have to believe the President, and I did believe him. He had never lied to me."[13] When Nixon ditched Haldeman, Ehrichman, and Dean, Ford said "I have the greatest confidence in the President, and I am absolutely positive he had nothing to do with this mess."[14] Ford was a loyalist, to a fault. As Hartmann observed: "Ford was a solid team player. If he had a major flaw it was excessive deference to the President."[15]

Ford's behavior might be seen as the desire for plausible deniability so he could serve a man he no longer respected, but it is likely that Ford's humility played a part. He simply could not believe Nixon could abuse power in a way he would never contemplate.

In his speech to Congress on assuming the vice presidency, he had told the nation: "I am a Ford, not a Lincoln."[16] On travels as vice president, he agreed to use an old plane so that Secretary of State Henry Kissinger could have the better aircraft. Not known for his speaking skills, Ford could also crack a joke at his own expense. On a flight to Washington, he asked the press crew what they thought of a speech he had just given. Since no one wanted to tell him how bad he was, Ford did it himself: "Not worth a damn, was it?" he said with a hearty laugh.[17]

Yet, in the end, Ford would acknowledge his gullibility: "My staff saw what was coming much earlier than I did...I always brushed it off...And now this [revelation of the "smoking gun"]...I was angry that Nixon hadn't told me the truth. The hurt was very deep."[18]

Ford Becomes President

On July 27, 1974, the House Judiciary Committee voted the first article of impeachment, for obstruction of justice, and on Sunday, August 4, under Supreme Court order, Nixon released the transcript of the June 23 tape. Ford had been informed by Chief of Staff Alexander Haig on the morning of August 1 that he should be prepared to assume the presidency, and in a private meeting that afternoon, Haig broached the subject of a Nixon pardon, without directly asking Ford to do so. After his key advisors erupted in anger at him for not dismissing the idea outright, Ford called Haig back and read him a statement, with witnesses present, "that I have no intention of recommending what the President should do about resigning or not resigning, and that nothing we talked about yesterday afternoon should be given any consideration in whatever decision the President may wish to make."[19]

With conviction in the Senate certain, and faced with the loss of his presidential pension unless he resigned, Nixon told the nation on the evening of August 8 that he would step down the next day. In an emotional ceremony in the East Room on the morning of August 9, he thanked his supporters, fondly recalled his parents, and demonstrated little sense of responsibility for creating the crisis that led to that moment.

Watergate had darkened the nation's mood, but public perceptions were gloomy for other reasons too. Ford would follow three "failed" presidencies—one destroyed by assassination, one by Vietnam, and the last by resignation. Both LBJ and Nixon had irrevocably damaged public trust.[20] Ford would begin his presidency not with a popular mandate but as a result of Congressional confirmation—and as vice president not president.

The economy was in its own foul mood. Wholesale prices had jumped 3.7 percent in July and would hit an annual rate of increase of 12.2 percent, nearly four times the figure in 1972.[21] The price of oil had risen from $3 to $12 a barrel as a result of the OPEC oil embargo launched when the United States supported Israel during the Yom Kippur War in October 1973. The nation had seen long gas lines. While the oil embargo had ended in March, Nixon's experiment with wage and price controls to halt surging inflation failed miserably.[22] Real GNP declined at an annual rate of 1.2 percent in the second quarter.[23] As Ford himself would later note, "I was the first president since Herbert Hoover to take office at a time of declining expectations about personal well-being."[24]

Just after 10 a.m., the Fords walked the Nixons down the red carpet toward *Army One*, the helicopter waiting on the South Lawn. As the helicopter rose, Ford waved good-bye, and according to a TV reporter on the scene, had tears in his eyes. As the Fords walked back inside, the vice president held his wife's hand, saying "We can do it."[25]

Chief Justice Warren Burger had flown back, at Ford's request, from a trip to the Hague, and over 270 guests filled the same East Room where Nixon had spoken just two hours before. With his children in the front row to his left and his cabinet and their wives to his right, Ford and Betty stood on the raised platform as the chief justice administered the oath. It was 12:03 p.m. After being sworn in, Ford kissed his wife on both cheeks and took a deep breath. Dressed in a dark blue suit and broad-striped tie, he stepped to the podium.

"Not an Inaugural Address"

At 850 words, Ford's "inaugural address" was the shortest for a first term in American history; only three inaugurals have been shorter. Eschewing policy or programmatic proposals, Ford needed just under eight minutes, in steady, measured tones to deliver it. While eight vice presidents had taken the oath upon the death of the president, Ford was the first to have taken it unelected after a president resigned.

He faced a cynical public. For this reason, he was clear that his remarks were, "Not an inaugural address, not a fireside chat, not a campaign speech—just a little straight talk among friends." His task—at this moment his only task—was to restore their faith in government and the presidency. He addressed this challenge in two ways. He evoked several key transition themes and he sought to embody a message about himself as a leader. But before concluding, he asked something of his audience.

The Themes of Transition

Position confers title, not legitimacy. Ford tackled that first. In his opening sentence, he mentioned the oath of office twice, George

Washington, "every other President," and the Constitution, linking himself to Article II and American presidential history. He returned to the need to establish his legitimacy in the fifth paragraph, reminding the audience that he *did* come into the presidency by way of the votes he received, to enter the vice presidency, from members of Congress "of both parties, elected by all the people and acting under the Constitution in their name." Invoking Jefferson and Lincoln, Ford pleaded for faith in the system that made him president.[26] Reminding his audience that "[o]ur Constitution works," he let them know that his vice presidency gave him a national perspective and credentials, coming from "recent visits to 40 States." He may have been a member of Congress, but he had gotten around. He ended with the solemn reminder that it was now his task—and his promise—"to uphold the Constitution."

He built his case for legitimacy carefully: "I am acutely aware that you have not elected me." He thus demonstrated his acceptance that the people would need to "confirm me," no matter what the Twenty-Fifth Amendment granted. He accepted the presidency as an obligation, not as a prize he sought, much as Washington (always the seemingly reluctant leader) had: "I have not sought this enormous responsibility."

In deferring to Congressional leadership, asking "if I could meet with you right after these remarks," Ford also took a key step to reverse the combative arrogance that marked Nixon's relations with the Hill.

Ford was also mindful that the presidency came with unpredictable yet inevitable burdens, which "I can only guess at" and potential "tragedies" that had already befallen three presidents and given others "lesser trials." Nonetheless, he would humbly "do the very best I can for America", and with God's help "I will not let you down."

Against the backdrop of Vietnam and Watergate, Ford could only plead for trust and try to demonstrate that he was trustworthy. He offered "a little straight talk" and asked his audience to believe that he had made no "secret promises" to become president, heading off the suspicion that he had agreed to pardon Nixon. Reusing a line from the opening statement of his Senate vice presidential confirmation hearings, Ford asked the American people to trust him, because "I believe that truth is the glue that holds government together." He would rely on that maxim in future acts, both "public and private," perhaps a reference to the nation's distaste for Nixon the man as well as Nixon the president. His truthfulness was among my "instincts of openness and candor with full confidence that honesty is always the best policy."

Ford appealed to his audience as "my dear friends, my fellow Americans." Leadership is a relationship and thus required an emotional not just a political connection. He sought straight talk "among friends" and a "compact with my countrymen." Members of Congress were also "my friends" as were the "friendly nations" of the world.

Continuing, Ford wanted to restore the frayed relationship between president and people. Thus, "there is no way we can go forward except together," and "We must go forward now together." There must be a "bond" that holds government together, and "let brotherly love purge our hearts of suspicion and hate." Borrowing from Lincoln's Second Inaugural, Ford urged his audience to join him to "bind up the internal wounds."

Ford wanted to move past Watergate, to govern not just occupy the office. He thus asked the Congressional leadership to allow him to speak to a joint session the following Monday, at which he would offer "my views on the priority business of the Nation, and to solicit your views." The need for moving forward was marked with the most strongly worded declaration of the speech: "our long national nightmare is over."

Anxious to move ahead, he nevertheless felt the need to assure continuity. He reminded foreign nations that the search for peace would go on and that they should not use this transition as a time to take advantage of the United States.

Embodying the Message

These themes—legitimacy, humility, trust, affection, transition, and continuity—were essential leadership work. Had Ford stopped there, the nation would probably have been relieved and grateful. They would have seen that he was intent on healing the nation. Indeed, Ford titled his own autobiography *A Time to Heal*.

But Ford had something else to say. He wanted the nation to pray for Richard Nixon. He did not have to say this. That he did embodied his healing message. As leadership writer and educator Howard Gardner has noted, the most effective leaders embody the story they tell.[27]

For his friends, such a statement came as little surprise. For most of the nation, it was a window into the character of their new president. To move past Watergate, it would have been easy to ignore its chief and tragic figure. Ford didn't have it in him. Nixon was still a friend. You remain loyal to friends when they need you most.

As he said "I asked you to pray for me. Before closing, I ask again your prayers, for Richard Nixon and for his family," Ford choked up for the only time in his speech. In faltering here, where the audience would have little inclination to be easy on the disgraced former president, Ford's compassion demonstrated an understanding of human frailty. He foreshadowed that, as president, he could marry strength with softness. He showed he had courage by taking this step that would be seen as unnecessary by some and unwelcome by others. This is a president, the American people could just dimly perceive, whose promise to "do what is right as God gives me to see the right" was more than rhetorical flourish. It was the first public inkling—and most missed it—that Ford could pardon Nixon.

There is no compelling evidence that he had already decided to grant Nixon a pardon. For the moment, this was just vintage Jerry Ford. When Hartmann showed him his draft of the inaugural, Ford bristled at only one line: "My fellow Americans, our long national nightmare is over." Hartmann was aghast, correctly viewing the line as central to the message and the key media sound bite. Yet Ford's comment was: "Isn't that a little hard on Dick?"[28] His empathy was directed more at his friend than the millions Nixon betrayed. They would get over it, Ford no doubt reasoned, but Nixon might not. This was Gerald Ford at his human best and politically naive worst.

A Very Difficult Request

As Ford allowed Americans to take his measure, he also asked something of them. Leadership, and his "compact" with Americans, implied a mutual set of obligations and actions. In return for his promise "to do the very best I can for America," Ford expected Americans to "purge our hearts of suspicion and hate." He expected them to show love and mercy, not just to demand justice for Nixon. In calling upon his "fellow Americans" to pray for him and to pray for Richard Nixon, he asked for a small act, but it was a beginning. As the nation would learn in a month's time, he would soon ask a lot more.

Turning Words into Acts

Ford's speedy delivery had not allowed—because he did not want— applause. As the Fords left the East Room, the nation, which had now heard two presidents in less than three hours, could not imagine what would happen next. Yet effective leaders pay attention to what comes next—the acts, images, artifacts, ceremonies, and stories that define their leadership.[29] Ford paid attention.

He chose the East Room for his inauguration, rather than the more expansive House chamber, because "it would be far more subdued and appropriate."[30] For the same reason, he asked that *Hail to the Chief* not be played.[31]

As he later noted, "One thing I wanted to do right away was eliminate the trappings of an 'imperial' Presidency."[32] He thus acknowledged the importance of leadership presence. Ford insisted that his living quarters in the White House be called "the residence," banishing Nixon's term, the "executive mansion." Ford wanted those who worked there to feel he was accessible. "I passed the word that I didn't want my agents to push people around. I said it was all right if they smiled once in a while."[33] He also made clear that the White House staff could reply if any of the Fords said hello, good-bye, or thank you—pleasantries the reclusive Nixon had banned.[34] Ford removed the portraits of Teddy Roosevelt and Woodrow Wilson in the Cabinet Room, replacing them with Lincoln and Harry Truman. Truman, as Hartmann observed: "was an inspired choice as well as a genuine tribute. Truman had been drafted as a substitute for a Vice President who had fallen from grace. Nobody knew much about him outside his home state, and nobody expected much of him."[35]

Ford's attention to symbolic leadership also defined the schedule for his first day. True to his inaugural remarks, his first meeting was in the Red Room with Congressional leaders. He then went to the press briefing area to announce Jerald terHorst, an old Grand Rapids friend and now D. C. bureau chief of the *Detroit News*, as his press secretary. To the press, he invited "the kind of rapport and friendship which we had in the past... We will have an open, we will have a candid Administration."[36] He would later ask that the press briefing area be redesigned to incorporate a slimmer podium that showed more of him than the one Nixon used. It would bring reporters' chairs closer to him, to "position me on the other side of the East Room before open doors that led to the red-carpeted Grand Entrance Hall"[37] to signal openness—an approach still in use. Ford also flew with the door to his cabin on *Air Force One* open, not closed as was the case with Nixon.

To end the day's symbolism, he went home—to Crown View Drive in Alexandria, because he had told the Nixon family (David and Julie

Nixon Eisenhower) to take all the time they needed to move out. The next morning, his first full day as president, he was "up before six, put on the water to boil for tea, sliced a melon and popped two halves of an English muffin in the toaster. Wearing baby-blue pajamas, he opened the front door of his Alexandria house to retrieve the *Washington Post*. It wasn't there yet, but a gaggle of news people already were."[38] Banishment of the imperial presidency seemed quite safe in the hands of Gerald Ford.

The Impact of the Inaugural Remarks

The media applauded the tone Ford set. The Chicago *Tribune* cited his "well-chosen, dignified and simple words." The LA *Times* carried the headline: "Smooth Transfer—Mood of Stability as Ford Moves In." The New York *Daily News* commented that his remarks were "simple and straight, without oratorical flourishes."[39] Two weeks later, Hugh Sidey of *Time*, said: "For ten years this nation has suffered from cardiac insufficiency. Now the heart is beginning to pump again under Jerry Ford...Ford's first days look like genius because they are so ordinary."[40]

The first national survey, published by Gallup on August 31, found his approval rating at 71 percent. Less than a month before, Nixon's stood at 24 percent.[41]

Ford's 32-minute speech to a joint session of Congress on Monday, August 12, continued the theme of his inaugural remarks. He received so much applause upon entering the chamber that he quipped "They're wasting good TV time" when he seemed incapable of quieting the audience. Interrupted by applause 32 times and laughter seven times, Ford told lawmakers that his "motto toward the Congress is communication, conciliation, compromise, and cooperation." "I do not want a honeymoon with you. I want a good marriage," he said. He delivered on his promise of straight talk by saying that "the state of our economy is not good." He also sent a signal that cooperation did not mean caving in—he would use the veto to keep spending under control.[42]

Ford's promise to work across the aisle led to both symbolic and substantive steps. He accepted a Democrat's proposal (Sen. Mike Mansfield, MT) for an economic summit and publicly gave him credit for it.[43] He met in the Oval Office with the Congressional Black Caucus, even though only one of its 16 liberal Democrats had voted to confirm him as vice president. He visited the Senate and the House to announce his desire to "officially inaugurate Pennsylvania Avenue as a two-way street."[44] Each week, he set aside "congressional hours" during which members could meet with him.[45]

Turning Good Will to Good Governance

Ford had many strengths in mid-August: low ego needs, accessibility, a reputation for honesty and compromise, the ability to build relationships, good will on Capitol Hill, the capacity to take criticism without vindictiveness, a life anchored in core values, and the fact that he had come into office without having campaign promises to keep. These would be useful in the days ahead. But would they be enough?

His initial steps were bold, and they broadened his support. On August 17, he asked Nelson Rockefeller to be his vice president, a move that showed he could accept a man of stature and independence (as well as someone who would anger the right wing of the party). On August 19, in his first major address outside Washington, Ford told the Veterans of Foreign Wars (VFW) in Chicago that he supported "earned reentry" for the 50,000 Americans who had been charged with desertion or draft evasion during the Vietnam War.[46] Recalling his inaugural remarks, in which he asked the nation to consider "not only righteousness but love, not only justice, but mercy," he said: "As I reject amnesty, so I reject revenge." Despite knowing the VFW would object (the convention voted unanimously to reject the idea), Ford chose this venue deliberately: "It would be a little...cowardice, you know, if we'd picked some audience that would have been ecstatic."[47]

In addition, Ford signaled his support of women's rights when he met with a delegation of 13 Congresswomen on August 22 and signed a proclamation backing the Equal Rights Amendment.[48] He also made good on his threat to Congress when he vetoed two appropriations bills in his first week as president because he thought they contained excessive spending that would fuel inflation.

Yet these were individual acts. They did not require a clear command of the executive management of the presidency. Ford was a politician who for 25 years had managed nothing larger than a Congressional caucus and his office staff. While he had acquired a broader perspective with increasing responsibility, especially in his eight months as vice president, his skills had been honed on a different stage. The White House was not Congress. Al Haig, Nixon's chief of staff, in a moment of telling hubris, would say to an aide that "we have to save Ford from his own inexperience."[49]

Ford had made a clean sweep of Agnew's staff when he assumed the vice presidency. But now he hesitated, caught between the desire to show continuity and get off to a quick start, which meant keeping Nixon loyalists, and the desire to become his own man, which argued for replacing them. At his inaugural day meeting with them, he took the path of least resistance and asked them to stay.

Robert Hartmann, writing later about the Nixon loyalists surrounding Ford, would note that the new president ignored one of the key principles laid out by his transition team: "Assumption of control which is firm and efficient." "Jerry Ford simply was not a control man,"[50] Hartmann observed. "There was never, for all thirty months he was President, a truly Ford Cabinet or Ford staff. There was an incompatible, uncontrolled, contentious collection of Praetorians" who "stubbornly shielded Jerry Ford from his better self."[51]

Ford made the problem worse by attempting a "hub and spokes" system of managing, in which many had access to him rather than coming through a chief of staff. While this worked in Congress, it could not survive the complexities of managing the entire Executive Branch, where the need for coordination among competing interests and departments would overwhelm any attempt at such a personal presidency.

Ford's management approach was driven by the same strength, unfortunately now carried so far as to become a weakness, that made his inaugural remarks so compelling: he trusted people. Hartmann reports on a conversation Ford had with Rockefeller, who tried to convince him that there were people who wanted to see the president fail. "Rocky named no names," Hartmann recalled, "Incredibly, Ford didn't demand them. He didn't even seem very interested in what amounted to a charge of high political treason…the President simply said he didn't believe that could be the case and went on to another topic."[52] "To put it bluntly," Hartmann observed later, "a President must be something of an SOB…Ford was simply too nice a guy; he boasted that he had adversaries but no enemies, and he really meant it. Sometimes he hurt people, but he hated it."[53]

Ford's struggle to find a "presidential" leadership approach was further compromised by his weakness in communicating to a national audience. His brand of politicking worked exceptionally well in a Congressional district, but it would fail him now. He did not write his own speeches and showed little interest in poring over drafts. As

Hartmann, his chief speechwriter, noted: "he rarely took the time to put his own thoughts on paper in more than note or outline form... it was frustrating that he was so unconsciously intolerant of the communication process... Ford rarely faced up to the fact that making a major address is *one of the most important things a President does*" (emphasis in the original).[54] Ford did not disagree: "I am the first to admit that I am no great orator or no person who got where I have gotten by any William Jennings Bryan technique. But I am not sure that the American people want that."[55]

The Path to the Pardon

For Gerald Ford, the "national nightmare" was not over. While he wished to fight inflation, promote energy independence, and address foreign affairs, the first weekend of his presidency found him in a dispute over who owned Nixon's White House papers and tapes. The day after the inauguration, Benton Becker—a member of Ford's transition team—saw boxes of Nixon's files being loaded on air force trucks on West Executive Avenue. With more moxy than authorization, he halted the shipment, a move that assured the controversy over ownership would now be owned by Gerald Ford. Custody of the Nixon materials accounted for 22 questions at terHorst's first press conference the following Monday.

As Ford prepared for his first press conference, scheduled for August 28, he bristled when his staff asked him to rehearse responses to questions about Nixon. He felt he was already on the public record, in his Senate confirmation hearings for vice president. When asked if a president could legally prevent or terminate any criminal investigation involving Nixon, Ford had replied that "I do not think he should." When pressed about whether he might take such action if Nixon resigned from office, Ford had said "I do not think the public would stand for it."[56]

Of 29 questions, 8 were about Nixon. "God dammit," Ford later recalled telling himself, "I am not going to put up with this. Every press conference from now on... will degenerate into a Q&A on, 'Am I going to pardon Mr. Nixon.'"[57] Ford, of course, made his own contribution to prolonging such speculation when he refused to take a pardon off the table. While stating at the press conference that "until any legal process has been undertaken, I think it is unwise and untimely for me to make any commitment," he also said that "I have asked for prayers for guidance on this very important point" and that

"I am not ruling it out. It is an option and a proper option for any President."[58] Frustrated, Ford recalled feeling that "I had to get the monkey off my back."[59]

Two days later, he told his senior staff that "I'm very much inclined to grant Nixon immunity from further prosecution."[60] He swore them to secrecy, and despite the efforts of some to have him reconsider or delay, Ford was unmoved. "The (Nixon) story would overshadow everything else," he recalled. "It would be virtually impossible for me to direct public attention to anything else."[61]

What remained was a question of timing. Ford wanted to complete the negotiations for access to Nixon's papers and tapes, and he wanted a statement of contrition—though he did not condition the pardon on either. By Sunday morning, September 8, Ford felt ready. As the nation returned from church, prepared for its Sunday NFL ritual, or otherwise relaxed in the welcome calm after Nixon's departure, Gerald Ford plunged them back into Watergate.

He faced an almost insurmountable challenge. A never-elected president who had defended Nixon until near the end and then asked the nation to pray for him when he resigned was now going to pardon him. A nation who had grown to distrust the two most recent presidents was going to be asked to trust that their new one had made no backroom deal. And a man not known for his ability to communicate was to give the speech that would define his career.

Grim faced, frequently looking at the speech on the desk in front of him, Ford delivered his unwelcome message, staring at the camera. Near the end, he paused as if preparing the nation and himself, signaling the tension of the moment. Then he forged ahead: "Now, therefore... " and read the key passage from the pardon proclamation. With his left hand, he signed the pardon. His judgment of Nixon was at an end. Now the nation would judge their new president.

Moral Courage

The pardon was a personal act—using a power given to the president alone. Declining counsel from his aides and keeping the decision secret even from his press secretary, Ford punctuated the opening of his speech with the clear message that this was his decision to make and that it was a matter of conscience that drove him to act. His first word was "I," and he used it seven times in the first three sentences. Whether the audience agreed or disagreed, it was evidence of moral courage. He took the politically most difficult of the paths before him. His party faced Congressional elections in two months. He had already decided he would seek the presidency in 1976. His phone calls to Congressional leaders just minutes earlier had disabused him of any hopes for widespread support for the pardon. Ford knew it would not be popular, even if he suspected (wrongly) that the political price would last only a short time.

He had promised "straight talk," and this was it. He had promised "to do what is right as God gives me to see the right," and thus his opening sentence concluded that, "it is the right thing to do." Acknowledging as well that he may have answered "hypothetical questions" too "freely and perhaps too fast on previous occasions," Ford nonetheless pressed on.

Values-Based Leadership and Ethics

Ford's speech demonstrates ethical reasoning in a complex moral dilemma. While he may not have been conscious of it, his speech touched on nearly all of the classical approaches to ethical thinking:

- *Virtue Ethics*: Aristotle argued that a virtuous man develops moral character by the lifelong cultivation of good habits. Ford's opening paragraphs, and much of the "My conscience tells me" and "I do believe" statements near the close grapple with what virtue requires. Ford struggled with identifying the right thing to do, and virtue requires that, having found it, he do it. Aristotle defined courage as the mean between two vices—timidity and rashness. Ford is seeking to do the courageous thing.
- *Divine Command*: Ford is conscious of the need for Divine guidance and the need to act in accordance with "the laws of God."
- *The Golden Rule*: In believing that he "will receive justice without mercy if I fail to show mercy," Ford seeks to do for Nixon as he would hope to have done for himself.
- *Principle-Based (Deontological) Reasoning*: Whether knowingly guided by Immanuel Kant or not, Ford has principles that he judges as universal "maxims," and he seeks a solution consistent with them. He must "do what is right" and believes that "right makes might." He believes in "equal justice for all Americans" and "equal treatment" for Nixon under the law. He believes in showing mercy—and respecting human dignity.
- *Ends-Based (Teleological) Reasoning*: Ford also believes that "my primary concern must always be the greatest good of all the people of the United States" as clear a utilitarian statement as philosopher Jeremy Bentham could expect.

Not surprisingly, these approaches did not always suggest the same answer to Ford's dilemma. A pardon to ensure the greater good for all Americans may not be seen as in the greater good by those Americans themselves. Mercy for Nixon is not necessarily consistent with the demands of justice. What God may require is not necessarily what the law expects. Ford's speech gives the impression of a conversation he has had with himself, but the conversation seems labored and—for the average listener—confused. His words may reflect the moral complexity he faces but they also lack a ringing moral clarity.

Ethicist Rushworth Kidder suggests that moral dilemmas can be analyzed through one or more of four pairs of conflicting values.[62] Should Ford give priority to *justice* (which would argue that Nixon be subject to the law) or *mercy*? Should he focus on the *truth* of Nixon's transgressions or *loyalty* to Nixon as his friend and former leader? Is it more important to attend to the *short-term* desire of the nation to extract revenge and a penalty on the former president or the *long-term* needs of the nation (as Ford saw them)? Finally, should Ford focus on the *individual* (Nixon and his family) or the *community* (the American people)? The values Ford seeks to honor conflict, and so his speech seems conflicted.

In the end, he does choose. Primacy cannot be given to all moral values, but Ford gives it to four: mercy, loyalty, community, and the long-term:

- *Mercy*: "Theirs is an American tragedy," he says, which "hang(s) like a sword over our former President's head." Indeed, the only change that Ford made to the draft of the pardon speech provided by Hartmann was to add this phrase: "threatening his health as he tries to reshape his life." Still further, "I feel that Richard Nixon and his loved ones have suffered enough", and "I do believe...that I...will receive justice without mercy if I fail to show mercy."
- *Loyalty*: Ford's loyalty to Nixon is a driver of his desire to show mercy. He says that he has "personal sympathy as a long-time friend of the former President," though disavowing that this shaped his decision making.
- *Community*: Ford's goal is "domestic tranquility," and in fact more than one person suggested that this goal of the Constitution's Preamble should have formed the core of Ford's argument.[63] Unfortunately for Ford, he ignored the advice.
- *Long-term*: As Ford makes clear, "My concern is the...future of this great country," thus ensuring the nation's need eclipses short-term considerations for Ford himself (such as the loss of trust and political support subsequent to the pardon).

Mercy and loyalty argue for the pardon, Ford suggests. But they are also consistent with the community and long-term health of the nation. What is best for the former president is best for the nation.

The Legal Argument

Ford also makes a legal argument. Though ostensibly eschewing his "judgment as a lawyer," he cites three ways that the "law is a respecter of reality:" (1) Nixon would be "cruelly and excessively penalized whether in preserving the presumption of innocence or in obtaining a speedy determination of guilt"; (2) a trial amid "ugly passions" might well harm the "credibility of our free institutions"; (3) "the courts might well hold that Richard Nixon had been denied due process" (if he could not receive a fair trial). In short, if Ford permitted a trial, there was no guarantee that it would be fair or render a conclusive and accepted judgment. The result: a "nation of laws" might suffer more than the man who broke them. Ford would not risk a "verdict of history [that] would be even more inconclusive with respect to these charges" against the former president.

Leadership and Persuasion

His speech suffers from no lack of moral reasons for pardoning Nixon. But there are also moral reasons not to do so. In ethical dilemmas, a decision is one of a number of morally justifiable choices. But what is justifiable is not necessarily justified in the minds of followers. Ford bears the responsibility to persuade. As we'll see, most of America was not persuaded, at least in the short term. In part, we can lay this at the feet of his audience, who was not ready to be forgiving. But in part, this is a failure of leadership.

Ford underestimated America's mood and tolerance, and his speech lacked a strong and morally clear central message. In laying bare his own reasoning, he sacrificed clarity for comprehensiveness. The argument that might have worked best—that he was anxious to heal the nation, for the sake of "domestic tranquility"—was lost amid his visible wrestling with his conscience, concern for Nixon's health and family, and worries over a fair and supportable legal process. In journalistic terms, Ford "buried the lead."

At the same time, the delivery lacked emotional power. David Hume Kennerly, White House photographer and a man Ford admired for his frankness as much as has facility with a camera, told Ford once that

"Your speeches are usually long, boring, and filled with rhetoric that turns people off."[64] Representative Wilmer "Vinegar Bend" Mizell (Republican-NC) said of Ford when he was minority leader that: "On the House floor, we were not swept away by his rhetoric."[65] And Bob Orben, who had been put on Ford's speechwriting staff to put some humor in the president's words, had written: "The President's main problem as concerns public speaking is the somewhat flat tone of his speaking voice... There is an absence of highs and lows and gradations of tonal qualities."[66] The collective judgment is evident in watching the pardon announcement. It was a solemn occasion, but Ford could not rise above a solemn delivery.

Most significantly, Ford missed the opportunity to frame what lay on the other side of the pardon. There is no promise of a better America, no soaring rhetoric that offers hope, no benefit other than that offered Nixon. It was as if Ford assumed that the public would be as relieved as he was that a pardon would allow the country to move forward.

At his first press conference following the pardon, on September 16, Ford tried to recover. In response to a question about the effect of Nixon's health on his decision, Ford said that: "The main concern I had at the time I made the decision was to heal the wounds throughout the United States... to reconcile the divisions in our country and to heal the wounds that had festered far too long."[67]

By Ford's own account, he fell short. In his autobiography, he said that "I have to confess that my televised talk failed to emphasize adequately that I wanted to give my full attention to grave economic and foreign policy matters. Nor did I explain as fully as I should have the strong judicial underpinnings, in particular, the Supreme Court's ruling that acceptance of a pardon means admission of guilt."[68]

Hartmann also faulted Ford for this misjudgment. Writing in 1980, he said that: "I believe the cloud that hangs over Ford's pardon... was largely of his own making. If he had been more candid and more articulate with his close advisers—and ultimately with the American people—about his real reasons, it would now have faded to a footnote in history."[69]

"I thought people would consider his resignation from the Presidency as sufficient punishment and shame," Ford said, "I thought there would be greater forgiveness."[70] In short, the president assumed that people would be as magnanimous as he was.

Ford failed to see that implementing the pardon involved more than signing it. Since he had not consulted Congress, he could not count on their support. He did not see that the public might suspect a link between the Nixon's resignation and the pardon, and so he planned no strategy to counter that suspicion. "In his haste," writer Barry Werth noted, "Ford lined up no surrogates, no congressional or party elders, no cabinet secretaries or editorialists or anyone else who could rally support, blunt criticism, and share the heat."[71]

Jerry Ford was being Jerry Ford. A leader has a story about himself, for good and ill—and it usually *is* both for good and ill. Ford's was that he was a man who did the right thing regardless of criticism. He admired the athlete's toughness. "Looking back," he would say in his autobiography, "I realize I was lucky to have competed in sports. As a football player, you have critics in the stands and critics in the press. Few of them have ever centered a ball, kicked a punt or thrown a touchdown pass with 100,000 people looking on, yet they assume they know all the answers. Their comments helped me to develop a thick hide, and in later years whenever critics assailed me, I just let their jibes roll off my back."[72] When LBJ criticized him in 1966 as someone "who can't walk and chew gum at the same time," Ford shrugged it off: "I knew he was wrong. I just made up my mind I was not going to let it bother me."[73]

So it is not surprising that Ford would tell Benton Becker, before the latter went to San Clemente to finish the pardon negotiations, that: "There have been too many decisions made in this office in the past few years because of politics. This question has nothing to do with politics. When the time is right, I'll do the right thing."[74]

As Jack Marsh, counselor to Ford for Congressional affairs put it: "The President's logic (on the pardon decision) was unassailable, yet I felt I was watching someone commit hara-kiri."[75] "As a man, my first consideration is to be true to my own convictions...My conscience tells me...that I cannot prolong the bad dreams," Ford had said. Yet, for Ford the "nightmare" he called attention to in his inaugural remarks would not be over.

However admirable it is to make the right decision, a leader has the additional responsibility to frame the decision and mitigate the negative consequences if he wants to preserve his legitimacy to lead. That Ford did little of either faults his leadership though his humanity remains intact and admirable.

Aftermath

Ford expected his decision would yield criticism, but he misjudged the depth and length of it. The first reaction was from his own press secretary, Jerald terHorst, who handed Ford a letter of resignation shortly before the pardon speech. "I couldn't defend a double standard of justice," his letter said, and then he later told the press that "I couldn't remain part of an act that I felt was ethically wrong."[76]

The initial press reaction was mostly negative. "This blundering intervention is a body blow to the President's own credibility and to the public's reviving confidence in the integrity of its government," claimed the *New York Times*. The *Washington Post* said: "However compassionate Ford's intentions," the effect is "nothing less than the continuation of a cover-up."[77] The *Baltimore Sun* said that "no man, not even an ex-President, should be placed above the law." And Bob Considine, a Hearst columnist, noted that: "In the first month of the honeymoon, the plate of Democratic presidential hopefuls was as bare as that of a poor-house dog...The President has saved the Democratic party the cost of a heart transplant."[78]

Politicians were quick to question the pardon. Sen. Sam Ervin (D-NC), chair of the Senate Watergate Committee, said: "President Ford ought to have allowed the legal processes to take their course, and not issued any pardon to former President Nixon until he had been indicted, tried, and convicted."[79] Four days after the pardon, Rep. Bella Abzug (D-NY) filed a Resolution of Inquiry, followed by a second from Rep. John Conyers (D-MI). These required Ford to respond to questions put to him about the pardon, and he testified in public in Congress, the first president since Lincoln to do so. The Senate passed a resolution opposing any more Watergate pardons until defendants had been found guilty and exhausted their appeals, and Congress slowed the approval process for Ford's vice presidential choice, not confirming Rockefeller until mid-December.

Ford fared no better with the public. At a speech in Pittsburgh the day after the pardon, protesters held signs saying "Jail Ford!"[80] In a Harris Poll released September 13, the percent who felt Ford was doing a good job as president had gone from 69–45 in the past month, and 60 percent disapproved of the pardon.[81] A Gallup Poll showed Ford's approval rating plummeting from 71 percent on September 1 to 50 percent on October 13, the biggest six week drop for a president in history to that time.[82] White House mail ran more than two and a half to one against the pardon, and overall messages received ran six to one against the decision.[83]

Rep. John Duncan of Tennessee's Second Congressional district wrote to Ford on September 13 that "I have found that many rank and file Republicans and just plain citizens are quite disturbed," and then added a thinly veiled alarm that "my district is the only district in the United States that has never had a Democrat in Congress."[84] The losses in the November 5 elections were in fact steep. The GOP dropped 40 seats in the House and 4 in the Senate.[85]

Not all reactions were negative. As early as September 10, CBS Radio Network commentator Nick Thimmesh said: "The President showed wisdom, courage, and compassion in this decision. He will be criticized for it but he will eventually be respected for it." The New Orleans *Times-Picayune* agreed in an editorial on the same day titled "Pardon Commendable."[86] On September 18, the *Wall Street Journal* acknowledged that: "Clearly, much of the anger vented on President Ford is in reality a cry for vengeance on Richard Nixon," finally noting that the country is "so inflamed that some think a President of the United States who speaks of mercy is immoral."[87]

As time passed, the reaction against Ford would soften, but not enough to prevent his loss of the presidency in 1976. The *Times* of London had criticized the pardon on September 10, but on September 14 printed a second editorial saying that: "What President Ford has done is to set against the claims of law the higher claims of mercy."[88] On October 16, Special Prosecutor Leon Jaworski told the *New York Times* that he thought the pardon was timely and legal.[89]

The damage to Ford emboldened the political right. Ronald Reagan challenged him for the Republican nomination. Ford beat Reagan by only 117 delegates, and thus went weakened into the general election against Democratic "outsider" Jimmy Carter. In an August 1, 1976, trial heat, Carter led by an astounding 62–29 percent, yet Ford flipped that result to a one point 47–46 percent advantage by November 1.[90] Still, Ford lost to Carter by 50–48 percent and a 297–240 electoral vote margin. Ford's own polls showed that 6 percent of the electorate had not forgiven him for the Nixon pardon and would vote against him for that reason alone. Betty recalled in 1978 "that we both believe the pardon, more than anything else, cost him the 1976 election."[91]

Ford's vindication, to the extent it came, awaited calmer times. The first words of President Carter's inaugural address paid homage to the sacrifice Ford had made: "For myself and for our nation,

I want to thank my predecessor for all he has done to heal our land." On August 11, 1999, President Clinton awarded Ford the Presidential Medal of Freedom, saying that "he guided our nation toward reconciliation and a reestablished confidence in our government."[92] On October 27, 1999, Ford received the Congressional Gold Medal for helping heal "a nation in torment."[93] On May 21, 2001, the John F. Kennedy Foundation gave Ford a Profile in Courage Award. Named after President Kennedy's Pulitzer Prize–winning book, the award was presented by Sen. Ted Kennedy, who said: "Unlike many of us at the time, President Ford recognized that the nation had to move forward...I was one of those who spoke out against his action then. But time has a way of clarifying past events, and now we see that President Ford was right."[94]

Even some in the press recanted. In 1975, Richard Reeves, former chief political correspondent of the *New York Times* had written a scathing book on the Ford presidency, which he titled (after Ford's vice presidential inaugural remarks) *A Ford, not a Lincoln*. In 1996, Reeves wrote a piece for *American Heritage* which he titled "I'm sorry, Mr. President." "Jerry Ford, perhaps the most accidental of American Presidents had done a better job than I had predicted or imagined," Reeves said. "Ford had the guts to take the hit. I, for one, did not have the sense to calm down and get beyond the obvious and into what he might have been thinking." "Presidents should be judged on the one, two, or five big things they do...He was right [about the pardon]. Whatever his failings as a leader...he was right about the big one."[95]

In the end, Gerald Ford—a lover of politics and master of the inside political game for nearly three decades—chose an act of statesmanship, not politics. Writing in preparation for his autobiography, he penned three paragraphs titled "The definition of a statesman as opposed to a politician." "A statesman is one who believes in the ultimate good judgment of the American people," he wrote. "A politician is interested in the next election. A statesman is concerned about the next generation."[96] A generation later, Tip O'Neill (D-MA), by then a former majority leader and Speaker of the House, agreed: "God has been good to America," he said, "especially during difficult times. At the time of the Civil War, he gave us Abraham Lincoln. And at the time of Watergate, he gave us Gerald Ford—the right man at the right time who was able to put the nation back together again."[97]

Fostering Statesmanship in Public Life

We began with two questions. What is statesmanship? How can leaders practice statesmanship—and how can we choose those who will—in the troubled present and the Black Swan future? It is time to return to these questions.

A caveat is essential. Thinkers have grappled with statesmanship at least since Socrates. The effort here is modest—to draw lessons across our leaders to define statesmanship in a way that offers help to those who aspire to it (and to all of us who choose them). Our sample is too small and not diverse enough to do more. Our conclusions are thus hypotheses for the American context.

Statesmanship, our cases suggest, is not identical to leadership. If it were, every act of leadership would be an act of statesmanship, a conclusion as illogical as it is disturbing. Our leaders did not always act as statesmen. George Marshall did not refuse to put Japanese citizens into internment camps; indeed, as chief of staff of the army he helped implement that policy. His deferral to civilian authority may have been an act of leadership, but it does not seem an act of statesmanship.

Nor do our leaders' stories sustain the view that some are statesmen and some are not. Statesmanship is a type of leadership in action, not a quality of the individual. Statesmanship is accessible to, though not practiced by, every leader and not practiced by even good leaders much of the time. A leader may engage in statesmanship in one situation and act far less statesmanlike in others. Jefferson practiced statesmanship when he delivered his First Inaugural but not when enforcing his 1807 embargo with a heavy hand that violated his own principles.

Nor is statesmanship dependent on success or public approval. An act of statesmanship may produce a positive result; but it may not. It may earn high ratings; but it may not. Washington's statesmanship helped forge a nation, but Lincoln's Second Inaugural fell mostly on deaf ears. Decades may go by before we can properly assess the impact of an act of statesmanship. Ford's pardon seemed a brazen political act to most at the time—a quid pro quo for Nixon's resignation. Only years later did many acknowledge it as an act of statesmanship. Some still debate whether it was.

Such debate is healthy. It means we are struggling to define the kind of leadership we need. So this chapter begins with a definition of statesmanship based on our case studies—an opening to a needed dialogue. A model of the character traits and skills required for statesmanship, as suggested by our seven cases, follows. The chapter ends with some reflections on how to prepare more leaders for statesmanship.

What is Statesmanship?

Action is my domain.

—*Gandhi*

Based on our cases, statesmanship is the moral act of a leader, which seeks to call forth the moral character of the nation, taken after prudential judgment, within our Constitutional framework, amid opposition and personal risk, aimed at achieving an important element of what, in the long term, constitutes a good society.

While a leader may *think* about statesmanship, there is no statesmanship without action. Washington's thoughts about leaving the presidency and how to preserve the nation's fragile republican government did not rise to an act of statesmanship until he stepped down and published his address.

Yet statesmanship is not just any leadership act. It must serve moral ends, though whether it does may often be the subject of debate. When Susan B. Anthony voted, she was acting under the presumption of rights based on natural law. Yet her opponents charged her with subverting the social order, and she was arrested for breaking the law. There are obvious boundaries to "moral ends." Action whose aim is to damage human dignity cannot be claimed as moral. Values embedded in the nation's founding culture and documents provide help in answering the question of whether a leadership act is anchored in moral ends.

An act of statesmanship also calls forth moral character in followers. When Lincoln asked for "...malice toward none; with charity for all," he was asking the nation to rise to a moral challenge, not just pledging to do so himself.

The kind of thinking the leader must do in an act of statesmanship is defined as prudential judgment. Aristotle called it *practical wisdom*—the ability to deliberate, based on experience not just facts. Practical wisdom can be acquired only with time and practice. When Washington said in his Farewell Address that he was offering "some sentiments which are the result of much reflection, of no inconsiderable observation," he was acting with prudential judgment.

In America, acts of statesmanship must be faithful to the U.S. Constitution, which serves as a foundation and set of boundaries. When Ford pardoned Nixon, he did so with the power granted under Article II, Section 2 as well as the Preamble's promise of domestic tranquility. When King violated a court injunction against marching in Birmingham, he acknowledged the city's right to arrest him (though he charged them with violating the *intent* of the Constitution). Naturally, there can be differences about whether an action is constitutional, and sometimes a leader will act without constitutional clarity. But with statesmanship as the goal, the leader must consider this question carefully.

Statesmanship occurs amid opposition and personal risk. In all of our cases, passionate and diverging interests characterized the decision-making context. Our leaders faced fierce attacks from opponents and, often, intense disagreement from presumed friends. Statesmanship would come at a cost. When Anthony and King violated the law, they were risking their leadership positions, their reputations, and their personal safety.

Finally, an act of statesmanship requires a conception of the good society. The leader acts in its interest, and thus sometimes against the interests of self, party, policy, power, and/or pet philosophy. When Marshall spoke at Harvard, he believed that peace and prosperity at home required a major commitment to European recovery and abandonment of America's traditional isolationism. He acted not to advance himself (*he* would never have called it the *Marshall* Plan), nor to aid Truman politically. He was laying out an approach based on principles that emerged from a thoughtful conception of what the good society required.

If statesmanship emerges from this definition as still elusive, that is both troubling and valuable. It is troubling because one man's statesmanship may be another's self-serving grab for power. What politician today might not convince himself that he is acting like a statesman? Fortunately, others are allowed to weigh in, and this chapter aims to help us do so. The definition is valuable because it gives us a place to start and questions to ask. It gives a standard to judge and debate. If defining statesmanship were simple, it would not have taken millennia to be where we are. There are hundreds of definitions of leadership, and we still struggle to pin *it* down.

A definition is like a scaffold. It is not much use until we erect something on it. The character traits and skills essential to statesmanship aim to do that.

The Character Traits and Skills of Statesmanship

Character is the only secure foundation of the state.

—*Calvin Coolidge*

Our definition is like a view from 30,000 feet, but we need a GPS to guide us. The model in Figure 8.1 suggests that statesmanship involves six interacting factors and is more likely (and more successful) when all are practiced well and mutually reinforcing. The model

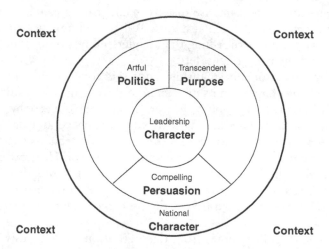

Figure 8.1 The components of statesmanship.

is presented briefly here and then explored in depth. There is no order of precedence; the leader moves among the six factors with dexterity in aiming for an act of statesmanship.

The first factor is the *context* in which the leader acts. Global and local trends, forces, and events shape the need for statesmanship and the way it is enacted. When King began his Birmingham campaign, he had a deep understanding of the African American experience and the post–World War II milieu for blacks and racism in the South. He soon learned, however, that he had misread the readiness of the black middle class in Birmingham to support him. He adjusted as he tried to shape the context to his advantage—a key task of statesmanship. The context can never be taken as a given.

Second, statesmanship is about the leader's *character*. Leadership may not require moral character (Hitler, Stalin) but statesmanship does. Virtue—not moral perfection—is a necessary condition for statesmanship. Take away Lincoln's penetrating self-criticism, and it is doubtful he could have authored the Second Inaugural. Take away Marshall's belief in selfless service, and it is unlikely he would have commanded the needed respect of Congress, the president and the American people to enact the European Recovery Program.

A leader must also master three sets of skills. First, the leader must be able to define a *transcendent purpose*. An act of statesmanship is generated by careful thought about the good society. This is more than just the "vision thing." It partakes of both purpose and program, with the former more central and less flexible than the latter. Anthony carried a deep sense of the American ideal within her. King could command the nation's attention from a jail cell because he could reconnect us to the purpose of America.

The leader must also have mastered the art of *politics*. Statesmanship is not above politics. It is political in the best sense of the term. Such leaders have a deep understanding of the history of the issues, people, and organizations central to accomplishing a transcendent purpose, and they seek and wield the tools of power. They have a realistic, yet hopeful view of human nature. They know how to manage productive dissent. They stay just enough above partisanship while at the same time using the tools of politics and party. Washington, though sometimes thought of as a man above politics, assembled arguably the best cabinet in American history, kept America out of a second war with England through moving the hated Jay Treaty through Congress, and managed to keep archrivals Hamilton and Jefferson within his administration for nearly five years.

Statesmanship also requires *compelling persuasion,* fueled by a powerful story that captures the transcendent purpose. Leaders tell the story in ways that gain followers. They know how to manage the emotions of their audiences, turning them into productive energy. King knew how to connect with core values, paint a vivid picture of a desired future, and move his audience to feel the pain of segregation (and the glorious sunlight of integration). In contrast, Ford's pardon speech did not connect with Americans, in part because he was unskilled at giving a compelling address. He was stiff and formal when the nation needed to feel his words not just hear them.

The leader's character, then, works with these three sets of skills in the context that he tries to alter to advantage. But those who aspire to statesmanship must shape the *nation's character* too. Unless people rise to the leader's moral vision, statesmanship is glorious in the attempt but remains, in Langston Hughes's words, a "dream deferred." The task is to invite, encourage, and pull the public toward a higher moral plane through what historian James MacGregor Burns called transformative leadership.[1] To do so, leaders engage in artful and difficult truth telling. They call forth what Lincoln so powerfully labeled in his First Inaugural as the "better angels of our nature."

Politics expects too little of the public; statesmanship expects much more. Anthony spent her life in the belief that woman suffrage would not only improve the lives of women but those of men as well. Her power came in part from the respect she gained by assuming that others would agree if only they understood. In time, most rose to the moral high ground she inhabited.

National character operates in tandem with the three skill sets, making them easier or harder to employ. When the public's values warp the national consciousness, this constrains the leader's ability to use skills in service to the public good. An angry North made Lincoln's call for magnanimity almost impossible to hear. Imagine Marshall's likelihood of success if Americans had insisted on returning to the isolationism that had characterized the previous century and a half of their history.

An act of statesmanship does not take the national character as a given. It must be shaped. Washington was especially conscious of this. He knew that the nation's character, more than his own, would determine the fate of the republican "experiment." His Farewell Address, as Spalding and Garrity so rightly note, was an exercise in character building.[2]

This model of statesmanship is a sketch. It needs detail.

Context

There are more things in heaven and earth, Horatio,
than are dreamt of in your philosophy.

—*Hamlet*

When George C. Marshall landed in Moscow for the Foreign Ministers' Conference, he had thoroughly prepared—for 45 years. By his own admission, he had "learned how to learn" when a student at the Army Staff College, and he was an avid learner even before. Though academically mediocre, he loved history. He learned about European history and sensitivities from his service during World War I, and he learned how the peace that ended that war created conditions for the next. He took his measure of Stalin and Molotov, not to mention the British and French, from working with them during World War II. He stopped in Britain and France to observe postwar conditions on his way to Moscow.

Throughout his career, he integrated his learning into a broad view of history to inform his understanding of the present. Speaking to Princeton University students on February 27, 1947, just days before departing for Moscow, he captured the critical importance of understanding the context:

> In order to take a full part in the life which is before you, I think you must in effect relive the past...Therefore, a deep understanding of history is necessary—not merely recent history...but an understanding...of what has created and what has destroyed great civilizations...One usually emerges from an intimate understanding of the past with its lessons and its wisdom, with convictions which put fire in the soul. I doubt seriously whether a man can think with full wisdom and with deep convictions regarding certain of the basic international issues today who has not at least reviewed in his mind the period of the Peloponnesian War and the Fall of Athens.

When Marshall laid out his macro- and microsystem views of the economic crisis in Europe, he drew from a deep understanding, as he put it, of "the entire fabric of European economy" and the "basis of modern civilization." Without that, he would risk action as damaging as the 1919 Treaty of Versailles. He would be like the watchman who ordered the Titanic to turn and so allowed the underwater portion of the iceberg to rip it bow to stern, when heading straight into it was the only chance for survival.

Context must be managed, as well as understood (see Figure 8.2). Anthony understood that women's subjugation had deep religious and cultural roots, that it was embedded in practices in homes, schools, and churches. A web of laws bound women, but they were built with the strands of prevailing social norms.

What she did with that understanding enabled her statesmanship. This meant a long campaign to change the way people—especially women—thought as well as acted. Enfranchisement would come only as a result of what she termed "subsoil plowing"—an endless series of letters, speeches, conventions, petitions, and canvasses. It included proposing legal changes and testifying on their behalf. It included efforts to get more women into higher education, the trades and professions, formal associations, informal networks—places where they could learn and acquire material, educational and psychological resources, and the political skills to achieve the vote. It is a testament to her will and wiles—and her understanding of the need to mange the context—that she mounted such an effort over 50 years.

It is also a testament to her self-understanding that she knew her limitations and could manage around them. Realizing that Elizabeth Cady Stanton was a more powerful writer, Anthony relied on her colleague for that, devoting her time to the organizing and political action at which she excelled.

Statesmanship also requires a tolerance for ambiguity. The context is often unclear, and leaders who force themselves to conclusions before they fully understand it dig very deep holes indeed.

Understand the context

- Understand the current situation—forces, people, organizations, events
- Place the current situation in historical context
- Identify underlying connections and structures—look beyond events for a systemic understanding

Be a continual learner

- Become self-aware, about strengths and weaknesses
- Be comfortable with ambiguity—stay in the question long enough to learn
- Love learning—about history, diverse fields, and from your own failures

Manage the context

- Take the context as a field upon which to act, not as a given
- Actively manipulate the environment to foster and support change

---

Figure 8.2   Context.

King came to Birmingham with a plan of action that soon proved ineffective. He accepted his own misreading of the level of black middle class and ministerial support—and adjusted accordingly. Had he failed to keep his mind open long enough to realize his mistake, Birmingham might have been the end of his leadership of the civil rights movement.

Indeed, statesmanship is much harder when context is poorly understood or mismanaged. Ford did not understand the context in which his pardon took place, believing the public's anger at the disgraced president would pass quickly. Thus, he did not prepare political support for the pardon—no consultation with political leaders and no communications strategy to sell it. He did not even manage to keep the support of his own press secretary, who resigned just before the pardon speech. While Ford engaged in an act of statesmanship, he executed it poorly. As a result, he weakened and lost his presidency.

Leadership Character

The source of this predominance was not barely his power of language, but...the reputation of his life, and the confidence felt in his character.

—*Plutarch on Pericles*[3]

Defining character (see Figure 8.3) is as difficult as defining statesmanship. We settle for identifying five character traits that shaped successful statesmanship. Careful readers may find others.

Great leaders, leadership writer Jim Collins found in *Good to Great,* his study of modern business executives, are characterized by great humility.[4] The same is true here.

It may not be surprising that Abraham Lincoln would be humble in defeat, but his Second Inaugural is a testament to humility in victory. As the Union's triumph neared, he scolded himself and chastised the nation. Lincoln's capacity to humble himself before the war, his country, and his God enabled his statesmanship and lent it power.

His humility was not calculated. It extended to matters of state that were far less visible. It was a way of being not a technique for leading. For example, he pardoned almost every solider sentenced to death for desertion, a fairly common crime for young farm boys forced into war. Their disloyalty in the field did not challenge his sense of command because he had command of himself.

Manage your ego
- Have a sense of humility in yourself and a sense of reverence for the world
- Be a citizen first, last, and always
- Manage your emotions

Be honorable
- Practice a sense of duty and obligation to society and its greater good
- Have responsible ambition

Lead through moral values
- Identify core moral values that call forth an act of statesmanship
- Have moral courage—persistence through danger—in service to core moral values

Passionately focus
- Dedicate your time and energy to core values, yet constrain your actions through humility and honor

Be resilient
- Live a life that is balanced, both physically and psychologically

Figure 8.3   Character.

Connected to humility in most of our leaders was a sense of reverence, of awe before something beyond themselves. For Lincoln this clearly was the God of Providence. King surely felt this, as did Ford, as can be seen by his moral struggle between the demands of justice and mercy for Nixon. For Marshall, it appears more as an acceptance of the powerful lessons of history and the forces of economic, social, and political change.

Jefferson, perhaps alone among our case subjects, lacked a deep sense of humility. While in his First Inaugural he said "that the task is above my talents," such an approach was a common rhetorical opening for the times. Indeed, the tone he set in that opening of the address, seeking to defuse the partisan rancor of the election period, may have succeeded only in part. Federalists gave him the benefit of the doubt, but not for long—and Jefferson himself seemed torn between magnanimity toward, and a desire to clean house of, his political opponents.

Second, our leaders exhibited a strong sense of public duty and concern with honor. In the founding generation, a call to serve one's country was an inescapable obligation. One's reputation as a gentleman depended on it. It was not just a rhetorical flourish when

Jefferson ended the Declaration with the phrase "we mutually pledge to each other our lives, our fortunes and our sacred honor." Honor meant something.

The notion of honor may seem quaint to modern readers, but it was as equally felt by George Marshall as it was by George Washington. In the spring of 1943, Marshall spoke to John Hilldring, a two star to whom he had just given the job of organizing military governments in occupied Europe. The Allies had yet to occupy any conquered territories, but Marshall had foresight. Years afterward, Hilldring reported what Marshall said:

> I'm turning over to you a sacred trust and I want you to bear that in mind every day and every hour you preside over this military government and civil affairs venture... we have a great asset and that is that our people, our countrymen, do not distrust us and do not fear us...This is a sacred trust that I turn over to you today...I don't want you to do anything...to damage this high regard in which the professional soldiers in the Army are held by our people, and it could happen, it could happen, Hilldring, if you don't understand what you are about.[5]

In Washington's case, he took command of the Continental Army out of a sense of honor, agreed to preside over the Federal Convention in 1787 for the same reason, and accepted the presidency to protect his honor. Honor is not inconsistent with ambition. All of our leaders were ambitious people, but their ambition was bounded by duty. This sense of honor also explains why Washington went to such lengths in the opening of the Farewell Address to seek approval from the public for his decision to step down, echoing the Roman emperor, Marcus Aurelius, who said: "whenever a man takes post...there he ought, as I think, to remain and abide the risk, taking into account nothing, whether death or anything else, in comparison to dishonor."[6]

Statesmanship is also driven by core moral values, a third element of character. In each case, one or two such values drove the act of statesmanship: Washington (union), Jefferson (representative government), Lincoln (love, forgiveness), Anthony (liberty), Marshall (peace), King (freedom, dignity), Ford (mercy). More than just platitudes, these values were a passionate focus in the leader's life and work.

Anthony spent the winter months traveling to speak for woman suffrage. This usually meant living in small, nearly unheated rooms or being marooned by snow. She traveled, struggling to meet expenses, despite the risk of small (or no) audiences or angry shouts from those who did attend. Her commitment can only be understood from her deep commitment to the core values for which she dedicated her life.

In each case, living core values also took moral courage. As ethicist Rushworth Kidder suggests in *Moral Courage*,[7] this involves more than having a moral principle at the center of one's thinking. It requires understanding the dangers one faces (to life, liberty, loss of power, reputation) and persevering anyway. In Anthony and King's cases, they faced arrest and imprisonment. In Lincoln's case (and King's), he risked public backlash and—in the end—an assassin's bullet.

Fourth, the acts of statesmanship in our cases were infused with passion. It was the passion for core values that fostered moral courage. Ford could easily have ended his speech with the lines: "My fellow Americans, our long national nightmare is over." Yet he continued, asking people to pray for Nixon when they were anxious to be rid of the disgraced president and Ford had nothing to gain by doing so. He was driven by his passion for mercy, even if it meant he might impair his presidency. Similarly, it is hard to explain Washington's address without seeing his passion for union, or Jefferson's without seeing his love of the rights of man. Yet passion was not irrational. In each case, humility and honor served as checks, ensuring statesmanship rather than the irresponsible exercise of power. The end did not justify every means.

Finally, statesmanship required personal resilience. Without the capacity to maintain psychological and physical balance in the midst of turmoil, leaders can easily succumb to pressures that compromise their ethics and behavior. As Max Weber put it, "Politics is a strong and slow boring of hard boards. It takes both passion and perspective... Only he has the calling for politics who is sure that he shall not crumble when the world from his point of view is too stupid or too base for what he wants to offer."[8]

Not crumbling required the ability to reset emotionally amid conflict and setbacks. Optimism and the tendency to psychologically reframe failures were essential to persevere. Anthony seemed able to see small victories even when state referenda continually defeated suffrage, and Lincoln's core faith in the promise of American republicanism saw him through one failed general after another.

For most of our leaders, resilience was also connected to personal habits that enabled them to recover. Marshall learned this early, through two breakdowns. As biographer Gerald Pops explains it: "Marshall had learned the importance of pacing himself and now was resolved to ride, play tennis, relax each day after work, and arrive home early…His routine during WWII sharply separated official and personal time…On a typical workday…he rode his horse in the early morning, departed the office at noon to have lunch with his wife at home, and often followed lunch with a brief nap…he felt he could perform much better with a fresh mind, broad interests, and his sense of humor intact."[9]

These traits of character seem essential for statesmanship. Their presence drew followers. Yet our leaders were not automatons. Marshall could get icily cold with subordinates. Washington could be petulant when his reputation was at risk. Anthony could be severe with women who left the movement for motherhood. What distinguished most of them was that they could acknowledge and moderate their shortcomings, because of their humility. Marshall, for example, would have a trusted aide read some of his letters before sending them, to ensure the tone was not overly harsh for the task at hand.

No doubt other character traits mattered in their leadership, such as persistence. One in particular—prudence—we will discuss under the rubric of skills. Yet our aim here is to argue first that character matters and second to suggest at least central elements of character in acts of statesmanship.

Transcendent Purpose

A constitution is a standard, a pillar, and a bond when it is understood, approved, and beloved. But without this intelligence and attachment, it might as well be a kite or balloon flying in the air.

—John Adams

Our leaders had a purpose, but it went beyond the immediate crisis they faced. They needed solutions, but their solutions were anchored in a long-term view of America's interests. Their acts of statesmanship were farsighted, not nearsighted. Their moral horizons extended well into the future, encompassing the nation as a whole (and sometimes beyond) (see Figure 8.4).

When Jefferson said in his First Inaugural that "it is proper you should understand what I deem the essential principles of our Government," he had a conception of the good society that drove

Be farsighted
- Think long term
- Think systemically
- Have a conception of the good society based on careful study

Be faithful to the American promise
- Act consistent with core founding values and documents
- Use the Constitution as a guide and boundary

Be hopeful
- Form a realistic, yet hopeful view of human nature

Figure 8.4   Transcendent purpose.

his statesmanship. He was focused on future generations even as his political action was in the present.

George Marshall won the Nobel Peace Prize for the Marshall Plan. At his Oslo ceremony in 1953, he was surprised that his being a soldier surprised people:

> There has been considerable comment over the awarding of a Nobel Peace Prize to a soldier...I am afraid this does not seem quite so remarkable to me...The cost of war is constantly spread before me, written neatly in many ledgers whose columns are gravestones. I am greatly moved to find some means or method of avoiding another calamity of war.[10]

In our cases, a conception of the good society certainly rested on core moral values, but it was more specific than that. For Jefferson it included a free press, checks on the size and scope of the national government, forgoing "entangling alliances" with foreign powers, respect for majority rule, reliance on a "well-disciplined militia" not a large standing army, and reduction of the federal debt. For King, it included a society where civil rights were protected, but the final goal was integration, a brotherhood of all people, not just desegregation.

The transcendent purpose was specific because it was the result of a lifetime of reflection. Washington was an astute observer of what he called the American "experiment." Jefferson was a polymath, once writing to his daughter that "there is not a sprig of grass that shoots uninteresting to me." He devoured books to construct his political philosophy. Lincoln was rarely without a book and had no problem discarding "the dogmas of the quiet past."[11]

Farsightedness also comes from a systemic view of society. Our leaders' statesmanship emerged from a complex understanding of how the world works. Marshall had not only a systems view of the European economy, but of what makes it possible—as he put his transcendent purpose—"to promote peace in the world."

As noted earlier, statesmanship must be faithful to the American promise. Part of this is fidelity to its founding documents. That is why Washington said that the Constitution was "sacredly obligatory" until changed. But the "American Promise" is not simply a rehash of the Declaration or Constitution. It rests on the spirit as well as the texts of these charters. Statesmanship requires the leader to seek a deep understanding of the American founding period. Washington and Jefferson could do this more easily; they lived through it. Lincoln demonstrated his grasp of founding values at Gettysburg, where he talked about the meaning of republication government. Anthony was thoroughly infused with founding doctrine in speaking to Judge Hunt, who seemed to lack the same grasp for natural law.

Ford may have used his Constitutional power to pardon Nixon, demonstrating that the Constitution was for him a guide, but here is what he also said: "As President, my primary concern must always be the greatest good of all the people of the United States whose servant I am." In short, he was struggling to do what was right for the America he believed in, and he acknowledged that the language of the Constitution alone could not give him the answer.

Napoleon said that "a leader is a dealer in hope." A transcendent purpose is nothing if not hopeful, and an act of statesmanship is nothing if not a belief in people. Acts of statesmanship are based on a positive view of human nature. That view may not always be justified, but it is always held, and it is not naive. Our leaders saw people for what they were, driven by self-interest. Washington once said that: "[W]e must make the best of mankind as they are, since we cannot have them as we wish." But our leaders believed people could be the best that they saw, and sometimes even better. How else can we explain Anthony's half-century slog through one defeat after another? How else can we explain Lincoln's determination to ask for charity?

Artful Politics

What the political leader requires is not policy science but good judgment—or, better, the union of virtue and wisdom that the ancients called prudence.

—Edward C. Banfield[12]

Purpose without the capacity to achieve it is failed statesmanship, and achievements in the public arena demand the capacity to act politically. Our leaders practiced political skills—artfully (see Figure 8.5).

Central among those skills is prudential judgment—the ability to apply, with wisdom, a careful decision process. None of our leaders started out with this ability. Aristotle explains why: "prudence deals with particular facts, with which experience alone can familiarize us...experience is the fruit of years."[13] Our leaders made mistakes along the way, but they learned from them because they were self-reflective about what they did.

Lincoln personifies this ability, as his "Meditation on the Divine Will" demonstrated. He sought to learn from the war to improve the peace. His learning extended as well to a conception of the legitimate rights of freed blacks, which he championed as the war ended even though he had shown little interest in them when the war began.

In *Judgment*, leadership authors Noel Tichy and Warren Bennis suggest that there are three phases in making "great calls" as leaders: preparation, call (the decision), and execution.[14] Our cases bear this out. Part of preparation is understanding context. Another part is involving others. Statesmanship is not a solitary adventure.

Practice prudential judgment

- Learn through self-reflection based on experience
- Be politically savvy
- Take informed risks

Shape decisions amidst countervailing pressures and unpalatable extremes

- Aim for, but do not expect, consensus on core values
- Engage in value trade-offs
- Frame the crisis and create tension when needed
- Use power, respectfully and ethically
- Pay attention to timing

Encourage and manage dissent

- Institutionalize dissent and eschew loyalty tests
- Invite opponents into the tent

Execute well

- Pay attention to execution—people, resources, support, timing
- Maintain flexibility
- Ensure that others are prepared to carry execution forward

Figure 8.5   Artful politics.

The ideal, almost never reached, is agreement around core values, among divergent constituencies, amid countervailing pressures, and despite flawed choices. The goal is not a perfect decision, widely applauded, but the right decision that stands a good chance of being executed.

Involving others may have multiple aims—getting input, testing ideas, finding landmines, forging coalitions, isolating opponents. Sometimes it is done through quiet consultation or even in secret. Often it involves tension, which the leader may create or accept to push the process forward. Always, the leader is finding appropriate value trade-offs and using power ethically—though forcefully when needed—to forge agreement. As King once put it: "A genuine leader is not a searcher for consensus but a molder of consensus." King led the Birmingham campaign this way. He took wide counsel in determining his course, changing it when the reliance on sit-ins and a boycott didn't work. His process engaged SCLC board members, lay and religious leaders in the black community, officials in the Kennedy Administration, personal counselors such as Stan Levison and Harry Belafonte, and his closest aides, such as Ralph Abernathy and Wyatt Walker. His explanation in the *Letter from Birmingham Jail* of the timing of the protests and the process involved showed a masterful understanding of how to shape consensus through both negotiation and confrontation, used as two ends of the seesaw of change.

Artful politics also requires a healthy respect for dissent, even for leaders who hate interpersonal conflict, like Jefferson. Politics without dissent is neither possible nor in most cases desirable, so the question is how to encourage and manage it. Indeed, Marshall counted on people to disagree with him to ensure he saw all points of view. This led him to remark, in a staff meeting shortly after Omar Bradley had joined his team: "Gentlemen, I am disappointed in you. You haven't yet disagreed with a single decision I've made." Lincoln was a master at managing dissent among his top advisors, as historian Doris Kearns Goodwin so well relates in *Team of Rivals*.[15]

In the preparation phase and in making decision calls, our leaders were also politically savvy. Politics and power were not dirty words for them. They relished practicing both because that's the way public purposes get served.

Social reform and politics were fields in which women were neither expected nor for the most part allowed to participate when Anthony thrust herself into temperance, antislavery and then suffrage work. Women lacked economic or political power. Yet, by the time of her trial, she had developed a sophisticated understanding of the male political world. She created networks, learned how to lead a movement, and knew how to use events to gain power and power to force events. That she kept a seating chart of Congress in her desk says how much she'd learned. She routinely challenged and chastised, cajoled, and pressured leaders in various groups. She could be sweet and supportive or tough and demanding. She could be, as Machiavelli put it, a lion and a fox.

Power was sometimes needed when no formal title was available to confer it. This was certainly true for Anthony and to a considerable degree for King. Acquiring power thus became a matter of drawing on one's expertise, interpersonal connections, information, and other forms of social power as opposed to positional power.[16] Often, an act of statesmanship required power for which even a title was insufficient. Ford was president, but he was not elected by the people. His positional power was not enough. He acknowledged that he needed to correct this perceived lack of legitimacy.

When making a decision call, statesmanship means taking a risk. Yet risks were usually well calculated because they were informed by "practical wisdom." George Marshall knew he was taking a risk in asking Truman to send the Marshall Plan to a Republican-led Congress, in a presidential election year, but he had courted Senator Arthur Vandenberg, Republican chair of the Foreign Relations Committee. He was astute enough to know to do this and politically skillful enough to know how.

Statesmanship also benefits from an exquisite sense of timing (and suffers from its absence). Had Lincoln preached forgiveness and joint responsibility for slavery while the war's outcome was uncertain, and before free blacks constituted a significant military advantage, he may never have gotten reelected. Had Ford prepared the nation for the pardon before he announced it, he may have had Lincoln's electoral good fortune.

An act of statesmanship is more than a decision. It requires execution. Leaders who do not pay attention to how they will implement their decisions have done a good thing—badly. Execution requires building support, ensuring resources to carry it out, and maintaining flexibility to adjust to conditions "on the ground." As noted, Ford's failure to orchestrate the politics of the pardon was a critical mistake. Jefferson, in contrast, selected a politically supportive cabinet and worked closely with the Republican leadership in Congress so that his decisions had ready support in the legislature.

Detailed procedures and plans help but can sometimes be counterproductive. It was in fact the very flexibility built into acts of statesmanship that gave them a chance to succeed. When Marshall's staff commented that there was no Marshall Plan but instead only "a plan for a plan," they were capturing a strength not a weakness. That flexibility provided negotiating room abroad and at home. It avoided the early commitment to specifics that might have built so much opposition that no execution could take place.

Similarly, Lincoln was masterful in his Second Inaugural in how he would bring states back into their "practical relation" with the Union. He avoided policies or conditions. Vagueness can be virtue when it comes to statesmanship. On the other hand, ignoring key elements of execution can be fatal. He let the Republican convention select his vice president, with the result that the nation ended up with the weak and unsympathetic Andrew Johnson. The result was Radical Reconstruction and an end to Lincoln's hopes for a peace without malice.

Compelling Persuasion

Oddly, perhaps, the rough-hewn Jackson understood the poetry of politics better than Calhoun, Clay, or Webster. His foes were speaking in prose, making technical arguments. Jackson was formulating a poetic narrative drama in which he was the hero defending the interests of the people against the powerful.[17]

—Jon Meacham on Andrew Jackson, from American Lion

Leaders must be storytellers (see Figure 8.6). Storytelling creates meaning out of often confusing and conflicting facts and emotions. As educator Howard Gardner showed in *Leading Minds*,[18] an effective story must communicate at a fairly simple level. Lincoln's Second Inaugural had only 703 words, 505 of which were one syllable. More importantly, Lincoln told a story about the war: its cause, the reason why it continued, and what needed to be done when God allowed it to end. His speech had a temporal construction, from troubled past to terrible present to brighter future. He did not confuse the story with the specifics of postwar policies.

Fashion a powerful story
- Create meaning out of disconnected facts
- Create a desired future

Tell the story in a compelling way
- Use language and symbols to convey the message
- Paint a picture
- Manage the emotions of followers

Be a teacher
- Use the story to transmit values and vision

Challenge followers
- Clarify what followers can and should do
- Release energy for creativity and change

Embody the story
- Ensure there is no disconnect between what you ask and who you are
- Live the story in concrete actions

Figure 8.6   Compelling persuasion.

King told several stories, perhaps the most compelling being that of the conditions under which blacks had lived for 340 years while being told to wait for their freedom. These stories worked because they touched profound human needs in vivid language.

Good statesmanship stories often contrast a desired future with a negative present. Ford in his inaugural remarks told a story of how he had followed in the line of all presidents—the American story—and would serve the people now that "our long national nightmare [a negative story] is over."

Statesmanship stories must be compelling—or they fail. In Ford's pardon speech, there was no clear story line—it was a confused mixture of legal and moral justifications that did not add up to a coherent narrative. It had elements that might have worked—the call for mercy, the plea for domestic tranquility—but they were assembled poorly.

Storytelling is one approach to something else our leaders shared: statesmanship involves teaching. It requires the leader to transmit essential wisdom. Washington sought to share the "counsels of an old and affectionate friend." Jefferson said he was offering "the essential principles of our Government." Marshall told his Harvard audience that "the very mass of facts presented to the public by press and radio make it exceedingly difficult for the man in the street to reach a clear appraisement of the situation" in Europe, so he proceeded to offer one.

One reason that stories work is that they challenge people. The challenge calls forth action to achieve the positive future in the leader's narrative. Washington suggested what Americans should do so that "heaven may continue to you the choicest tokens of its beneficence." Some of his challenge was subtle, such as the opening where he suggested that being a citizen required responding to the call of duty. Some was more direct, such as his statement that, in regard to their new Constitution: "[R]espect for its authority, compliance with its laws, acquiescence in its measures, are duties enjoined by the fundamental maxims of true liberty."

A key part of the challenge is a call for creativity. Acts of statesmanship are not self-implementing. Jefferson's call for a return to republican principles, Lincoln's for forgiveness, Anthony's for suffrage—could only be accomplished by millions whose inventiveness would need to surmount certain obstacles. The leader cannot—and should not try—to spell out all the actions that are needed. That is another reason for flexibility and vagueness in what the leader says.

Powerful stories channel, build, and release energy for change. When Lincoln began the Second Inaugural with a paragraph whose tone was somber, he was quieting the vengeful emotions of his audience. When he ended with a paragraph of hope, he was trying to generate the positive emotion needed for the work ahead. King's Letter from Birmingham Jail was an effort to move from calm reasonableness to contained outrage, leaving the audience with what the French writer George Sand called "this indignation which is one of the most passionate forms of love."

Compelling communication also requires that the leader embody the story, as Gardner has suggested. Ford's inaugural was a call for a return to integrity and simplicity in the presidency. In his first twenty-four hours, he lived that message. He talked frankly to the press corps, abolished the use of Nixon's reference to the "Executive Mansion," calling it simply "the residence," and then left the White House to live at home in Alexandria, where he came outside the next morning in his pajamas to retrieve the *Washington Post*.

The most powerful embodiment, of course, comes from the leader's character. It is not manufactured by an image consultant. Anthony could tell a story about the need to sacrifice to gain the vote because she was doing so in her life. Marshall could talk about America's need to be selfless because he lived a life of selfless service.

National Character

What the statesman is most anxious to produce is a certain moral character in his fellow citizens, namely a disposition to virtue and the performance of virtuous actions.

—*Aristotle*

While political leadership may at times call upon people's fears and hatreds, statesmanship calls upon their hopes and encourages common bonds among citizens. Our acts of statesmanship called upon the best in people, not the worst (see Figure 8.7). If statesmanship requires virtue in the leader, an act of statesmanship is more likely to succeed if it calls forth virtue in others as well. In the terms of old-style Black Baptist preaching, evoking national character in support of an act of statesmanship involves both call and response. The leader must ask, and the public must act.

Conversely, where an act of statesmanship failed, at least in the short term, such as revengeful Reconstruction after Lincoln's death, continued opposition to woman suffrage after Stanton's trial, or angry rejection of Ford and his pardon—it demonstrated that the national character was not yet up to the challenge.

Even in failure, an act of statesmanship may nudge the national character in a positive direction. Factional strife did not end through Washington's Farewell Address, but his words set a standard that still demands attention, one reason it is read aloud each year in the Senate. King did not achieve meaningful desegregation in the short term, but he moved many Americans off the moral sidelines, shaping the national character in the direction of inclusion.

Recall the national character and ideals
  • Call forth high moral values and cultural ideals

Shape the national character
  • Prepare the public to hear the truth
  • Tell a profound truth
  • Offer a way to act in responsible citizenship

Figure 8.7   National character.

An act of statesmanship also seeks to speak a truth. When Lincoln told Thurlow Weed that his Second Inaugural was "a truth which I thought needed to be told," he was capturing two central elements in drawing forth the national character. First, statesmanship aims at a profound truth, anchored in core values.[19] This truth emerges from the leader's own character, an astute understanding of the context, and prudent judgment. And, as Lincoln noted, it has to be told even if unwelcome. Ford recognized this as well, in preparing his autobiography: "A statesman is one who stands before an antagonistic audience and disagrees with conviction, strength and persuasion."[20]

Second, those who engage in statesmanship believe that, properly led, the public can handle the truth. This is where the leader's on-balance, hopeful view of human nature matters. It is impossible to conceive of Lincoln's address if he did not trust the public to respond. Similarly, Ford said that "A statesman is one who believes in the ultimate good judgment of the American people."[21] While the people may fall short, dooming the act of statesmanship to either fail or wait years to lend it power, citizenship without citizens is a logical impossibility.

Schools for Statesmanship

It was preeminently a school for statesmen and as such, on the North American continent, its product has never been excelled.

—*Dumas Malone*[22]

At 17, Jefferson left the limited intellectual and social world of his boyhood home in rural Shadwell for the colonial capitol of Williamsburg to attend the College of William and Mary and, as he put it, to "get a more universal Acquaintance." His learning encompassed not just academics but government in the General Court and House of Burgesses. He dined with the Royal Governor, his professor (William Small), and George Wythe, one of the colony's most eminent legal minds, forging networks that would enrich his learning and his capacity to lead. He witnessed the deliberations and decisions that sought to turn Enlightenment values into republican governance.

Without such an education in Williamsburg, the "school for statesmen," strengthened by later service in the legislature, Continental

Congress, and posts of increasing responsibility, it is doubtful Jefferson would have ever had the chance to practice presidential acts of statesmanship.

It bears asking, then, who should be schooled for statesmanship and what would constitute a "curriculum."

Our seven leaders include four elected politicians, one presidential appointee (and general officer) and two activists who led social movements. In the preface, we suggested as well that modern business leaders were increasingly actors on the public stage who might benefit from schooling in statesmanship—not to block their profit-making focus but to provide them a broader perspective as they integrate profit with other societal expectations. Career civil service leaders also need the character and skills of statesmanship. Many have massive and global responsibilities, managing multibillion dollar programs and large staffs. While under political direction, they still have wide latitude to act. In the world they inhabit, they shape policy, design, and execute programs, and often adjudicate public disputes. As Virginia Tech professor John Rohr put it, public administrators: "should learn to think like judges as well as legislators and executives because they are all three of these. In a regime of separation of powers, administrators must do the work of statesmen."[23]

Content areas for schooling for statesmanship are suggested by each of the six factors in the framework offered in this chapter (and in the figures that summarize key skills and traits of statesmanship). Some of this content is already taught in colleges and universities, especially graduate schools of government and public administration, and in leadership and executive education programs. Some is not, especially in the curriculum of professional schools (e.g. law, engineering, medicine, business administration, etc.) from which most of the future leaders in public and private organizations will come. Nor does it mean that it is taught with sufficient gravity or depth, as is the case with the teaching of ethics, when it is taught at all, in MBA programs.[24]

The aim here is not to fashion a comprehensive curriculum but to highlight three aspects of schooling for statesmanship that seem to need more attention than they receive.

Developing Character

We tend to take character as a given, yet it's worth asking whether we do enough to shape character in a child's early years and beyond.

Parents and elementary/secondary schools play primary roles in the formation of character, and many programs exist to help them do so. These programs may not be widespread enough, or given enough attention, especially with the heavy focus on "the basics" and testing in contemporary educational reform. For example, the Common Core Standards adopted by 41 states focus on language arts and mathematics but do not address character development as an important outcome, though the materials students study to achieve these outcomes offer multiple opportunities to focus on it.[25]

At the postsecondary level, the current intense focus on career preparation downplays the importance of character development. The National Consortium for Character-Based Leadership of the Center for the Study of the Presidency and Congress, as one example, aims to change that.[26] Much more is needed.

Once we get past the collegiate level, it is even harder to find institutional efforts aimed at character development. The Aspen Institute's programs in values-based leadership offer one such approach for both young adults and those at mid-career.[27]

In government service, attention to character development plays an important role in the service academies and in military leadership education. Indeed, officer evaluations in the military include assessments of character. The army, for example, evaluates an officer's attention to honor, integrity, courage, loyalty, respect, selfless service, and duty. In the civil service, character development is given far less attention. Character traits are not considered "objective" enough for performance-based appraisal systems. While government-wide leadership competencies fashioned by the U.S. Office of Personnel Management include integrity/honesty, resilience, and public service motivation, they tend to be addressed in courses only briefly, not as a primary focus.

One avenue for character development is the study of moral exemplars. As public administration professor David K. Hart notes, "The testimony of history is clear that a free people must have moral exemplars. They give confidence in public leadership, they serve as moral guides, and they provide a necessary encouragement for individual moral development."[28] For Washington and Jefferson, *Plutarch's Lives* was one source of moral exemplars. For today's students, Washington and Lincoln often serve this purpose, though it is not clear how much of the time devoted to them is focused on their character, as opposed to battles and dates. As a society, when we turn the birthdays of noted Americans into shopping extravaganzas, we diminish their power as moral exemplars.

The study of moral exemplars is a worthy pursuit well past the early years. Those aspiring to statesmanship should seek exemplars in their lives, as George Marshall did in Gen. John J. "Black Jack" Pershing. Marshall served under him and modeled aspects of his own character on his mentor—including the laser focus on mission, the cool demeanor at work, and the welcoming of dissent. Not surprisingly, when Marshall became chief of staff, he hung a portrait of Pershing above his desk.

Transcendent Purpose

Acts of statesmanship should be informed by a conception of the good society. As noted in the preface, an understanding of American history and government is essential for this, but we do a poor job of transferring that knowledge. If we expect future leaders to act for a better America (not to mention a better world), then we had best give them a better grounding in the ideas and ideals that produced the one we have.

In the American context, a deep understanding of the founding period is especially important. This requires going beyond a surface reading of the Declaration and the Constitution. Will Harris, founding director of the Center for the Constitution at James Madison's Montpelier, argues for the need to understand that the words and structure of the Constitution rest on primary documents of the founding, which include *theories* of constitution-making (the *Federalist Papers* and antifederalist writings) and the *processes* of constitution-making (Madison's *Notes* on the Constitutional Convention). Going even further back, Harris notes the importance of the basic science of constitutions itself—what forming a constitution means. Most leaders today, in both the public and private sectors, content themselves with invoking the Constitution, often as part of an argument for a preferred course of action, not with understanding it at this level.

For public leaders, the need to understand the Constitution is even greater. They take a solemn oath to "support and defend" it. Unfortunately, this oath is often administered their first day at work, sandwiched between signing personnel forms and giving out office supplies. What they need is a serious understanding of the oath, including the circumstances under which fidelity to it might be tested and how that test implies the need to subordinate personal or organizational loyalties.

John Rohr suggests that faithfulness to the oath requires deep study. He argues in *Public Service, Ethics and Constitutional Practice* that the curriculum for civil servants should include, in addition to the oath, institutional literacy (the statutory foundation, administrative history, and leading court decisions affecting one's agency or program) and presidential politics (the political vision of the president). In *Ethics for Bureaucrats*, he argues that the study of Supreme Court cases should also include those that cut across agencies and touch deep "regime values" for which the study of agency-specific cases is not enough.[29]

Ethical Decision Making

Many methods and courses exist for teaching decision making, but they often lack a focus on ethics. Public and private sector ethical failures in recent years have been numerous. Leaders with good character, a conception of the good society, and ethical decision-making skills might well have prevented these failures through acts of statesmanship. The current movement for an "MBA Oath" in schools of business administration is an acknowledgment of this failure in management education.[30] Unfortunately, for practicing public administrators the tendency has been to hammer away at codes of conduct that focus on what *not* to do (e.g. do not accept a gift from a government contractor) but offer little help in choosing what one *should* do. Instead, the focus on not breaking rules signals a drive to the lowest common denominator in which being legal is equated with being ethical.

Rohr, in *Ethics for Bureaucrats*, explains why studying Supreme Court cases can be used effectively to foster ethical judgment. In doing so, he offers key principles for an ethical decision-making process that can be learned from examining the Court's approach. According to Rohr, examining court cases: (a) shows values in action and acting on values—what precedent has allowed and rejected; (b) reinforces attention to the law and using the law for moral reflection; (c) impresses upon one the need to consider not just the current situation but the implications of a potential decision for the future (i.e. a long-term perspective); (d) stresses the value of circulating proposed decisions for comment; (e) builds in a way to provide for thoughtful dissent and attention to it; (f) demonstrates the value of subjecting decisions to public scrutiny; and (g) establishes valuable decision-making criteria, such as whether a decision passes

Constitutional muster and the need to balance political, organizational, and constitutional demands.

A Final Word

Here, at the end, it is worth saying that we have just begun. We have a canvas on which to paint statesmanship, not a finished work. Lines may be redrawn, features removed. More details wait to be added. But our work in progress invites our imagination and serves as a source for the application of our talents. Statesmanship is in need of both.

With this beginning, we can have a fruitful conversation—about leadership, statesmanship, the differences between them, the importance of character, the requisite skills, how to develop and encourage statesmanship, and how, as citizens, to appreciate its contributions and its calls for sacrifice. We need this conversation.

The statesmanship we have viewed did not come from great men and women. It came from men and women who did exemplary things. Statesmanship is not reserved for presidents, the titans of business, and for leaders of social movements. It is accessible to all of us, for citizenship is the obligation of all of us. If we can set aside the "great man" or "great woman" theory of moving us forward, then we can get busy with expanding the presence of statesmanship and move closer to the good society we seek. We can all engage in statesmanship. We all need to do so. We are tied together in this confusing present and in our Black Swan future. Author and former priest, James Carroll, perhaps put the argument for expanding statesmanship best when he said: "In the end, as in the beginning, we are responsible to each other and for each other. It is that kind of island, this earth."

Appendices

These appendices provide six of the nine core documents that form the foundation for the first seven chapters of this book. Reading these texts in the course of reading the chapters will, hopefully, both enrich the chapters and deepen understanding of the leader's exercise of statesmanship.

Three documents could not be included here, due to both length and copyright considerations. All of these are easily accessible on the Internet, and links to them can be found as indicated below.

Washington's Farewell Address can be found at: http://www.access.gpo.gov/congress/senate/farewell/sd106–21.pdf

King's Letter from Birmingham Jail can be found at:
http://www.mlkonline.net/jail.html

The Letter from Eight Alabama Clergy, to which King was nominally responding, can be found at:
http://www.stanford.edu/group/King//frequentdocs/clergy.pdf

Appendix A

Thomas Jefferson's First Inaugural Address: March 4, 1801

Friends and Fellow-Citizens:

Called upon to undertake the duties of the first executive office of our country, I avail myself of the presence of that portion of my fellow-citizens which is here assembled to express my grateful thanks for the favor with which they have been pleased to look toward me, to declare a sincere consciousness that the task is above my talents, and that I approach it with those anxious and awful presentiments which the greatness of the charge and the weakness of my powers so justly inspire. A rising nation, spread over a wide and fruitful land, traversing all the seas with the rich productions of their industry, engaged in commerce with nations who feel power and forget right, advancing rapidly to destinies beyond the reach of mortal eye—when I contemplate these transcendent objects, and see the honor, the happiness, and the hopes of this beloved country committed to the issue, and the auspices of this day, I shrink from the contemplation, and humble myself before the magnitude of the undertaking. Utterly, indeed, should I despair did not the presence of many whom I here see remind me that in the other high authorities provided by our Constitution I shall find resources of wisdom, of virtue, and of zeal on which to rely under all difficulties. To you, then, gentlemen, who are charged with the sovereign functions of legislation, and to those associated with you, I look with encouragement for that guidance and support which may enable us to steer with safety the vessel in which we are all embarked amidst the conflicting elements of a troubled world.

During the contest of opinion through which we have passed the animation of discussions and of exertions has sometimes worn an aspect which might impose on strangers unused to think freely and to speak and to write what they think; but this being now decided by the voice of the nation, announced according to the rules of the Constitution, all will, of course, arrange themselves under the will of the law, and unite in common efforts for the common good. All, too, will bear in mind this sacred principle, that though the will of the majority is in all cases to prevail, that will to be rightful must be reasonable; that the minority possess their equal rights, which equal laws must protect, and to violate would be oppression. Let us, then, fellow-citizens, unite with one heart and one mind. Let us restore to social intercourse that harmony and affection without which liberty and even life itself are but dreary things. And let us reflect that, having banished from our land that religious intolerance under which mankind so long bled and suffered, we have yet gained little if we countenance a political intolerance as despotic, as wicked, and capable of as bitter and bloody persecutions. During the throes and convulsions of the ancient world, during the agonizing spasms of infuriated man, seeking through blood and slaughter his long-lost liberty, it was not wonderful that the agitation of the billows should reach even this distant and peaceful shore; that this should be more felt and feared by some and less by others, and should divide opinions as to measures of safety. But every difference of opinion is not a difference of principle. We have called by different names brethren of the same principle. We are all republicans, we are all federalists. If there be any among us who would wish to dissolve this Union or to change its republican form, let them stand undisturbed as monuments of the safety with which error of opinion may be tolerated where reason is left free to combat it. I know, indeed, that some honest men fear that a republican government can not be strong, that this Government is not strong enough; but would the honest patriot, in the full tide of successful experiment, abandon a government which has so far kept us free and firm on the theoretic and visionary fear that this Government, the world's best hope, may by possibility want energy to preserve itself? I trust not. I believe this, on the contrary, the strongest Government on earth. I believe it the only one where every man, at the call of the law, would fly to the standard of the law, and would meet invasions of the public order as his own personal concern. Sometimes it is said that man can not be trusted with the government of himself. Can he, then, be trusted with the government of others? Or have we found angels in the form of kings to govern him? Let history answer this question.

Let us, then, with courage and confidence pursue our own Federal and Republican principles, our attachment to union and representative government. Kindly separated by nature and a wide ocean from the exterminating havoc of one quarter of the globe; too high-minded to endure the degradations of the others; possessing a chosen country, with room enough for our descendants to the thousandth and thousandth generation; entertaining a due sense of our equal right to the use of our own faculties, to the acquisitions of our own industry, to honor and confidence from our fellow-citizens, resulting not from birth, but from our actions and their sense of them; enlightened by a benign religion, professed, indeed, and practiced in various forms, yet all of them inculcating honesty, truth, temperance, gratitude, and the love of man; acknowledging and adoring an overruling Providence, which by all its dispensations proves that it delights in the happiness of man here and his greater happiness hereafter—with all these blessings, what more is necessary to make us a happy and a prosperous people? Still one thing more, fellow-citizens—a wise and frugal Government, which shall restrain men from injuring one another, shall leave them otherwise free to regulate their own pursuits of industry and improvement, and shall not take from the mouth of labor the bread it has earned. This is the sum of good government, and this is necessary to close the circle of our felicities.

About to enter, fellow-citizens, on the exercise of duties which comprehend everything dear and valuable to you, it is proper you should understand what I deem the essential principles of our Government, and consequently those which ought to shape its Administration. I will compress them within the narrowest compass they will bear, stating the general principle, but not all its limitations. Equal and exact justice to all men, of whatever state or persuasion, religious or political; peace, commerce, and honest friendship with all nations, entangling alliances with none; the support of the State governments in all their rights, as the most competent administrations for our domestic concerns and the surest bulwarks against antirepublican tendencies; the preservation of the General Government in its whole constitutional vigor, as the sheet anchor of our peace at home and safety abroad; a jealous care of the right of election by the people—a mild and safe corrective of abuses which are lopped by the sword of revolution where peaceable remedies are unprovided; absolute acquiescence in the decisions of the majority, the vital principle of republics, from which is no appeal but to force, the vital principle and immediate parent of despotism; a well disciplined militia, our best reliance in peace and for the first moments of war, till regulars may relieve them; the supremacy of the civil over the military authority; economy in the public expense, that labor may be lightly burthened; the honest payment of our debts and sacred preservation of the public faith; encouragement of agriculture, and of commerce as its handmaid; the diffusion of information and arraignment of all abuses at the bar of the public reason; freedom of religion; freedom of the press, and freedom of person under the protection of the habeas corpus, and trial by juries impartially selected. These principles form the bright constellation which has gone before us and guided our steps through an age of revolution and reformation. The wisdom of our sages and blood of our heroes have been devoted to their attainment. They should be the creed of our political faith, the text of civic instruction, the touchstone by which to try the services of those we trust; and should we wander from them in moments of error or of alarm, let us hasten to retrace our steps and to regain the road which alone leads to peace, liberty, and safety.

I repair, then, fellow-citizens, to the post you have assigned me. With experience enough in subordinate offices to have seen the difficulties of this the greatest of all, I have learnt to expect that it will rarely fall to the lot of imperfect man to retire from this station with the reputation and the favor which bring him into it. Without pretensions to that high confidence you reposed in our first and greatest revolutionary character, whose preeminent services had entitled him to the first place in his country's love and destined for him the fairest page in the volume of faithful history, I ask so much confidence only as may give firmness and effect to the legal administration of your affairs. I shall often go wrong through defect of judgment. When right, I shall often be thought wrong by those whose positions will not command a view of the whole ground. I ask your indulgence for my own errors, which will never be intentional, and your support against the errors of others, who may condemn what they would not if seen in all its parts. The approbation implied by your suffrage is a great consolation to me for the past, and my future solicitude will be to retain the good opinion of those who have bestowed it in advance, to conciliate that of others by doing them all the good in my power, and to be instrumental to the happiness and freedom of all.

Appendix B

Lincoln's Second Inaugural*:
March 4, 1865

Fellow-Countrymen:

At this second appearing, to take the oath of the presidential office, there is less occasion for an extended address than there was at the first. Then a statement, somewhat in detail, of a course to be pursued, seemed fitting and proper. Now, at the expiration of four years, during which public declarations have been constantly called forth on every point and phase of the great contest which still absorbs the attention, and engrosses the energies of the nation, little that is new could be presented. The progress of our arms, upon which all else chiefly depends, is as well known to the public as to myself; and it is, I trust, reasonably satisfactory and encouraging to all. With high hope for the future, no prediction in regard to it is ventured.

On the occasion corresponding to this four years ago, all thoughts were anxiously directed to an impending civil war. All dreaded it—all sought to avert it. While the inaugural address was being delivered from this place, devoted altogether to saving the Union without war, insurgent agents were in the city seeking to destroy it without war— seeking to dissolve the Union, and divide effects, by negotiation. Both parties deprecated war; but one of them would make war rather than let the nation survive; and the other would accept war rather than let it perish. And the war came.

One-eighth of the whole population were colored slaves, not distributed generally over the Union, but localized in the Southern part of it. These slaves constituted a peculiar and powerful interest. All knew that this interest was, somehow, the cause of the war. To strengthen, perpetuate, and extend this interest was the object for which the insurgents would rend the Union, even by war; while the Government claimed no right to do more than to restrict the territorial enlargement of it. Neither party expected for the war. the magnitude, or the duration, which it has already attained. Neither anticipated that the <u>cause</u> of the conflict might cease with, or even before, the conflict itself should cease. Each looked for an easier triumph, and a result less fundamental and astounding. Both read the same Bible, and pray to the same God; and each invokes His aid against the other. It may seem strange that any men should dare to ask a just God's assistance in wringing their bread from the sweat of other men's faces; but let us judge not that we be not judged. The prayers of both could not be answered; that of neither has been answered fully. The Almighty has His own purposes. "Woe unto the world because of offenses! for it must needs be that offenses come; but woe to that man by whom the offense cometh!" If we shall suppose that American slavery is one of those offenses which, in the providence of God, must needs come, but which, having continued through His appointed time, He now wills to remove, and that He gives to both North and South this terrible war, as the woe due to those by whom the offense came, shall we discern therein any departure from those divine attributes which the believers in a living God always ascribe to Him? Fondly do we hope— fervently do we pray—that this mighty scourge of war may speedily pass away. Yet, if God wills that it continue, until all the wealth piled by the bondsman's two hundred and fifty years of unrequited toil shall be sunk, and until every drop of blood drawn with the lash, shall be paid by another drawn with the sword, as was said three thousand years ago, so still it must be said "the judgments of the Lord, are true and righteous altogether."

With malice toward none; with charity for all; with firmness in the right, as God gives us to see the right, let us strive on to finish the work we are in; to bind up the nation's wounds; to care for him who shall have borne the battle, and for his widow, and his orphan—to do all which may achieve and cherish a just and a lasting peace, among ourselves, and with all nations.

*Punctuation and underlining as in the original

Appendix C

Speech Before the Circuit Court in the Sentencing of Susan B. Anthony*: June 19, 1873

Judge Hunt—(Ordering the defendant to stand up), "Has the prisoner anything to say why sentence shall not be pronounced?"

Miss Anthony—Yes, your honor, I have many things to say; for in your ordered verdict of guilty, you have trampled under foot every vital principle of our government. My natural rights, my civil rights, my political rights, my judicial rights, are all alike ignored. Robbed of the fundamental privilege of citizenship, I am degraded from the status of a citizen to that of a subject; and not only myself individually, but all of my sex, are, by your honor's verdict, doomed to political subjection under this, so-called, form of government.

Judge Hunt—The Court cannot listen to a rehearsal of arguments the prisoner's counsel has already consumed three hours in presenting.

Miss Anthony—May it please your honor, I am not arguing the question, but simply stating the reasons why sentence cannot, in justice, be pronounced against me. Your denial of my citizen's right to vote, is the denial of my right of consent as one of the governed, the denial of my right of representation as one of the taxed, the denial of my right to a trial by a jury of my peers as an offender against law, therefore, the denial of my sacred rights to life, liberty, property and—

Judge Hunt—The Court cannot allow the prisoner to go on.

Miss Anthony—But your honor will not deny me this one and only poor privilege of protest against this high-handed outrage upon my citizen's rights. May it please the Court to remember that since the day of my arrest last November, this is the first time that either myself or any person of my disfranchised class has been allowed a word of defense before judge or jury—

Judge Hunt—The prisoner must sit down—the Court cannot allow it.

Miss Anthony—All of my prosecutors, from the 8th ward corner grocery politician, who entered the compliant, to the United States Marshal, Commissioner, District Attorney, District Judge, your honor on the bench, not one is my peer, but each and all are my political sovereigns; and had your honor submitted my case to the jury, as was clearly your duty, even then I should have had just cause of protest, for not one of those men was my peer; but, native or foreign born, white or black, rich or poor, educated or ignorant, awake or asleep, sober or drunk, each and every man of them was my political superior; hence, in no sense, my peer. Even, under such circumstances, a commoner of England, tried before a jury of Lords, would have far less cause to complain than should I, a woman, tried before a jury of men. Even my counsel, the Hon. Henry R. Selden, who has argued my cause so ably, so earnestly, so unanswerably before your honor, is my political sovereign. Precisely as no disfranchised person is entitled to sit upon a jury, and no woman is entitled to the franchise, so, none but a regularly admitted lawyer is allowed to practice in the courts, and no woman can gain admission to the bar—hence, jury, judge, counsel, must all be of the superior class.

Judged Hunt—The Court must insist—the prisoner has been tried according to the established forms of law.

Miss Anthony—Yes, your honor, but by forms of law all made by men, interpreted by men, administered by men, in favor of men, and against women; and hence, your honor's ordered verdict of guilty; against a United States citizen for the exercise of "that citizen's right to vote," simply because that citizen was a woman and not a man. But, yesterday, the same man made forms of law, declared it a crime punishable with $1,000 fine and six months imprisonment, for you, or me, or any of us, to give a cup of cold water, a crust of bread, or a night's shelter to a panting fugitive as he was tracking his way to Canada. And every man or woman in whose veins coursed a drop of human sympathy violated that wicked law, reckless of consequences, and was justified in so doing. As then, the slaves who got their freedom must take it over, or under, or through the unjust forms of law, precisely so, now, must women, to get their right to a voice in this government, take it; and I have taken mine, and mean to take it at every possible opportunity.

Judge Hunt—The Court orders the prisoner to sit down. It will not allow another word.

Miss Anthony—When I was brought before your honor for trial, I hoped for a broad and liberal interpretation of the Constitution and its recent amendments, that should declare all United States citizens under its protecting aegis—that should declare equality of rights the national guarantee to all persons born or naturalized in the United States. But failing to get this justice—failing, even, to get a trial by a jury not of my peers—I ask not leniency at your hands—but rather the full rigors of the law.

Judge Hunt—The Court must insist—

(Here the prisoner sat down.)

Judge Hunt—The prisoner will stand up.

(Here Miss Anthony arose again.)

The sentence of the Court is that you pay a fine of one hundred dollars and the costs of the prosecution.

Miss Anthony—May it please your honor, I shall never pay a dollar of your unjust penalty. All the stock in trade I possess is a $10,000 debt, incurred by publishing my paper—*The Revolution*—four years ago, the sole object of which was to educate all women to do precisely as I have done, rebel against your manmade, unjust, unconstitutional forms of law, that tax, fine, imprison, and hang women, while they deny them the right of representation in the government; and I shall work on with might and main to pay every dollar of that honest debt, but not a penny shall go to this unjust claim. And I shall earnestly and persistently continue to urge all women to the practical recognition of the old revolutionary maxim, that "Resistance to tyranny is obedience to God."

Judge Hunt—Madam, the Court will not order you committed until the fine is paid.

*Gordon, Ann D. *The Selected Papers of Elizabeth Cady Stanton and Susan B. Anthony: Volume II, Against and Aristocracy of Sex, 1866 to 1873*. Copyright © 2000 by Rutgers, the State University of New Jersey. Reprinted by permission of Rutgers University Press.

Appendix D

The Marshall Plan Speech: June 5, 1947

Mr. President, Dr. Conant, members of the Board of Overseers, Ladies and Gentlemen:

I am profoundly grateful, touched by the great distinction and honor and great compliment accorded me by the authorities of Harvard this morning. I am overwhelmed, as a matter of fact, and I am rather fearful of my inability to maintain such a high rating as you've been generous enough to accord to me. In these historic and lovely surroundings, this perfect day, and this very wonderful assembly, it is a tremendously impressive thing to an individual in my position.

But to speak more seriously, I need not tell you that the world situation is very serious. That must be apparent to all intelligent people. I think one difficulty is that the problem is one of such enormous complexity that the very mass of facts presented to the public by press and radio make it exceedingly difficult for the man in the street to reach a clear appraisement of the situation. Furthermore, the people of this country are distant from the troubled areas of the earth, and it is hard for them to comprehend the plight and consequent reactions of the long-suffering peoples of Europe and the effect of those reactions on their governments in connection with our efforts to promote peace in the world.

In considering the requirements for the rehabilitation of Europe, the physical loss of life, the visible destruction of cities, factories, mines, and railroads was correctly estimated, but it has become obvious during recent months that this visible destruction was probably less serious than the dislocation of the entire fabric of European economy. For the past ten years conditions have been highly abnormal. The feverish preparation for war and the more feverish maintenance of the war effort engulfed all aspects of national economies. Machinery has fallen into disrepair or is entirely obsolete. Under the arbitrary and destructive Nazi rule, virtually every possible enterprise was geared into the German war machine. Long-standing commercial ties, private institutions, banks, insurance companies, and shipping companies disappeared through loss of capital, absorption through nationalization, or by simple destruction. In many countries, confidence in the local currency has been severely shaken. The breakdown of the business structure of Europe during the war was complete. Recovery has been seriously retarded by the fact that two years after the close of hostilities a peace settlement with Germany and Austria has not been agreed upon. But even given a more prompt solution of these difficult problems, the rehabilitation of the economic structure of Europe quite evidently will require a much longer time and greater effort than had been foreseen.

There is a phase of this matter which is both interesting and serious. The farmer has always produced the foodstuffs to exchange with the city dweller for the other necessities of life. This division of labor is the basis of modern civilization. At the present time it is threatened with breakdown. The town and city industries are not producing adequate goods to exchange with the food-producing farmer. Raw materials and fuel are in short supply. Machinery, as I have said, is lacking or worn out. The farmer or the peasant cannot find the goods for sale which he desires to purchase. So the sale of his farm produce for money which he cannot use seems to him an unprofitable transaction. He, therefore, has withdrawn many fields from crop cultivation and he's using them for grazing. He feeds more grain to stock and finds for himself and his family an ample supply of food, however short he may be on clothing and the other ordinary gadgets of civilization.

Meanwhile, people in the cities are short of food and fuel, and in some places approaching the starvation levels. So, the governments are forced to use their foreign money and credits to procure these necessities abroad. This process exhausts funds which are urgently needed for reconstruction. Thus, a very serious situation is rapidly developing which bodes no good for the world. The modern system of the division of labor upon which the exchange of products is based is in danger of breaking down. The truth of the matter is that Europe's requirements for the next three or four years of foreign food and other essential products—principally from America—are so much greater than her present ability to pay that she must have substantial additional help or face economic, social, and political deterioration of a very grave character.

The remedy seems to lie in breaking the vicious circle and restoring the confidence of the people of Europe in the economic future of their own countries and of Europe as a whole. The manufacturer and the farmer throughout wide areas must be able and willing to exchange their product for currencies, the continuing value of which is not open to question.

Aside from the demoralizing effect on the world at large and the possibilities of disturbances arising as a result of the desperation of the people concerned, the consequences to the economy of the United States should be apparent to all. It is logical that the United States should do whatever it is able to do to assist in the return of normal economic health in the world, without which there can be no political stability and no assured peace. Our policy is directed not against any country or doctrine but against hunger, poverty, desperation, and chaos. Its purpose should be the revival of a working economy in the world so as to permit the emergence of political and social conditions in which free institutions can exist.

Such assistance, I am convinced, must not be on a piecemeal basis, as various crises develop. Any assistance that this Government may render in the future should provide a cure rather than a mere palliative. Any government that is willing to assist in the task of recovery will find full cooperation, I am sure, on the part of the United States Government. Any government which maneuvers to block the recovery of other countries cannot expect help from us. Furthermore, governments, political parties, or groups which seek to perpetuate human misery in order to profit there from politically or otherwise will encounter the opposition of the United States.

It is already evident that before the United States Government can proceed much further in its efforts to alleviate the situation and help start the European world on its way to recovery, there must be some agreement among the countries of Europe as to the requirements of the situation and the part those countries themselves will take in order to give a proper effect to whatever actions might be undertaken by this Government. It would be neither fitting nor efficacious for our Government to undertake to draw up unilaterally a program designed to place Europe on its feet economically. This is the business of the Europeans. The initiative, I think, must come from Europe. The role of this country should consist of friendly aid in the drafting of a European program and of later support of such a program so far as it may be practical for us to do so. The program should be a joint one, agreed to by a number, if not all, European nations.

An essential part of any successful action on the part of the United States is an understanding on the part of the people of America of the character of the problem and the remedies to be applied. Political passion and prejudice should have no part. With foresight, and a willingness on the part of our people to face up to the vast responsibility which history has clearly placed upon our country, the difficulties I have outlined can and will be overcome.

I am sorry that on each occasion I have said something publicly in regard to our international situation, I have been forced by the necessities of the case to enter into rather technical discussions. But, to my mind, it is of vast importance that our people reach some general understanding of what the complications really are, rather than react from a passion or a prejudice or an emotion of the moment.

As I said more formally a moment ago, we are remote from the scene of these troubles. It is virtually impossible at this distance merely by reading, or listening, or even seeing photographs and motion pictures, to grasp at all the real significance of the situation. And yet the whole world of the future hangs on a proper judgment. It hangs, I think, to a large extent on the realization of the American people, of just what are the various dominant factors. What are the reactions of the people? What are the justifications of those reactions? What are the sufferings? What is needed? What can best be done? What must be done?

Thank you very much.

Appendix E

Gerald Ford's Remarks on Taking the Oath of Office: August 9, 1974

Mr. Chief Justice, my dear friends, my fellow Americans:

The oath that I have taken is the same oath that was taken by George Washington and by every President under the Constitution. But I assume the Presidency under extraordinary circumstances never before experienced by Americans. This is an hour of history that troubles our minds and hurts our hearts.

Therefore, I feel it is my first duty to make an unprecedented compact with my countrymen. Not an inaugural address, not a fireside chat, not a campaign speech—just a little straight talk among friends. And I intend it to be the first of many.

I am acutely aware that you have not elected me as your President by your ballots, and so I ask you to confirm me as your President with your prayers. And I hope that such prayers will also be the first of many.

If you have not chosen me by secret ballot, neither have I gained office by any secret promises. I have not campaigned either for the Presidency or the Vice Presidency. I have not subscribed to any partisan platform. I am indebted to no man, and only to one woman—my dear wife—as I begin this very difficult job.

I have not sought this enormous responsibility, but I will not shirk it. Those who nominated and confirmed me as Vice President were my friends and are my friends. They were of both parties, elected by all the people and acting under the Constitution in their name. It is only fitting then that I should pledge to them and to you that I will be the President of all the people.

Thomas Jefferson said the people are the only sure reliance for the preservation of our liberty. And down the years, Abraham Lincoln renewed this American article of faith asking, "Is there any better way or equal hope in the world?"

I intend, on Monday next, to request of the Speaker of the House of Representatives and the President pro tempore of the Senate the privilege of appearing before the Congress to share with my former colleagues and with you, the American people, my views on the priority business of the Nation and to solicit your views and their views. And may I say to the Speaker and the others, if I could meet with you right after these remarks, I would appreciate it.

Even though this is late in an election year, there is no way we can go forward except together and no way anybody can win except by serving the people's urgent needs. We cannot stand still or slip backwards. We must go forward now together.

To the peoples and the governments of all friendly nations, and I hope that could encompass the whole world, I pledge an uninterrupted and sincere search for peace. America will remain strong and united, but its strength will remain dedicated to the safety and sanity of the entire family of man, as well as to our own precious freedom.

I believe that truth is the glue that holds government together, not only our Government but civilization itself. That bond, though strained, is unbroken at home and abroad.

In all my public and private acts as your President, I expect to follow my instincts of openness and candor with full confidence that honesty is always the best policy in the end.

My fellow Americans, our long national nightmare is over.

Our Constitution works; our great Republic is a government of laws and not of men. Here the people rule. But there is a higher Power, by whatever name we honor Him, who ordains not only righteousness but love, not only justice but mercy.

As we bind up the internal wounds of Watergate, more painful and more poisonous than those of foreign wars, let us restore the golden rule to our political process, and let brotherly love purge our hearts of suspicion and of hate.

In the beginning, I asked you to pray for me. Before closing, I ask again your prayers, for Richard Nixon and for his family. May our former President, who brought peace to millions, find it for himself. May God bless and comfort his wonderful wife and daughters, whose love and loyalty will forever be a shining legacy to all who bear the lonely burdens of the White House.

I can only guess at those burdens, although I have witnessed at close hand the tragedies that befell three Presidents and the lesser trials of others.

With all the strength and all the good sense I have gained from life, with all the confidence my family, my friends, and my dedicated staff impart to me, and with the good will of countless Americans I have encountered in recent visits to 40 States, I now solemnly reaffirm my promise I made to you last December 6: to uphold the Constitution, to do what is right as God gives me to see the right, and to do the very best I can for America.

God helping me, I will not let you down.

Thank you.

Appendix F

Ford's Speech Announcing the Pardon of Richard Nixon: September 8, 1974

Ladies and gentlemen:

I have come to a decision which I felt I should tell you and all of my fellow American citizens, as soon as I was certain in my own mind and in my own conscience that it is the right thing to do.

I have learned already in this office that the difficult decisions always come to this desk. I must admit that many of them do not look at all the same as the hypothetical questions that I have answered freely and perhaps too fast on previous occasions.

My customary policy is to try and get all the facts and to consider the opinions of my countrymen and to take counsel with my most valued friends. But these seldom agree, and in the end, the decision is mine. To procrastinate, to agonize, and to wait for a more favorable turn of events that may never come or more compelling external pressures that may as well be wrong as right, is itself a decision of sorts and a weak and potentially dangerous course for a President to follow.

I have promised to uphold the Constitution, to do what is right as God gives me to see the right, and to do the very best that I can for America.

I have asked your help and your prayers, not only when I became President but many times since. The Constitution is the supreme law of our land and it governs our actions as citizens. Only the laws of God, which govern our consciences, are superior to it.

As we are a nation under God, so I am sworn to uphold our laws with the help of God. And I have sought such guidance and searched my own conscience with special diligence to determine the right thing for me to do with respect to my predecessor in this place, Richard Nixon, and his loyal wife and family.

Theirs is an American tragedy in which we all have played a part. It could go on and on and on, or someone must write the end to it. I have concluded that only I can do that, and if I can, I must.

There are no historic or legal precedents to which I can turn in this matter, none that precisely fit the circumstances of a private citizen who has resigned the Presidency of the United States. But it is common knowledge that serious allegations and accusations hang like a sword over our former President's head, threatening his health as he tries to reshape his life, a great part of which was spent in the service of this country and by the mandate of its people.

After years of bitter controversy and divisive national debate, I have been advised, and I am compelled to conclude that many months and perhaps more years will have to pass before Richard Nixon could obtain a fair trial by jury in any jurisdiction of the United States under governing decisions of the Supreme Court.

I deeply believe in equal justice for all Americans, whatever their station or former station. The law, whether human or divine, is no respecter of persons; but the law is a respecter of reality.

The facts, as I see them, are that a former President of the United States, instead of enjoying equal treatment with any other citizen accused of violating the law, would be cruelly and excessively penalized either in preserving the presumption of his innocence or in obtaining a speedy determination of his guilt in order to repay a legal debt to society.

During this long period of delay and potential litigation, ugly passions would again be aroused. And our people would again be polarized in their opinions. And the credibility of our free institutions of government would again be challenged at home and abroad.

In the end, the courts might well hold that Richard Nixon had been denied due process, and the verdict of history would even more be inconclusive with respect to those charges arising out of the period of his Presidency, of which I am presently aware.

But it is not the ultimate fate of Richard Nixon that most concerns me, though surely it deeply troubles every decent and every compassionate person. My concern is the immediate future of this great country.

In this, I dare not depend upon my personal sympathy as a long-time friend of the former President, nor my professional judgment as a lawyer, and I do not.

As President, my primary concern must always be the greatest good of all the people of the United States whose servant I am. As a man, my first consideration is to be true to my own convictions and my own conscience.

My conscience tells me clearly and certainly that I cannot prolong the bad dreams that continue to reopen a chapter that is closed. My conscience tells me that only I, as President, have the constitutional power to firmly shut and seal this book. My conscience tells me it is my duty, not merely to proclaim domestic tranquility but to use every means that I have to insure it. I do believe that the buck stops here, that I cannot rely upon public opinion polls to tell me what is right. I do believe that right makes might and that if I am wrong, 10 angels swearing I was right would make no difference. I do believe, with all my heart and mind and spirit, that I, not as President but as a humble servant of God, will receive justice without mercy if I fail to show mercy.

Finally, I feel that Richard Nixon and his loved ones have suffered enough and will continue to suffer, no matter what I do, no matter what we, as a great and good nation, can do together to make his goal of peace come true.

Now, therefore, I, Gerald R. Ford, President of the United States, pursuant to the pardon power conferred upon me by Article II, Section 2, of the Constitution, have granted and by these presents do grant a full, free, and absolute pardon unto Richard Nixon for all offenses against the United States which he, Richard Nixon, has committed or may have committed or taken part in during the period from July [January] 20, 1969 through August 9, 1974.

In witness whereof, I have hereunto set my hand this eighth day of September, in the year of our Lord nineteen hundred and seventy-four, and of the Independence of the United States of America the one hundred and ninety-ninth.

Notes

Preface

1. Abigail Adams to John Quincy Adams, January 19, 1780. For the full text, go to: http://www.masshist.org/JQA/05-mother_advises_son/aatojqa 17800119p1.html. (January 9, 2012).
2. See http://en.wikipedia.org/wiki/Black_swan_theory,(January 9, 2012).
3. Reuters/Ipsos Poll, August 4–8, 2011, http://www.pollingreport.com/right. htm
4. Gallup Poll, July 2010, see http://www.pollingreport.com/institut.htm
5. See, A National Study on Confidence in Leadership, Center for Public Leadership, Kennedy School of Government, Harvard University, 2010 at: http://www.centerforpublicleadership.org/index.php?option=com_flipping book&view=book&id=24&Itemid=301 (January 9, 2012).)
6. I use the generic terms "statesmen" and "statesmanship" throughout, for ease of language only. Stateswomen are just as badly needed and offer just as much hope for our collective future.
7. See, for example, Willingham (2009).
8. See Neustadt and May (1986).
9. See http://www.isi.org/media/content/constitutionday_9–15.pdf (January 9, 2012).
10. See http://www.americancivicliteracy.org/2006/major_findings.html (January 9, 2012).
11. Public speeches became more common, at least in presidential rhetoric, as democracy advanced and both demanded and encouraged appeals to the public. Washington's Farewell Address was not a speech at all, and Jefferson's First Inaugural was delivered mostly to Congress. Early leaders viewed speaking to the public as unneeded at best and demagoguery at worst, threatening rule by the mob. Jeffrey Tulis's work on *The Rhetorical Presidency* (1987) charts this change well.

I Washington Steps Down: The Farewell Address

1. Smith (1993), p. 278 and Spalding and Garrity (1996), p. 45.
2. Washington refused pecuniary honors throughout his career. When Virginia gave him a gift after the war, he gave it to charity. See Flexner (1969), p. 194.

3. Letter to Benjamin Lincoln from Mount Vernon, October 26, 1788.
4. Letter to Catherine Macaulay Graham, January 9, 1790.
5. Weisberger (2000), p. 73.
6. James Madison, "Substance of a Conversation with the President," May 5–25, 1792.
7. Thomas Jefferson to George Washington, May 23, 1792.
8. Alexander Hamilton to George Washington, July 30, 1792.
9. Quoted in Paltsits (1935), p. 31.
10. George Washington to Alexander Hamilton, May 15, 1796.
11. Flexner (1969), p. 5.
12. Smith (1993), p. 4.
13. Quoted in Wood (2006), p. 33.
14. George Washington to Alexander Hamilton, August 10, 1796.
15. Paltsits (1935), p. 49.
16. "Certification of David C. Claypoole," February 22, 1826, *Memoirs of the Historical Society of Pennsylvania* Vol. 1, 1826.
17. Circular to the States, June 12, 1783.
18. Letter to Alexander Hamilton, from Philadelphia, May 15, 1796.
19. Spalding and Garrity (1996), p. 34.
20. Throughout this analysis, I treat the address as Washington's product. While Hamilton (and Madison) helped, they relied on Washington's guidance. The final manuscript was in Washington's hand and includes changes from Hamilton's major draft, which of course was based on Washington's earlier draft.
21. Speech to the Continental Congress, June 16, 1775.
22. To Martha Washington, from Philadelphia, June 18, 1775.
23. Quoted in Spalding and Garrity (1996), p. 28.
24. Letter to Gouverneur Morris, December 22, 1796.
25. Quoted in Smith (1993), p. 23.
26. Ellis (2005), p. 12.
27. Flexner (1969), p. 38.
28. Ellis (2005), p. 26.
29. Flexner (1969), p. 37.
30. Ibid., p. 170.
31. Washington's final manuscript of the Farewell Address, contained in Paltsits (1935), p. 159.
32. Quote in Wood (2006), p. 42.
33. Leaving power is still rare for leaders who bring about revolutionary change, as the examples of Vladimir Putin and Robert Mugabe demonstrate. Nelson Mandela is one of the few parallels to Washington that we have today.
34. Smith (1993), p. 12.
35. Quoted from Flexner (1965), Vol. 1, p. 250.
36. For a thorough analysis of Washington's use of language in the Farewell Address, see Ryan Halford, "The Rhetoric of George Washington's Farwell Address," *Speaker and Gavel*, Vol. 38, (2001), pp. 1–15. Halford explores the use of rhetorical questions as well as other devices in the Address.
37. George Washington to Henry Knox, March 8, 1787—commenting on the prospects of the forthcoming Federal (Constitutional) Convention. Knox

was Secretary of War under the Articles of Confederation and then again under Washington after the Constitution was ratified.

38. Spalding (1996), p. 67.
39. George Washington to John Jay, May 8, 1796.
40. I am indebted to Will Harris, founding director of the Montpelier Foundation's Center for the Constitution, for the notion that many of the framers, especially James Madison, appealed to the country with the two contrasting visions—the dream and the nightmare.
41. Circular Address to the States, June 18, 1783.
42. Greenleaf (1977).
43. Spalding and Garrity (1996), p. 5.
44. Ibid., p. 10.
45. See "Washington and Entangling Alliances" by Roland Usher (p. 55) in Kaufman (1969).
46. The Courier of New Hampshire at Concord was the first to reprint the text, on October 11, 1796, with the title "Washington's Farewell Address," as it has since become known.
47. Quoted in Paltsits (1935), p. 57.
48. Ibid. p. 60.
49. Quoted in Spalding and Garrity (1996), p. 3.
50. Paltsits (1935), p. 72.
51. Ibid., p. 62.
52. Quoted in Smith (1993), p. 285.
53. Quoted in Ellis (2005), p. 245.
54. Paltsits (1935), p. 63.
55. Quoted in Spalding and Garrity (1996), p. 143.
56. Smith (1993), p. 288.
57. Paltsits (1935), p. 64.
58. First Inaugural Address, Thomas Jefferson, March 4, 1801.
59. The quote is from the Webster-Hayne debates between Senator Daniel Webster of Massachusetts and Senator Robert Y. Hayne of South Carolina that took place on January 19–27, 1830.
60. Quoted in Spalding and Garrity (1996), p. 147.
61. See Gilbert (1961).
62. State of the Union address, January 4, 1939 (for the full text, go to: http://www.infoplease.com/t/hist/state-of-the-union/150.html)
63. Spalding and Garrity (1996), p. 165.
64. For the history of this practice and senators' comments, go to: http://www.senate.gov/artandhistory/history/minute/Washingtons_Farewell_Address.htm (January 9, 2012).

2   The Electoral Crisis of 1801: Jefferson's First Inaugural

1. Jefferson to Francis Hopkinson, March 13, 1789.
2. The clash of principles between Jefferson and Adams persists as the clash of federalist and antifederalist views on the nature of man and government.

3. Jefferson to John Taylor, June 4, 1798, *The Papers of Thomas Jefferson Digital Edition*, 2008.
4. Ferling (2004), pp. 140–142.
5. Ibid., pp. 151–154.
6. Quoted in Weisberger (2000), p. 259.
7. Quoted in Ferling (2004), p. 180.
8. Jefferson to James Monroe, February 15, 1801. *The Papers of Thomas Jefferson Digital Edition*, 2008. Several excellent accounts of the election of 1800 exist. See, for example: Weisberger (2000), Ferling (2004), and Ackerman (2007).
9. Jefferson to James Madison, February 17, 1801.
10. *American Sphinx* by Joseph Ellis (2007), *Thomas Jefferson: A Strange Case of Mistaken Identify* by Alf Mapp, Jr. (1987), and *The Inner Jefferson*, by Andrew Burstein (1995).
11. For details on Jefferson's inauguration, see The *National Intelligencer's* account, published March 6, 1801, as well as The Papers of Thomas Jefferson, First Inaugural Address, at http://www.princeton.edu/~tjpapers /inaugural/inednote.html (January 9, 2012). While some accused Adams of snubbing Jefferson, it is also likely he left at 4 a.m. because that's when the stage departed.
12. Dunn (2004), p. 236.
13. Ibid., p. 236.
14. Weisberger (2000), p. 30.
15. An Editorial Note to the three versions of the Inaugural Address speculates that this, the third draft, was the speaking copy. See http://www.princeton .edu/`tjpapers/inaugural.inednote.html (January 9, 2012).
16. Weisberger (2000), p. 279.
17. Horn et al. (2002), p. 32.
18. Jefferson to James Monroe, March 7, 1801. *The Papers of Thomas Jefferson Digital Edition*, 2008.
19. Jefferson to Thomas Jefferson Smith, February 21, 1825, from Padover (1956), p. 337. Jefferson did not avoid conflict, as evident in his revolutionary writings. He just preferred to engage in it indirectly, often through proxies, leaving himself free to maintain the image and ease of a calm, private life.
20. Jefferson to Robert Morris, March 6, 1801. *The Papers of Thomas Jefferson Digital Edition*, 2008.
21. Jefferson to James Madison, September 6, 1789.
22. Jefferson to William Bache, February 2, 1800. *The Papers of Thomas Jefferson Digital Edition*, 2008.
23. Jefferson to Spencer Roane, September 6, 1819, http://teachingamerican history.org/library/index.asp?document=2192 (January 9, 2012).
24. Ferling (2004), p. 170.
25. Ackerman (2007).
26. Jefferson to Joseph Priestley, March 21, 1801. *The Papers of Thomas Jefferson Digital Edition*, 2008.

27. Jefferson to John Adams, April 8, 1816.
28. Horn et al., (2002), p. 39.
29. Browne (2003) and T. Jefferson to Henry Lee, May 8, 1825.
30. Jefferson to Elbridge Gerry, January 26, 1799. *The Papers of Thomas Jefferson Digital Edition*, 2008.
31. Jefferson to John Wise, February 12, 1798. *The Papers of Thomas Jefferson Digital Edition*, 2008.
32. Jefferson to John Taylor, June 4, 1798. *The Papers of Thomas Jefferson Digital Edition*, 2008.
33. Jefferson to Henry Knox, March 27, 1801. *The Papers of Thomas Jefferson Digital Edition*, 2008.
34. Jefferson to James Monroe, March 7, 1801. *The Papers of Thomas Jefferson Digital Edition*, 2008.
35. Onuf and Sadosky (2002), p. 50.
36. Ibid., p. 77.
37. Browne (2003), p. 34.
38. Quoted in Ellis (2007), p. 54.
39. The portico of the Rotunda of Jefferson's University of Virginia, which he built in his retirement years, also faces southwest. Thanks to Dr. James Sofka, Jefferson Scholar, for this point.
40. Wilson(1989), p. 56.
41. Jefferson to Robert Skipwith, August 3, 1771.
42. For Jefferson's *Literary Commonplace Book*, see Wilson (1989).
43. Malone (1948), p. 60.
44. Malone(1948)., p. 73.
45. T. Jefferson to Robert Skipwith, August 3, 1771, *The Papers of Thomas Jefferson Digital Edition*, 2008.
46. Bailey (2007), p. 132.
47. Jefferson to William C. Jarvis, September 28, 1820. See http://wiki.monticello.org/mediawiki/index.php/Quotations_on_Education (January 9, 2012).
48. Unlike today, in Jefferson's time the oath was administered first, followed by the address.
49. For details of the events, see The Papers of Thomas Jefferson, First Inaugural Address, Editorial Note at: http://www.princeton.edu/`tjpapers/inaugural.inednote.html (January 9, 2012). For the size of the common table, see Malone (1970), p. 492.
50. Cunningham (2001), pp. 17–20 and *The Papers of Thomas Jefferson*, First Inaugural Address, Editorial Note, p. 3.
51. Cunningham (2001), p. 41.
52. Dunn (2004), pp. 225, 230.
53. McDonald (1976), p. 38.
54. Dunn (2004), p. 235. The Bill of Rights to the Constitution protected the press against federal, not state, restrictions.
55. Ackerman (2007), p. 204.
56. Weisberger (2000), p. 288.
57. McDonald (1976), p. 34.

58. Weisberger (2000), p. 290.
59. Ibid., pp. 297–298.
60. John Adams to James Lloyd, February 6, 1815, quoted in Dunn (2004), p. 230.
61. Jefferson to William Duane, March 28, 1811. Quoted in Mayer (1994) p. 126.
62. Jefferson to Spencer Roane, September 6, 1819, http://teachingamerican history.org/library/index.asp?document=2192 (January 9, 2012).
63. Malone (1970), p. 28.
64. Jefferson to John Colvin, September 20, 1810. See http://press-pubs.uchicago .edu/founders/documents/a2_3s8.html (January 9, 2012).
65. See Wood (2006) for a discussion of how the revolutionary generation hastened the demise of the rule by gentlemen.
66. Quoted in Golden and Golden (2002), p. 280. Toffel (2005) speculates that this story may have been apocryphal, p. 8, 194 footnote.

3 Healing the Wounds of Civil War: Lincoln's Second Inaugural

1. Nicolay (1949), pp. 224–225.
2. White (2002), pp. 29–32.
3. Collected Works of Abraham Lincoln (1953), Vol. 7, p. 514.
4. McPherson (1988), p. 742.
5. Brooks (1958), p. 211.
6. White (2002), p. 39.
7. Brooks (1958), p. 210.
8. Ibid., p. 212.
9. New York Herald, March 5, 1865, p. 1.
10. Letter from Benjamin Brown French to his son, April 24, 1865. See http:// memory.loc.gov/cgi-bin/query/r?ammem/pin:@field(NUMBER+pin2205)) (January 9, 2012)
11. For an excellent analysis of the text and language of the Second Inaugural, see White (2002).
12. Description by George Haven Putnam, quoted in Donald (1995), p. 238.
13. New York Herald, March 5, 1865, p. 1.
14. Brooks (1958), p. 213.
15. Ibid.
16. Quoted in Donald (1995), p. 98.
17. England had considered recognizing the Confederacy and thus might wonder what the United States would do with its massive, battle-tested army and navy after the war. While it seems unthinkable today, the young United States had tried to take Canada during the Revolution and the War of 1812.
18. Wilson (2006), p. 263.
19. White (2002), pp. 52–54.

20. See, especially, Collins and Porras (1994) for a discussion of the importance of "big, hairy, audacious goals" to leadership success.
21. Douglas Wilson speculates that Lincoln may have written this last paragraph first. From a leadership standpoint, having the end in mind must have been essential to Lincoln's calculation of how he would get his audience prepared for his (most likely unwelcome) challenge. See Wilson (2006), p. 273.
22. Collected Works of Abraham Lincoln, letter to Cuthbert Bullitt, New Orleans, LA, July 28, 1862.
23. White (2002), pp. 170–171.
24. Quoted in Donald (1995), p. 102.
25. This analysis contains many conclusions also reached by White (2002). His insightful analysis of the second inaugural is perhaps the most thorough ever completed, though his focus is not primarily on Lincoln as leader.
26. Collected Works of Abraham Lincoln, Vol. 4, p. 60.
27. John Locke Scripps to William Herndon, June 24, 1865, Herndon-Weik Collection, Library of Congress, as quoted in Donald (1995), p. 19.
28. William Herndon and Jesse Weik, Herndon's Life of Lincoln, ed. Paul M. Angle (Cleveland: World Publishing, 1949 (1930), p. 473. Quoted in Wilson (1998).
29. Quoted in Donald (1995), p. 541.
30. Gardner (1995) offers a well-crafted set of examples of the power of story to persuade others to act.
31. Miller (2008) offers a powerful portrayal of Lincoln as statesman, driven by the duty inherent in his solemn oath.
32. Quoted in White (2002), p. 210.
33. Lincoln's capacity for learning as a result of the Civil War is captured nicely in Tackach (2002). See pp. 154–155.
34. Quoted in Miller (2002), p. 44.
35. John Hanks, interview with William H. Herndon, September 15, 1865, Herndon's Informants, p. 121 (quoted in Wilson (1998)).
36. Sarah Bush Johnston Lincoln, William H. Herndon interview, September 8, 1865, Herndon's Informants, p. 107 (quoted in Wilson (1998)).
37. Collected Works of Abraham Lincoln, Vol 7, p. 281.
38. Quoted in Donald (1995), p. 134.
39. Collected Works of Abraham Lincoln, Speech at Peoria, Illinois, October 16, 1854.
40. Quoted in Donald (1995), p. 270.
41. For an excellent treatment of Lincoln's views on slavery and blacks, see What Lincoln Believed by Michael Lind (2004). For example, in his debate with Stephen Douglas on September 18, 1858, Lincoln said: "I am not, nor ever have been, in favor of bringing about in any way the social and political equality of the white and black races...I am not nor ever have been in favor of making voters or jurors of negroes, nor of qualifying them to hold office, nor to intermarry with white people." Source: Collected Works of Abraham Lincoln, Vol 3, p. 145.

42. Wilson (2006, p. 275) makes the point as well—that the last paragraph of the address is a response to this question, anticipated at the end of the third paragraph.

43. Hansen (2004) focuses on the question of human agency in the Second Inaugural. "the Second Inaugural centers on the question of who has done what leading to the Civil War and what can now be done... Although all inaugurals seek to outline what should be done in the future, Lincoln's Second Inaugural is perhaps unique in that it asks us to consider who has acted as an agent and who can act as an agent in the past, present, and future, and does so in the smallest details of the text." (p. 231).

44. Quoted in Miller (2002), p. 255.

45. Burns (1978).

46. Heifetz (1994).

47. Wills (1999).

48. Lind (2004) makes the point that Lincoln may deserve the title of Great Democrat, not Great Emancipator, for he was reluctantly brought to championing abolition but was always steadfast in preserving the Union to maintain the idea of democracy as viable in a world where few such experiments existed and most had failed. See, especially, pp. 272 (from which this quote is taken)–284.

49. Brooks (1998), pp. 167–169.

50. Letter to Thurlow Weed, March 15, 1865.

51. The source is Elizabeth Keckley, Behind the Scenes, pp. 156–161 (cited from: http://www.mrlincolnswhitehouse.org/inside.asp?ID=38&subjectID=2) (January 9, 2012). It seems corroborated by Frederick Douglass's account, to be described later.

52. Brooks (1958), p. 213.

53. New York Herald, March 5, 1865, p. 1.

54. Allen Thorndike Rice, editor, Reminiscences of Abraham Lincoln by Distinguished Men of His Time, pp. 191–193 (cited from: http://www.mrlincolnswhitehouse.org/inside.asp?ID=38&subjectID=2) (January 9, 2012).

55. On March 27, 1865, Lincoln issued General Order No. 50, which stated that at noon on April 14, 1865, the same U.S. flag that flew over Ft. Sumter when it was evacuated on April 14, 1861 would be raised at the fort again. Less than 12 hours after this symbolic end to the war, Lincoln would lay mortally wounded.

56. Harper's Weekly, March 18, 1865.

57. Boston Daily Evening Transcript, March 6, 1865, p. 2.

58. The Tribune's view is cited in Harper's Weekly, March 18, 1865.

59. New York Herald, March 5, 1865, p. 2.

60. Ibid.

61. These and the following other press accounts are taken from a short summary, titled "Context Preview for Abraham Lincoln's 'Second Inaugural Address,'" which was prepared for a communications course at the University of Washington. The original was posted with no designation of author (but is no longer posted) at: http://www.com.washington.edu/program/courses/com435/contextpreviews/Lincoln%202nd%20Inaug%20cp.doc.

62. Ibid.
63. Miller (2008), p. 368.
64. On March 2, 1861, at the request of outgoing President Buchanan, Congress enacted a Thirteenth Amendment that would prevent any amendment from interfering with the "domestic institutions" of any state. While sent to the states for ratification, this version of a Thirteenth Amendment died with the start of the war.
65. American Presidency Project, Executive Order of February 13, 1865, http://www.presidency.ucsb.edu (January 9, 2012).
66. Donald (1995), p. 572.
67. Ibid., p. 574.
68. Ward (1990).
69. Tarbell, Ida M., "Lincoln's Last Day on Earth," *The New York Times*, December 27, 1908.
70. Winik (2001).
71. Wills (1999).

4   The Struggle for Woman Suffrage: The Trial of Susan B. Anthony

1. Descriptions quoted from the *New York World* (1866) and the Adrian, Michigan *Times and Expositor* (1870). See, Sherr (1995), p. 147.
2. Partly to attract women to a territory overbalanced with men, and partly because they doubted it would be enacted, the territorial legislature passed an act enfranchising women. To their surprise, the territorial governor signed it.
3. Before 1878, in most states criminal defendants were not permitted to testify in their own defense.
4. The phrases "woman's rights" and "woman suffrage" were used at the time, instead of our more common "women's rights." Since "man" was used to refer to all men, "woman" was used in the same way. "Woman" also signaled the individuality of each person. See, http://womenshistory.about.com/od/suffrageoverview/a/woman.htm (January 9, 2012).
5. Ward and Burns (1999), p. 42.
6. Sherr (1995), pp. xviii–xix, and Ward and Burns (1999), p. ix.
7. Harper (1899), p. 40.
8. Sherr (1995), p. xix.
9. Ward and Burns (1999), p. 38.
10. Quoted in Gordon (1997), p. 134.
11. Quoted in Harper (1899), p. 57.
12. Ibid., pp. 62–64.
13. Ibid., p. 77.
14. Ward and Burns (1999), p. 72.
15. Ibid., p. 77.
16. Griffith (1984), p. 74.
17. Harper (1899), p. 130.

18. Ibid., p. 152.
19. Ibid., p. 96.
20. Quoted in Sherr (1995), p. 20.
21. Quoted in Griffith (1984), p. 91.
22. Harper (1899), p. 166.
23. Letter to Lydia Mott, quoted in Harper (1899), p. 172.
24. Harper (1899), pp. 185.
25. Ward and Burns (1999), pp. 103–104.
26. Sherr (1995), p. 69.
27. Stanton campaigned in the state as well. Negro suffrage failed by nearly the same 3–1 margin.
28. Ward and Burns (1999), p. 110.
29. Quoted in Harper (1899), p. 243.
30. Quoted in Gordon (2000), p. 399.
31. Sherr (1995), p. 66.
32. Ibid., p. 48. Singularity of focus can warp understanding, and Anthony was not immune. When Frederick Douglass remarried in 1884 (his first wife had died), and controversy erupted because his new wife was white and twenty years younger, Stanton publicly congratulated him, but Anthony would not. She told Stanton that such a public step "has no place in our platform...Your sympathy has run away with your judgment." (Sherr (1995), p. 31). Anthony would also allow black women to be barred from launching chapters of the National American Woman Suffrage Association for fear of losing the political support of whites.
33. Sherr (1995), p. 209.
34. Quoted in Harper (1899), p. 257.
35. Sherr (1995), p. 240.
36. Ibid., p. 241.
37. Sherr (1995), p. 90.
38. Gordon (2000), pp. 101–102.
39. Dorr (2008), p. 243.
40. Sherr (1995), p. 120.
41. Dorr (2008), pp. 194–195.
42. Sherr (1995), pp. 227–228.
43. Ibid., p. 94.
44. Ibid., pp. 95.
45. Ibid., p. 202.
46. Woodhull was one of the first female brokers on Wall Street, used that fortune to start a newspaper and, in 1872, make an aborted run for president as head of a new political party. Anthony strongly objected to the unauthorized use of her name in this effort, believing that a new party would be useless. In May 1872, Woodhull tried to take the stage at the New York convention of the National Woman Suffrage Association to push her candidacy. Incensed, Anthony turned off the lights to force her off the stage.
47. Harper (1899), p. 284.
48. Gordon (2005), p. 57. http://www.fjc.gov/history/docs/susanbanthony.pdf (January 9, 2012)

49. Harper (1899), p. 315.
50. Gordon (2000), p. 548.
51. Dorr (2008), p. 254.
52. A full account of Anthony's voting and trial, from which much of this account is taken, can be found at: http://www.law.umkc.edu/faculty /projects/ftrials/anthony/sbahome.html (January 9, 2012).
53. Letter to Elizabeth Cady Stanton, November 5, 1872 (Gordon, 2005, p. 61).
54. Linder (2001), unpaginated: http://www.law.umkc.edu/faculty/projects /ftrials/anthony/sbaaccount.html (January 9, 2012).
55. She was charged with violating federal law in voting for an at-large member of Congress and a member from her own district.
56. Letter to Hon, B. F. Butler, April 27, 1873, as found in The Trail of Susan B. Anthony: A 100-Year Chronology, at: http://www.law.umkc.edu/faculty /projects/ftrials/anthony/trialrecord.html (January 9, 2012).
57. Most trials in the nineteenth century did not have official transcripts, though segments of a transcript from Anthony's trial were found recently in a home in Rochester. However, no account of her speech is included in these records. There were three accounts of Anthony's remarks. The one used here is the longest and is hers.
58. Ward and Burns (1999), p. 21.
59. Sherr (1995), p. 135.
60. Ibid. p. 131.
61. Earl Warren, speech, 1962, New Haven, Connecticut, quoted in: Gilman, Stuart C., Joseph, Joshua, and Raven. Cheryl L., "Conflicts of Interest; Balancing Appearances, Intentions and Values," Ethics Resource Center, Washington, DC (2002).
62. In contrast, the three inspectors were jailed in early 1874 for refusing to pay their fines. On learning this, Anthony arranged for their bail. They were pardoned shortly thereafter by President Grant.
63. Gordon (2000), p. 617. Anthony here links her case to the infamous decision in *Dred Scott v. Sanford* by Justice Taney, which held that blacks were not citizens and thus not protected by the Constitution.
64. Undeterred, Anthony voted again in the March 4, 1873 city election, without incident. When she tried to vote the next November, Sylvester Lewis (the man whose complaint led to her earlier arrest) told her that her name had been removed from the registration rolls.
65. Harper (1899), p. 337.
66. Quoted in Ward and Burns (1999), p. 148.
67. Quoted in Harper (1899), p. 335.
68. Quoted in Gordon (2005), p. 36. In time, Hunt's behavior would produce legislation (that Grant vetoed) allowing appeal of a federal criminal conviction to the Supreme Court as well as two court rulings. The first, in a circuit court case in 1882, ruled that Hunt's decision was a clear violation of the guarantee of trial by jury. The second, by the Supreme Court in 1895 (*Sparf et al. v. United States*) held that federal courts could not direct a jury to return a guilty verdict in a criminal trial (Gordon (2005), p. 19).
69. Harper (1899), p. 342.

70. See *Minor v. Happersett* at: http://caselaw.lp.findlaw.com/scripts/getcase
    .pl?navby=case&court=us&vol=88&invol=162 (Janaury 9, 2012).
71. Gordon (2000), p. 145.
72. Quoted in Ward and Burns (1999), p. 150.
73. Ferry, as President Pro Tem of the Senate, became next in line of succession
    when Vice President Henry Wilson died on November 22, 1875.
74. Quoted in Sherr (1995), pp. 289–290.
75. Ward and Burns (1999), p. 172.
76. Sherr (1995), pp. 321–322.
77. Dorr (2008), pp. 332–333.
78. Ibid. p. 337.
79. Ibid., p. 340.
80. Sherr (1995), p. 324.
81. Ward and Burns (1999), p. 212.

5   Saving Postwar Europe (and America): The Marshall Plan Speech

1. Smith, Robert E., "Harvard Hears of the Marshall Plan," *The Harvard Crimson Review* (May 4, 1962) p. 2.
2. Cray (1990), pp. 20–21.
3. Ibid., pp. 25–27.
4. Pogue Interview, Tape 3, Recorded March 6, 1957, George C. Marshall Foundation Research Library, pp. 108–109.
5. Cray (1990), p. 139.
6. *Report on the Army*, July 1, 1939—June 30, 1943, Biennial Reports of General George C. Marshall, Washington, DC: The Infantry Journal, 1943 and Uldrich (2005), p. 12.
7. In early 1945, Prime Minister Winston Churchill cabled British Field Marshal Henry "Jumbo" Wilson, Chief of the British Joint Staff Mission in Washington: "Pray give General Marshall my warmest congratulations...what a joy it must be to him to see how the armies called into being by his own genius have won immortal renown. He is the true 'organizer of victory.'" Pops (2009), p. 111.
8. *Sinews of Peace*, by Winston Churchill, delivered on March 5, 1956, at Westminster College, Fulton, Missouri. For the full text, go to: http://en.wikisource.org/wiki/Sinews_of_Peace. (January 9, 2012).
9. Behrman (2007), p. 27.
10. Stafford, Neal, *The Christian Science Monitor*, Box 157, Item 2, George C. Marshall Papers, The George C. Marshall Research Library, Lexington, Virginia.
11. Cray (1990), p. 588.
12. Pogue Interview, Tape 19, Recorded November 20, 1956, George C. Marshall Foundation Research Library, p. 562.
13. Cray (1990), p. 591.
14. Behrman (2007), p. 23 and Cray (1990), p. 29.

15. Behrman (2007), p. 39.
16. Jones (1955), pp. 223–224.
17. Fossedal (1993), p. 221.
18. Behrman (2007), p. 52.
19. Interview IV with Barry Price and Roy Foulke, October 30, 1952, p. 1. For a full text of the interview, go to: http://marshallfoundation.org/library /documents/Price_and_Foulke_1_000.pdf (January 12, 2012).
20. Pogue (1987), p. 209.
21. Smith, Robert E., "Harvard Hears of the Marshall Plan," *The Harvard Crimson Review* (May 4, 1962), p. 4.
22. John F. Kennedy School of Government, Case Number C14–82–480, *George Marshall*, p. 13.
23. China needed help too, but Marshall's strategic sense was that the European situation was far more threatening to the United States.
24. Pogue Interview, Tape 19, Recorded November 20, 1956, George C. Marshall Foundation Research Library, pp. 556–557.
25. Jones (1955), pp. 226–232.
26. Cray (1990), p. 415.
27. Pogue Interview, Tape 11, Recorded November 15, 1956, George C. Marshall Foundation Research Library, pp. 343–344.
28. Marshall (1946), p. 250.
29. Memorandum, May 23, 1947, Director, Policy Planning Staff to Under Secretary of State Acheson, U.S. Department of State, *Foreign Relations of the United States*, 1947, Volume III, Washington, DC: U.S. Government Printing Office. p. 225.
30. Ibid., p. 231.
31. Address by Mr. Bernard Baruch, George C. Marshall Day, Virginia Military Institute, May 15, 1951.
32. Marshall (1946), p. 143.
33. Memorandum, May 23, 1947, Director, Policy Planning Staff to Under Secretary of State Acheson, U.S. Department of State, *Foreign Relations of the United States*, 1947, Volume III, Washington, DC: U.S. Government Printing Office. p. 226.
34. Memorandum, May 27, 1947, Under Secretary of State for Economic Affairs, Will Clayton to Under Secretary Acheson, *Foreign Relations of the United States*, 1947, Volume III, Washington, DC: U.S. Government Printing Office. p. 232.
35. Heifetz (1994).
36. Behrman (2007), p. 74.
37. Memorandum Prepared by the Policy Planning Staff, July 21 (?), 1947, *Foreign Relations of the United States*, 1947, Volume III, Washington, DC: U.S. Government Printing Office. p. 335.
38. Quoted in Cray (1990), p. 73.
39. Pogue Interview, Tape 19, Recorded November 20, 1956, George C. Marshall Foundation Research Library, p. 558.
40. Ibid., p. 558.
41. Jones (1955), pp. 252–253.

42. Interview V with Barry Price and Roy Foulke, February 18, 1953, p. 1. For a full text of the interview, go to: http://marshallfoundation.org/library /documents/Price_and_Foulke_2_000.pdf. (January 9, 2012).

43. Memorandum, May 27, 1947, Under Secretary of State for Economic Affairs, Will Clayton to Under Secretary Acheson, *Foreign Relations of the United States,* 1947, Volume III, Washington, DC: U.S. Government Printing Office., p. 231.

44. Interview IV with Barry Price and Roy Foulke, October 30, 1952, p. 3. For a full text of the interview, go to: http://marshallfoundation.org/library /documents/Price_and_Foulke_1_000.pdf (January 9, 2012).

45. Pogue Interview, Tape 19, Recorded November 20, 1956, George C. Marshall Foundation Research Library, pp. 560.

46. Cray (1990), p. 611.

47. Jones (1955), p. 233.

48. Ibid., p. 106.

49. Marshall (1946), p. 9.

50. Cray (1990), p. 106.

51. Ibid., p. 114.

52. Acheson, Dean, "Homage to General Marshall," *The Reporter,* November 26, 1959.

53. Speech at Princeton University, February 22, 1947.

54. Pogue Interview, Tape 18, Recorded November 19, 1956, George C. Marshall Foundation Research Library, p. 527.

55. Behrman (2007), pp. 73–74.

56. "BBC Correspondent Leonard Miall and the Marshall Plan Speech: An Interview," George C. Marshall Foundation, September 19, 1977. For the full text, go to: www.marshallfoundation.org/library/oral_histories_miall _interview.html (January 9, 2012).

57. *New York Times,* April 2, 1949, p. 4.

58. BBC Coorespondent Leonard Miall and the Marshall Plan Speech: An Interview," George C. Marshall Foundation, September 19, 1977. For the full text, go to: www.marshallfoundation.org/library/oral_histories_miall _interview.html (January 9, 2012).

59. Behrman (2007), p. 80.

60. Isaacson and Thomas (1986), p. 424. "Politicians were a race that Marshall got along with but did not understand," Chip Bohlen recalled." Marshall resisted at first but then got very close to Vandenberg. "We could not have gotten much closer unless I sat in Vandenberg's lap or he sat in mine," Marshall recalled.

61. Interview IV with Barry Price and Roy Foulke, October 30, 1952, p. 2. For a full text of the interview, go to: http://marshallfoundation.org/library /documents/Price_and_Foulke_1_000.pdf (January 9, 2012).

62. Behrman (2007), p. 74.

63. Ibid., p. 76.

64. Ibid., p. 101.

65. *The Gallup Poll* (1972), p. 683.

66. Pogue Interview, Tape 19, Recorded November 20, 1956, George C. Marshall Foundation Research Library, p. 556.
67. Behrman (2007), p. 122.
68. "The Marshall Plan: Origins and Implementation," U.S. Department of State, Washington, DC, June 1982, p. 7.
69. Behrman (2007), pp. 115–116.
70. For an account of the committee, see, Bonds (2002), Chapter 9.
71. "European Recovery Program, Hearings Before the Committee on Foreign Relations, United States Senate," January 8, 1947.
72. Presentation Speech by Carl Joachim Hambro, The Nobel Peace Prize 1953 (for the full text see, http://nobelprize.org/nobel_prizes/peace /laureates/1953/press.html (January 9, 2012).
73. Behrman (2007), p. 333.
74. "The Marshall Plan: Origins and Implementation," U.S. Department of State, Washington, DC, June 1982, p. 16.
75. Behrman (2007), p. 226
76. "Government's Greatest Achievements of the Past Half-Century" can be found at: http://www.brookings.edu/papers/2000/11governance_light.aspx. (January 9, 2012).
77. Quoted in Behrman (2007), p. 337.
78. Ibid., p. 334.
79. Time, "The Year of Decision," January 5, 1948.
80. Gilbert (2005), p. 389.
81. "Statement by the Former President of the United States, Harry S. Truman," October 20, 1959, courtesy of the George C. Marshall Foundation Research Library, Lexington, Virginia.
82. Address at Trinity College, Hartford, Connecticut, June 15, 1941, pp. 5–6. Courtesy of the George C. Marshall Foundation Research Library, Lexington, Virginia.
83. Nobel Lecture, December 11, 1953, the Nobel Peace Prize, George C. Marshall. For the full text go to: http://nobelprize.org/nobel_prizes/peace /laureates/1953/marshall-lecture.html. (January 9, 2012).

6   The Movement in Crisis: King's Letter from Birmingham Jail

1. Carson (1998), p. 182.
2. Branch (1988), p. 728.
3. King (1969), p. 222.
4. Carson (1998), p. 5.
5. When he was five, his father changed both their names to "Martin" upon return from a trip to the Holy Land. "Martin Luther" would be a namesake the younger King would say it took years to earn.
6. Letter to Miss Joan Thatcher, August 7, 1959, quoted in Warren (2001), p. 29.

7. Carson (1998), p. 7.
8. Ibid. p. 10.
9. King (1958), p. 7.
10. Application for Admission, February 1948.
11. King (1958), pp. 7–8.
12. Ibid., p. 8.
13. The degree to which *Brown* actually propelled the civil rights movement can still be debated. King certainly saw it as creating the necessary groundwork on which to base demands for more broad-based change. Gerald Rosenberg, in *The Hollow Hope* (2008) argues that the court strategy realized less change than King's approach, primarily because the Court is more restrained by the Constitution and its place in the federal system.
14. King (1958), pp. 47–48.
15. Martin Luther King Jr. Speech at the Holt Street Baptist Church, December 5, 1955. (for full text, go to:http://www.stanford.edu/group/King/papers /vol3/551205.004-MIA_Mass_Meeting_at_Holt_Street_Baptist_Church .htm (January 10, 2012).
16. Branch (1988), p. 185.
17. The term "Negro" was far more commonly used than "Black" until the mid-1960s. It is used in this chapter whenever doing so would be more faithful to King's work and words.
18. King (1963), p. 5.
19. For a vivid account of the early days of the ACMHR, see, Eskew (1997), pp. 121–151.
20. King (1958), p. xxx.
21. For the full text of King's speech, go to: http://www.stanford.edu/group /King/papers/vol4/570517.004-Give_Us_the_Ballot.htm (January 10, 2012).
22. King (1969), p. 160.
23. Quoted in Garrow (1986), pp. 84–85.
24. Branch (1988), p. 195.
25. Historians have documented that Mayor Asa Kelley secretly arranged to have King's fine paid to make sure he could not continue to keep Albany in the headlines. See, Garrow (1986), p. 204.
26. Quoted in Branch (1988), p. 557.
27. Ibid., p. 631.
28. Ibid.,
29. King (1958), p. 71.
30. See his article in *Christian Century*, No. 74, February 6, 1957 (pp. 165–167 in Washington (1986)).
31. Carson (1998), p. 26.
32. Quoted in Garrow (1986), p. 47.
33. Quoted in Branch (1988), p. 83.
34. "Man of the Year: Martin Luther King Jr., Never Again Where He Was," *Time*, January 3, 1964.
35. Carson (1998), p. 168.

36. Warren (2001), p. 22.
37. Quoted in Branch (1988), p. 632.
38. Bass (2001), p. 98.
39. King (1963), p. 49.
40. Eskew (1997), p. 11.
41. Ibid., p. 12.
42. Bass (2001), p. 87.
43. "Fear and Hatred Grip Birmingham," by Harrison E. Salisbury, *The New York Times*, April 12, 1960.
44. Branch (1988), p. 650.
45. King (1969), p. 219.
46. King (1963), p. 56.
47. *Lest We Forget*, Volume 2, Birmingham, Alabama Mass Meeting, 1963, Folkways Records.
48. Eskew (1997), p. 230.
49. Garrow (1986), p. 240.
50. Branch (1988), p. 704.
51. Quoted in Branch (1988), p. 711 and *The Washington Post*, Friday, April 12, 1963, p. A6.
52. Branch (1988), p. 711.
53. King (1969), p. 88.
54. Quoted in Eskew (1997), p. 240.
55. Quoted in Branch (1988), pp. 729–730.
56. Eskew (1997), p. 240.
57. Carson (1998), p. 183 and Branch (1988), pp. 729–730.
58. Bass (2001), p. 111.
59. Eskew (1997), p. 242.
60. Branch (1988), p. 735.
61. Ibid., p. 736.
62. *The Washington Post*, Sunday, April 14, Outlook, p. E6.
63. Bass (2001), p. 117.
64. Ibid., p. 116.
65. King (1958), p. 204.
66. Eskew (1997), p. 244.
67. Bass (2001), pp. 135–136. Interestingly, Wyatt Walker did not maintain any of King's original notes or revisions, despite what would seem compelling historical reasons to do so.
68. Quoted in King (1969), p. 80.
69. King (1969), p. 80.
70. Quoted in Rieder (2008), p. 14.
71. Quoted in Garrow (1986), p. 35.
72. King (1969), p. 6.
73. Branch (1988), p. 76.
74. Rieder (2008), p. 301.
75. As Bass (2001, p. 24) notes, "As King fasted that Good Friday before his march to jail, the white religious leaders ate lunch. The black ministers

stayed at the only lodging available to them, the Gaston Motel; the white clergy met at the finest hotel in Birmingham" to compose their letter.

76. King drew this statement from one he attributed to Abraham Lincoln: "As Lincoln said, 'If I answered all criticism, I'd have time for nothing else.'" See *Playboy* interview, 1965, as included in Washington (1986), p. 348.
77. http://en.wikipedia.org/wiki/Justice_delayed_is_justice_denied(January 10, 2012).
78. Ahmann (1963), pp. 155–169.
79. French and Raven (1959).
80. Thomas Jefferson to Henry Lee, May 8, 1825 (http://edsitement.neh.gov/view_lesson_plan.asp?id=723) (January 10, 2012).
81. In addition to drawing from the Bible, Martin Buber, Paul Tillich, Thomas Aquinas, Paul, Jefferson, Lincoln, Earl Warren and W. E. B. Dubois, King also drew from his own prior work, especially: (a) an Address delivered to the annual meeting of the Fellowship of the Concerned, Nov 16, 1961 and printed in *New South* in December 1961, (b) an early sermon titled "Mental and Spiritual Slavery" and later retitled "Transformed Nonconformist,"(c) and his speech on "A Challenge to the Churches and Synagogues in 1962 (see Ahmann (1963)).
82. John Adams to Hezekiah Niles, February 13, 1818, http://en.wikiquote.org/wiki/John_Adams#What_do_we_mean_by_the_American_Revolution.3F_.281818.29 (January 10, 2012).
83. *Liberation*, April 1956 (quoted in Washington (1986), p. 75).
84. King (1958), p. 24.
85. Quoted in Rieder (2008), p. 221.
86. King (1968), p. 44.
87. Eskew (1997), p. 255.
88. Branch (1988), pp. 754–755.
89. Carson (1998), pp. 207–208.
90. Eskew (1997), p. 268.
91. Garrow (1986), p. 251.
92. Branch (1988), p. 774.
93. Ibid. p. 777.
94. Quoted in Eskew (1997), p. 292.
95. Branch (1988), p. 791.
96. Eskew (1997), p. 293.
97. See King (1969), p. 234, Branch (1988), pp. 804–805, 823–825, 856, King (1963), p. 144, *Time*, January 3, 1964.
98. Gallup (1972), pp. 1812, 1842.
99. Bass (2001), pp. 135–144.
100. Ibid., p. 176.
101. Ibid., p. 167.
102. Ibid., p. 226.
103. Ibid., p. 183.
104. Ibid., pp. 190, 193.
105. Ibid., p. 213.

106. Ibid., p. 206.
107. Ibid., pp. 231–232.

7   Constitutional Crisis: Ford Assumes the Presidency and Pardons Nixon

1. Details of the president's schedule are courtesy of the Gerald Ford Presidential Library in Ann Arbor, Michigan.
2. *The Washington Post*, September 8, 1974, p. A3.
3. *The Washington Post*, September 8, 1974, p. A1.
4. Cannon (1994), pp. 13–15.
5. Ibid., p. 38.
6. Ford (1979), p. 62.
7. Cannon (1994), p. 64.
8. Ibid., p. 70.
9. Ibid., p. 75.
10. Ibid., p. 205.
11. Hartmann (1980), p. 48.
12. Ibid., p. 59.
13. Cannon (1994), p. 152.
14. Ibid., p. 159.
15. Hartmann (1980), p. 47.
16. "Remarks of Gerald R. Ford After Taking the Oath of Office as Vice President," December 6, 1973.
17. DeFrank (2007), p. 3.
18. Ford (1979), pp. 5–6.
19. Ibid., p. 13.
20. The National Election Studies, conducted every two years since the late 1950s, routinely ask "To what extent do you trust the government in Washington to do the right thing?" In 1964, the percentage of the public saying "just about always" or "most of the time" was 76 percent. By 1970, it was 53 percent and by 1976, it was 33 percent. It has rarely gotten much above 30 percent ever since.
21. Mieczkowski (2005), p. 99.
22. Ibid., p. 102.
23. *Facts on File* (1974), New York: Facts on File Inc, pp. 644–645.
24. Ford (1979), p. 154.
25. Ibid., pp. 39–40.
26. The reference to Jefferson comes from a 1787 letter to James Madison: "Educate and inform the whole mass of the people. Enable them to see that it is their interest to preserve peace and order, and they will preserve them. And it requires no very high degree of education to convince them of this. They are the only sure reliance for the preservation of our liberty." The reference to Lincoln comes from his own First Inaugural: "Why should there

not be a patient confidence in the ultimate justice of the people? Is there any
better or equal hope in the world?"

27. Gardner (1995).
28. Hartmann (1980), p. 164.
29. Bolman and Deal (2008) argue that leaders must understand and work
    in four "frames" to lead effectively. These include the structural, human
    resource, political and symbolic.
30. Ford (1979), p. 30.
31. Cannon (1994), pp. 347–348.
32. Ford (1979), p. 126.
33. Ibid., p. 127.
34. Ibid., p. 204.
35. Hartmann (1980), p. 180.
36. "Remarks of the President Upon Appointment of J. F. terHorst as Press
    Secretary to the President," The Briefing Room, August 9, 1974, 1:04 p.m.
37. Ford (1979), p. 157.
38. Hartmann (1980), p. 181.
39. Ibid., pp. 181–182.
40. Ibid., pp. 238–239.
41. Werth (2006), p. 254.
42. "Address to a Joint Session of the Congress," August 12, 1974. For the
    full text, see: http://www.presidency.ucsb.edu/ws/index.php?pid=4694#
    axzz1ju2noudY (January 19, 2012).
43. Hartmann (1980), p. 233.
44. Werth (2006), p. 149.
45. Mieczkowski (2005), p. 29.
46. Ford signed a proclamation on September 16, 1974, announcing "A Program
    for the Return of Vietnam-Era Draft Evaders and Military Deserters."
    While some claim to see in this effort a political calculation that a Nixon
    pardon would be more acceptable if accompanied by a "pardon" of sorts
    for draft evaders and deserters, there is no compelling evidence that the lat-
    ter was crafted as political "cover" for the former.
47. Werth (2006), p. 128.
48. Ford (1979), p. 144 and Werth (2006), p. 159.
49. Werth (2006), p. 13.
50. Hartmann (1980), p. 166.
51. Ibid., p. 220.
52. Ibid., p. 350.
53. Ibid., p. 424.
54. Ibid., p. 384.
55. Mieczkowski (2005), p. 55.
56. "Hearings Before the Committee on Rules and Administration," U.S. Senate,
    First Session on the Nomination of Gerald R. Ford of Michigan to be Vice
    President of the United States, November 1, 5, 7, and 14, 1973, p. 124.
57. Werth (2006), p. 221.
58. President Gerald R. Ford's News Conference, August 28, 1974, transcript
    courtesy of the Gerald R. Ford Presidential Library.

59. Ford (1979), p. 159.
60. Werth (2006), p. 243.
61. Ford (1979), p. 161.
62. Kidder (1995).
63. In what appears to be a draft of Ford's pardon statement for Nixon, speech-writer Robert Hartmann included the line, "They tell me that to restore domestic tranquility it will be not enough simply to proclaim it, but that I must use every means I have to ensure it." Gerald R. Ford Presidential Library, Robert Hartmann Papers, Box 145.
64. Quoted in Schlesinger (2009), p. 260.
65. Ibid., p. 249.
66. Ibid., p. 246.
67. "President Gerald R. Ford's News Conference #2," East Room, the White House, September 16, 1974.
68. Ford (1979), p. 179. In 1998, when being interviewed by Bob Woodward, Ford pulled out a portion of the 1915 Supreme Court ruling in *Burdick vs. United States* that backed up the point that acceptance of a pardon is an admission of guilt. "I've got it in my wallet here because anytime anybody challenges me I pull it out," he said.
69. Hartmann (1980), p. 270.
70. Quoted in Werth (2006), p. 330.
71. Werth (2006), p. 313.
72. Ford (1979), p. 53.
73. Cannon (1994), p. 93.
74. Werth (2006), p. 315.
75. Ibid., p. 245.
76. Cannon (1994), pp. 383, 385.
77. *New York Times, The Washington Post*, September 9, 1974.
78. Gerald R. Ford Presidential Library, Hartmann Papers, Nixon Pardon, Box 145.
79. Quoted in Cannon (1994), p. 384.
80. Werth (2006), p. 331.
81. Harris Poll, September 13, 1974, taken from: Gerald R. Ford Presidential Library, Dean Burch Files, Box 4. Gerald Ford Library, Transmittal of Poll results by Richard Wirthlin, President, Decision Making Information, to Dean Burch, September 25, 1974.
82. *The Gallup Poll: Public Opinion 1972–1977, Volume One*, Wilmington, DE: Scholarly Resources Inc., 1978.
83. Memorandum to Mr. Hartmann from Anne Higgins, January 4, 1975, Gerald R. Ford Presidential Library, Robert Hartmann Papers, Box 145, and Mieczkowski (2005), p. 30.
84. Gerald R. Ford Presidential Library, Dean Burch Files, Memoranda-White House Staff, Box 4.
85. Rep. Duncan held his seat and continued to do so until 1988, when he died in office. His son, John Duncan, Jr., succeeded him and still serves in Congress.
86. Gerald R. Ford Presidential Library, Robert Hartmann Papers, Nixon Pardon, Box 145.

87. "A Bitter Spirit That Won't Die," by Vermont Royster, *The Wall Street Journal*, September 18, 1974.
88. Gerald R. Ford Presidential Library, John Marsh Files, Box 25, Letter to Jack Marsh dated September 16, 1974 from George Feldman.
89. "The Pardon of Nixon was Timely, Legal, Jaworski Believes," *The New York Times*, October 16, 1974.
90. *The Gallup Poll: Public Opinion 1972–1977, Volume Two*, Wilmington, DE: Scholarly Resources Inc., 1978. pp. 801, 899.
91. Cannon (1994), p. 414 and Ford (1978), p. 181.
92. See: http://www.fordlibrarymuseum.gov/images/avproj/pop-ups/P75131 -13a.html (January 11, 2012).
93. The Congressional Medal of Freedom was awarded the Betty Ford in the same ceremony. See: http://artandhistory.house.gov/house_history/gold Medal.aspx (January 11, 2012).
94. Remarks by Sen. Edward M. Kennedy, 2001 Profile in Courage Award, May 21, 2001.
95. *American Heritage*, Vol. 47, No. 8, December 1996, pp. 52–54.
96. "The definition of a statesman as opposed to a politician," Materials from the writing of *A Time to Heal*, 1977–1979, Gerald R. Ford Presidential Library.
97. Quoted in Mieczkowski (2005), p. 45.

8   Fostering Statesmanship in Public Life

1. Burns (1978) defines transformative leadership as: "leaders inducing followers to act for certain goals that represent the values and the motivations— the wants and needs, the aspirations and expectations—*of both leaders and followers.*" p. 19.
2. Spalding and Garrity (1996).
3. Plutarch, edited by Clough (2001), p. 215.
4. Collins (2001).
5. Pops (2009), p. 127.
6. Farquharson and Rutherford (2008), p. 62.
7. Kidder (2005).
8. Max Weber, *Politics as a Vocation*, http://www2.selu.edu/Academics /Faculty/jbell/weber.pdf , p. 27. (January 11, 2012).
9. Pops (2009), pp. 30, 81, 82.
10. For Marshall's full speech, go to: http://nobelprize.org/nobel_prizes/peace /laureates/1953/marshall-lecture.html (January 15, 2012).
11. Annual Message to Congress, December 1, 1862: "The dogmas of the quiet past are inadequate to the stormy present. The occasion is piled high with difficulty, and we must rise—with the occasion. As our case is new, so we must think anew, and act anew. We must disenthrall ourselves, and then we shall save our country." See http://showcase.netins.net/web/creative /lincoln/speeches/congress.htm (January 15, 2012).
12. Goldman (1980), p. 19.

13. Peters (1891), p. 194.
14. Tichy and Bennis (2007).
15. Goodwin (2006).
16. French and Raven (1959).
17. Meacham (2008), p. 288.
18. Gardner (1995).
19. Some acts of statesmanship may be taken in secret since public exposure could threaten success, especially in international affairs. In such cases, public persuasion may be unnecessary at the outset, though persuading a small set of intimates still is. For example, Kennedy could not tell the public (including the Europeans) that he had offered to remove missiles from Turkey if the Soviets removed missiles from Cuba. It would have made him appear to be trading off European for American security. However, we should be careful in too freely assuming that secrecy is required for "national security." Secrecy can be used as an excuse to clothe acts of questionable leadership in the mantle of statesmanship. Also, in many cases, acts of statesmanship taken in secret will later need to be made public in the process of seeking Congressional and/or citizen support for actions and resources essential to execution.
20. Gerald R. Ford, Materials for the writing of A Time to Heal, 1977–79, Gerald R. Ford Library, Ann Arbor, MI.
21. Ibid.
22. Malone (1948), p. 60.
23. Rohr (1998), p. 91.
24. Anderson and Escher (2010).
25. The Common Core State Standards Initiative is a state-led effort coordinated by the National Governors Association Center for Best Practices (NGA Center) and the Council of Chief State School Officers (CCSSO). See http://www.corestandards.org.
26. See: http://www.thepresidency.org/what-we-do/current-programs/national-consortium-for-character-based-leadership (Januay 15, 2012).
27. See: http://www.aspeninstitute.org/policy-work/business-society (January 15, 2012). The Giving Voice to Values program of the Aspen Institute focuses specifically on how to act, not just thin, ethically.
28. Cooper and Wright (1992), p. 13.
29. Rohr (1998) and Rohr (1989).
30. Anderson and Escher (2010).

Selected Bibliography

Ackerman, Bruce. 2007. *The Failure of the Founding Fathers: Jefferson, Marshall, and the Rise of Presidential Democracy.* Cambridge, MA: Belknap Press.

Ahmann, Matthew. Editor. 1963. *Race: Challenge to Religion*, Chicago, IL: H. Regency Co.

Anderson, Max and Peter Escher. 2010. *The MBA Oath: Setting a Higher Standard for Business Leaders.* New York, NY: Penguin.

Bailey, Jeremy. 2007. *Thomas Jefferson and Executive Power.* New York, NY: Cambridge University Press.

Bass, S. Jonathan. 2001. *Blessed are the Peacemakers: Martin Luther King, Jr. Eight White Religious Leaders, and the "Letter from Birmingham Jail."* Baton Rouge, LA: Louisiana State University Press.

Behrman, Greg. 2007. *The Most Noble Adventure: The Marshall Plan and the Time When America Helped Save Europe.* New York, NY: Free Press.

Bolman, Lee and Terrence Deal. 2008. *Reframing Organizations: Artistry, Choice and Leadership.* San Francisco, CA: Jossey-Bass Publishers.

Bonds, John Bledsoe. 2002. *Bipartisan Strategy: Selling the Marshall Plan.* Westport, CT: Prager.

Branch, Taylor. 1988. *Parting the Waters: America in the King Years 1964–1963.* New York, NY: Simon and Schuster Paperbacks.

Brooks, Noah. Edited with an Introduction by Herbert Mitgang. 1958. *Washington in Lincoln's Time.* New York, NY: Rinehart & Company.

Brooks, Noah. 1998. *Lincoln Observed: Civil War Dispatches of Noah Brooks.* Edited by Michael Burlingame. Baltimore, MD: The Johns Hopkins University Press.

Browne, Stephen Howard. 2003. *Jefferson's Call for Nationhood.* College Station, TX: Texas A&M University Press.

Burns, James McGregor. 1978. *Leadership.* New York, NY: Harper Collins.

Burstein, Andrew. 1996. *The Inner Jefferson: Portrait of a Grieving Optimist.* Charlottesville, VA: University Press of Virginia.

Cannon, James. 1994. *Time and Chance: Gerald Ford's Appointment with History.* Ann Arbor, MI: The University of Michigan Press.

Carson, Clayborne. 1998. *The Autobiography of Martin Luther King, Jr.* New York, NY: Grand Central Publishing.

Chinard, Gilbert. 1926. *The Commonplace Book of Thomas Jefferson.* Baltimore, MD: The Johns Hopkins Press.

Clough, Arthur Hugh. Editor. 2001. *Plutarch's Lives, Volume 1, The Dryden Translation.* New York, NY: The Modern Library.

Collected Works of Abraham Lincoln. This collection is digitized and can be located at: http://quod.lib.umich.edu/l/lincoln/. Accessed on February 29, 2012.

Collins, James and Jerry Porras. 1994. *Built to Last: Successful Habits of Visionary Companies.* New York, NY: HarperCollins.

Collins, James. 2001. *Good to Great: Why Some Companies Make the Leap...and Others Don't.* New York, NY: HarperBusiness.

Cooper, Terry L. and N. Dale Wright. 1992. *Exemplary Public Administrators: Character and Leadership in Government.* San Francisco, CA: Jossey-Bass.

Cray, Ed. 1990. *General of the Army George C. Marshall, Soldier and Statesman.* New York, NY: Cooper Square Press.

Cunningham, Noble. 2001. *The Inaugural Address of President Thomas Jefferson, 1801 and 1805.* Columbia, MO: University of Missouri Press.

DeFrank, Thomas M. 2007. *Write It When I'm Gone: Remarkable Off-the-Record Conversations with Gerald R. Ford.* New York, NY: G. P. Putnam's Sons.

Donald, David Herbert. 1995. *Lincoln.* New York, NY: Simon and Schuster.

Dorr, Rheta Childe. 2008. *Susan B. Anthony: The Woman Who Changed the Mind of a Nation.* Whitefish, NY: Kessinger Publishing.

Dunn, Susan. 2004. *Jefferson's Second Revolution: The Election Crisis of 1800 and the Triumph of Republicanism.* New York, NY: Houghton Mifflin.

Ellis, Joseph J. 2005. *His Excellency George Washington.* New York, NY: Vintage Books.

———. 2007. *American Sphinx: The Character of Thomas Jefferson.* New York, NY: Alfred A. Knopf.

Eskew, Glenn. 1997. *But for Birmingham: The Local and National Movements in the Civil Rights Struggle.* Chapel Hill, NC: University of North Carolina Press.

Facts on File, Vol. XXXIV. 1974. New York: Facts on File Inc.

Farquharson, A. S. L. and R. B. Rutherford. 2008. *The Meditations of Marcus Aurelius Antoninus.* New York, NY: Oxford University Press.

Ferling, John. 2004. *Adams vs. Jefferson: The Tumultuous Election of 1800.* New York, NY: Oxford University Press.

Flexner, James Thomas. 1965–1972. *George Washington, 4 Volumes.* Boston, MA: Little, Brown and Company.

Flexner, James Thomas. 1969. *Washington: The Indispensable Man.* Boston, MA: Little, Brown and Company.

Ford, Betty. 1978. *The Times of My Life.* New York, NY: Harper and Row.

Ford, Gerald R. 1979. *A Time to Heal: The Autobiography of Gerald R. Ford.* New York, NY: Harper and Row.

Fossedal, Gregory A. 1993. *Our Finest Hour: Will Clayton, the Marshall Plan, and the Triumph of Democracy.* Stanford, CA: Hoover Institution Press.

French, J. and B. Raven. 1959. *Studies on Social Power.* Ann Arbor, MI: University of Michigan Press.

Gardner, Howard. 1995. *Leading Minds: An Anatomy of Leadership*. New York, NY: Basic Books.

Garrow, David J. 1986. *Bearing the Cross: Martin Luther King, Jr., and the Southern Christian Leadership Conference*. New York, NY: Vintage Books.

———. 1989. *Martin Luther King, Jr.: Civil Rights Leader, Theologian, Orator*. Brooklyn, NY: Carlson Publishing.

Gilbert, Felix. 1961. *To the Farwell Address: Ideas of Early America Foreign Policy*. Princeton, NJ: Princeton University Press.

Gilbert, Martin. 2005. *Churchill and America*. New York, NY: Free Press.

Golden, James L. and Alan L. Golden. 2002. *Thomas Jefferson and the Rhetoric of Virtue*. Lanham, MD: Rowman & Littlefield.

Goldman, Robert. Editor. 1980. *Bureaucrats, Policy Analysts, Statesmen: Who Leads?* Washington, DC: American Enterprise Institute for Public Policy Research

Goodwin, Doris Kearns. 2006. *Team of Rivals: The Political Genius of Abraham Lincoln*. New York, NY: Simon & Schuster.

Gordon, Ann D. Editor. 1997. *In the School of Anti-Slavery, 1840–1866. Volume 1 of The Selected Papers of Elizabeth Cady Stanton and Susan B. Anthony*. New Brunswick, NJ: Rutgers University Press.

———. 2000. *Against an Aristocracy of Sex, 1866–1873. Volume 2 of The Selected Papers of Elizabeth Cady Stanton and Susan B. Anthony*. New Brunswick, NJ: Rutgers University Press.

———. Editor. 2005. *The Trial of Susan B. Anthony*. The Papers of Elizabeth Cady Stanton and Susan B. Anthony. Federal Judicial Center, Federal Judicial History Office.

Greenleaf, Robert. 1977. *Servant Leadership*. New York, NY: Paulist Press.

Griffith, Elizabeth. 1984. *In Her Own Right: The Life of Elizabeth Cady Stanton*. New York, NY: Oxford University Press.

Hansen, Andrew C. 2004. "Dimensions of Agency in Lincoln's Second Inaugural." *Philosophy and Rhetoric* 37 (3), pp. 223–254.

Harper, Ida Husted. 1899. *The Life and Work of Susan B. Anthony (Volume 1 and 2)—Including Public Addresses, Her Own Letters and Many from Her Contemporaries During Fifty Years*. Indianapolis, IN: The Bowen-Merrill Company.

Hartmann, Robert. 1980. *Palace Politics: An Inside Account of the Ford Years*. New York, NY: McGraw-Hill.

Heifetz, Ron. 1994. *Leadership Without Easy Answers*. Cambridge, MA: Harvard University Press.

Herndon, William H. and Jesse Weik. 1949. *Herndon's Life of Lincoln*. Edited by Paul M. Angle. Cleveland, OH: World Publishing.

Horn, James, Jan Ellen Lewis, and Peter Onuf. 2002. *The Revolution of 1800: Democracy, Race & the New Republic*. Charlottesville, VA: University of Virginia Press.

Isaacson, Walter and Evan Thomas. 1986. *The Wise Men: Six Friends and the World They Made: Acheson, Bohlen, Harriman, Kennan, Lovett, McCloy*. New York, NY: Simon and Schuster.

Jones, Joseph Marion. 1955. *The Fifteen Weeks: An Inside Account of the Genesis of the Marshall Plan.* New York, NY: Viking Press.

Kaufman, Burton Ira. 1969. *Washington's Farewell Address: The View from the 20th Century.* Chicago, IL: Quadrangle Books.

Kidder, Rushworth. 1995. *How Good People Make Tough Choices: Resolving the Dilemmas of Ethical Living.* New York, NY: Fireside Books.

———. 2005. *Moral Courage.* New York, NY: Harper Paperbacks.

King, Coretta Scott. 1969. *My Life with Martin Luther King, Jr.* New York, NY: Holt, Rinehart and Winston.

King, Jr., Martin Luther. 1958. *Stride Toward Freedom: The Montgomery Story.* Boston, MA: Beacon Press.

———. 1963. *Why We Can't Wait.* New York, NY: Signet Classics.

———. 1968. *Where Do We Go From Here: Chaos or Community?.* Boston, MA: Beacon Press.

Linder, Doug. 2001. *The Trial of Susan B. Anthony for Illegal Voting.* http://www.law.umkc.edu/faculty/projects/ftrials/anthony/sbaaccount.html. Accessed on February 29, 2012.

Lind, Michael. 2004. *What Lincoln Believed: The Values and Convictions of American's Greatest President.* New York, NY: Anchor Books.

Malone, Dumas. 1948. *Jefferson the Virginian.* Boston, MA: Little, Brown and Company.

———. 1970. *Jefferson the President.* Boston, MA: Little, Brown and Company.

Mapp, Alf J., Jr. 1987. *Thomas Jefferson: A Strange Case of Mistaken Identity.* New York, NY: Madison Books.

Marshall, Katherine Tupper. 1946. *Together: Annals of an Army Wife.* New York, NY: Tupper and Love.

Mayer, David N. 1994. *The Constitutional Thought of Thomas Jefferson.* Charlottesville, VA: University Press of Virginia.

McDonald, Forrest. 1976. *The Presidency of Thomas Jefferson.* Lawrence, KS: University Press of Kansas.

McPherson, James M. 1988. *Battle Cry of Freedom: The Civil War Era.* New York, NY: Ballentine Books.

Meacham, Jon. 2008. *American Lion.* New York, NY: Random House.

Mieczkowski, Yanek. 2005. *Gerald Ford and the Challenges of the 1970s.* Lexington, KY: The University Press of Kentucky.

Miller, William Lee. 2002. *Lincoln's Virtues: An Ethical Biography.* New York, NY: Vintage Books.

———. 2008. *President Lincoln: The Duty of a Statesman.* New York, NY: Alfred E. Knopf.

Neustadt, Richard and Ernest May. 1986. *Thinking in Time: The Uses of History for Decision Makers.* New York, NY: Free Press.

Nicolay, Helen. 1949. *Lincoln's Secretary: A Biography of John G. Nicolay.* New York, NY: Longmans, Green and Company.

Onuf, Peter and Leonard Sadosky. 2002. *Jeffersonian America.* Malden, MA: Blackwell Publishers Inc.

Padover, Saul. 1956. *A Jefferson Profile: As Revealed in His Letters*. New York, NY: The John Day Company.

Paltsits, Victor Hugo. 1935. *Washington's Farewell Address*. New York, NY: New York Public Library.

Peters, F. H. 1891. *The Nichomachean Ethics of Aristotle*. London: Kean, Paul, Trench, and Trubner.

Pogue, Forrest. 1987. *George C. Marshall: Statesman*. New York: Penguin Books.

Pops, Gerald M. 2009. *Ethical Leadership in Turbulent Times: Modeling the Public Career of George C. Marshal*. Lanham, MD: Lexington Books.

Reeves, Richard. 1996. "I'm Sorry, Mr. President." *American Heritage*. pp. 52–54.

Rieder, Jonathan. 2008. *The Word of the Lord is Upon Me: The Righteous Performance of Martin Luther King, Jr*. Boston, MA: The Belknap Press of Harvard University Press.

Rohr, John A. 1989. *Ethics for Bureaucrats: An Essay on Law and Values. Second Edition*. New York, NY: Marcel Dekker, Inc.

———. 1998. *Public Service, Ethics & Constitutional Practice*. Lawrence, KS: University Press of Kansas.

Rosenberg, Gerald. 2008. *The Hollow Hope: Can Courts Bring About Social Change. Second Edition*. Chicago, IL: University of Chicago Press.

Ryan, Halford. 2001. "The Rhetoric of George Washington's Farewell Address." *Speaker and Gavel* 38, pp. 1–15.

Schlesinger, Robert. 2009. *White House Ghosts: Presidents and Their Speechwriters, from FDR to George W. Bush*. New York, NY: Simon and Schuster Paperbacks.

Sherr, Lynn. 1995. *Failure is Impossible: Susan B. Anthony in Her Own Words*. New York, NY: Times Books.

Smith, Richard Norton. 1993. *Patriarch: George Washington and the New American Nation*. New York, NY: Houghton Mifflin Co.

Spalding, Matthew. 1996. "George Washington's Farewell Address." *Wilson Quarterly* (Autumn), 20 (4), pp. 65–71.

Spalding, Matthew and Patrick Garrity. 1996. *A Sacred Union of Citizens: George Washington's Farewell Address and the American Character*. Boston, MA: Rowman and Littlefield Publishers, Inc.

Tackach, James. 2002. *Lincoln's Moral Vision: The Second Inaugural Address*. Jackson, MS: The University Press of Mississippi.

The Gallup Poll: Public Opinion, 1935–1971, Volume 1. 1972. New York, New York Random House.

The Gallup Poll: Public Opinion 1972–1977, Volume One. 1978. Wilmington, DE: Scholarly Resources Inc.

The Gallup Poll: Public Opinion 1972–1977, Volume Two. 1978. Wilmington, DE: Scholarly Resources Inc.

The Papers of Thomas Jefferson Digital Edition. 2008. Edited by Barbara B. Oberg and J. Jefferson Looney. Charlottesville, VA: University of Virginia Press, Rotunda.

Tichy, Noel M. and Warren G. Bennis. 2007. *Judgment: How Winning Leaders Make Great Calls*. New York, NY: Portfolio.

Toffel, Richard J. 2005. *Sounding the Trumpet: The Making of John F. Kennedy's Inaugural Address*. Chicago, IL: Ivan R. Dee.

Tulis, Jeffrey. 1987. *The Rhetorical Presidency*. Princeton, NJ: Princeton University Press.

Uldrich, Jack. 2005. *Soldier Statesman Peacemaker: Leadership Lessons from George C. Marshall*. New York, NY: Amacom.

Ward, Geoffrey C. 1990. *The Civil War: An Illustrated History*. New York, NY: Alfred A. Knopf.

Ward, Geoffrey C. and Ken Burns. 1999. *Not for Ourselves Alone: The Story of Elizabeth Cady Stanton and Susan B. Anthony*. New York, NY: Alfred A. Knopf.

Warren, Mervyn A. 2001. *King Came Preaching: The Pulpit Power of Dr. Martin Luther King, Jr.* Downers Grove, IL: InterVarsity Press.

Washington, James M. Editor. 1986. *A Testament of Hope: The Essential Writings and Speeches of Martin Luther King, Jr.* New York, NY: Harper One.

Weisberger, Bernard A. 2000. *America Afire: Jefferson, Adams, and the Revolutionary Election of 1800*. New York, NY: William Morrow.

Werth, Barry. 2006. *31 Days: Gerald Ford, The Nixon Pardon, and a Government in Crisis*. New York, NY: Anchor Books.

White Jr., Ronald C. 2002. *Lincoln's Greatest Speech: The Second Inaugural*. New York, NY: Simon and Schuster.

Willingham, Dan. 2009. *Why Don't Students Like School?* San Francisco: Jossey-Bass.

Wills, Gary. 1999. "Lincoln's Greatest Speech?" *The Atlantic Monthly*. September 1999.

Wilson, Douglas L. 1989. *Jefferson's Literary Commonplace Book*. Princeton, NJ: Princeton University Press.

———. 1998. *Honor's Voice: The Transformation of Abraham Lincoln*. New York, NY: Alfred A. Knopf.

. 2006. *Lincoln's Sword: The Presidency and the Power of Words*. New York, NY: Vintage Books.

Winik, Jay. 2001. *April 1865: The Month That Saved America*. New York, NY: HarperCollins.

Wood, Gordon S. 2006. *Revolutionary Characters: What Made the Founders Different*. New York, NY: The Penguin Press.

Index

Note: Page numbers in **bold** are used to indicate a large section of text devoted to a topic (e.g. **1–26**); subheads break out details within that large section.